THE POWER OF IDEALS

THE POWER
OF IDEALS

THE REAL STORY
OF MORAL CHOICE

WILLIAM DAMON

AND

ANNE COLBY

OXFORD
UNIVERSITY PRESS

OXFORD
UNIVERSITY PRESS

Oxford University Press is a department of the University of
Oxford. It furthers the University's objective of excellence in research,
scholarship, and education by publishing worldwide.

Oxford   New York
Auckland   Cape Town   Dar es Salaam   Hong Kong   Karachi
Kuala Lumpur   Madrid   Melbourne   Mexico City   Nairobi
New Delhi   Shanghai   Taipei   Toronto

With offices in
Argentina   Austria   Brazil   Chile   Czech Republic   France   Greece
Guatemala   Hungary   Italy   Japan   Poland   Portugal   Singapore
South Korea   Switzerland   Thailand   Turkey   Ukraine   Vietnam

Oxford is a registered trademark of Oxford University Press
in the UK and certain other countries.

Published in the United States of America by
Oxford University Press
198 Madison Avenue, New York, NY 10016

Library of Congress Cataloging-in-Publication Data
Damon, William, 1944–
The power of ideals: the real story of moral choice / William Damon, Anne Colby.
pages cm
Summary: "The Power of Ideals examines the lives and work of six 20th century moral
leaders who pursued moral causes ranging from world peace to social justice and human
rights and uses these six cases to show how people can make choices guided by their
moral ideals rather than by base emotion or social pressures"—Provided by publisher.
ISBN 978-0-19-935774-1 (hardback)
1. Ethics.   2. Moral development.   3. Leaders.   I. Colby, Anne, 1946–   II. Title.
BF723.M54D363 2015
155.2′5—dc23
2014035161

1 3 5 7 9 8 6 4 2
Printed in the United States of America
on acid-free paper

*This book is dedicated to our beloved family
and friends, and especially to our mothers,
Emily Jane Colby and Helen Damon.*

CONTENTS

ACKNOWLEDGMENTS

This book was made possible by generous support from the John Templeton Foundation. We benefitted from the help of three thoughtful program officers at the Foundation—Kent Hill, Craig Joseph, and Sarah Clement. Abby Gross of Oxford University Press and Jim Levine of Levine Greenberg Rostan Literary Agency offered excellent suggestions both at the outset and at several points during our writing, as did reviewer John Gibbs. Two Stanford graduate students, Brandy Quinn and Hyemin Han, helped to collect and make sense of the historical data on the leaders we studied, and they also assisted in coding those data. Pamela King, Jenni Mariano, Lee Shulman, and William Sullivan conducted further expert coding of the historical data on the moral leaders in order to check our interpretations, and they used their own knowledge of the historical figures to help us better understand the cases. Lisa Staton expertly managed financial and administrative aspects of the project. Finally, we are grateful to Elissa Hirsh, who gave us superb help with many aspects of the research project and the manuscript preparation, and who always maintained her patience and good cheer in the face of intense time pressure and other challenges.

INTRODUCTION

This is a book about *moral commitment*—how it develops, why some people are able to sustain it in the face of pressure, and what it looks like when played out in large public arenas by world leaders. What is moral commitment? Although we don't wish to begin this book with an effort as difficult and distracting as an attempt to define "moral," neither do we want to cloud our subject matter by ignoring the question entirely. We consider morality to be the vast realm of social actions, intentions, emotions, and judgments aimed at providing benefits (and preventing damage) to people, society, and the world beyond the self. It's a multilayered system of prosocial acts, with "acts" understood to mean mental and physiological as well as behavioral acts. Morality covers both the *means* and the *ends* of human activity—that is, not only *what* people aim to do but also *how* they go about doing it—and the finer the moral sense, the more likely that both means and ends will be morally driven.

As for the focus on moral *commitment*, this signifies our interest in sustained dedication to a moral cause (or causes) rather than single and isolated acts. Moral commitment can be as ordinary as a parent making sacrifices for the well-being of a child or a worker determined to conduct a job with integrity, responsibility, and a sense of public mission. It can be as heroic as a civic leader taking risky stands in favor of human rights or a charity worker undergoing years of personal privation in the service of the needy. Moral commitment can be inspired by a desire to serve God or other transcendent truths, or it can be directed toward strictly humanistic concerns. Whether ordinary or extraordinary, spiritual or mundane, moral commitment enables civilized societies to become havens of common decency for most of their members.

For as long as we can recall, we two authors (Bill and Anne) have been intrigued, fascinated, inspired, and humbled by examples of moral commitment that we've seen in public and private lives. We have tried to understand the workings of moral commitment through the lens of moral psychology, a scholarly discipline that has produced insights for business, education, and professional training. Each of us has written about many issues in moral psychology related to character development over the lifespan. Our one previous book together (*Some Do Care: Contemporary Lives of Moral Commitment*) was our first attempt, more than twenty years ago, to apply what we knew about moral psychology to the mysteries of deep moral commitment.

Yet some recent work in moral psychology has taken a strange and disturbing direction, and due to widespread media attention, this is the direction now shaping public impressions of what humans are (and are not) capable of when confronted with moral concerns. The reason we find this direction strange is that we can't find in this work anything that we (or virtually everyone else through the ages) have recognized as moral commitment—or even, to put a stronger point on it, as authentic moral concerns. The reason we find the direction disturbing is that its lack of authenticity and its "game-playing" approach to moral scholarship have conveyed a dispiriting picture of the human moral sense that contributes to the cynicism and negativity of our contemporary public discourse.

We both grew up in the United States in the 1950s and 1960s. It was a time when the word "moral" in American parlance was taking on enhanced meanings. In the early part of that period, as children subject to the socializing guidance of parents and other on-guard adults, we heard the term mostly in connection with proper dating behavior. Then suddenly, it seemed, the great social causes of the 1960s arose, offering new and more captivating images of what moral commitment can look like. Bill remembers the civil rights movement as his first experience with a moral cause that captured his imagination. For Anne, it was the Vietnam War: Indeed, that war triggered

Anne's decision to devote her career to studying morality and moral education. The urgent, compelling, and spiritually enlarging nature of the concerns we experienced in those early years brought the study of morality to the center of both our lives, individually and in our long partnership (the two of us met in the course of our moral development work and married over thirty years ago). The concerns we encountered were easy to identify with: human rights, justice, world peace, compassion, honor, integrity—ideals that have ennobled human life through the ages, even in the toughest spots and darkest times.

In Chapter 1, we review studies from what some have called the "new science" school of moral psychology. It is an approach that relies on presenting unusual hypothetical scenarios to research subjects (often college students) and then examining how those subjects respond to the scenarios: what choices they make, how their brains react while they think about their choices, and so on. It's a fascinating line of work that has produced new information about how certain patterns of cognition and affect are reflected in distinctive patterns of brain functioning. No doubt some lines of this work will turn out to be important for advancing the understanding of moral psychology and development, and in this book we signal our bets regarding which lines of the recent neuroscience work hold most promise for such a contribution.

But here the question that concerns us is whether findings from the "new science" and related approaches are providing an adequate, or even accurate, account of the human capacity for moral commitment. For this is the claim that many of the scientists and journalists who report the findings to the public are making—to the serious detriment of public expectations regarding human moral potential.

One recent missive in the new science vein, published after we had written the main parts of this book, is *Moral Tribes* by Harvard professor Joshua Greene.[1] We found *Moral Tribes* to be informative and interesting, and if asked we would endorse it as a good and worthwhile read. But Greene's book doesn't need our endorsement: it's been praised by several distinguished colleagues, who call it a "masterpiece," "a landmark work," "dazzling," "groundbreaking," and a "rare" source of new ideas "after two and a half millennia" of writings on morality(!). Certainly such notice demands the attention of anyone trying to understand how the human moral sense works, right?

What revealing window on morality does *Moral Tribes* offer? We agree that it's a "rare" view, if by rare one means that it looks at behaviors that are unusual and have little to do with people's actual experience. Here is a quick summary of the pivotal instrument that Greene uses to elicit what he considers to be moral responses from experimental subjects: *You are standing on a bridge watching a runaway trolley car heading towards five people. You can prevent this calamity by throwing a man off the bridge in the path of the trolley. Is this morally OK to do?* There are alternate versions of this dilemma, such as imagining yourself as the conductor of the trolley, as we note in Chapter 1. What all the versions have in common is their remoteness from ordinary experience. Not only do such events rarely (actually, *never*) happen in real life, but neither do they come close to emulating the mental and emotional fabric of the human moral response. Such experiments are academic games, no more, no less. They may trigger patterns of brain activity that reveal something interesting about how people with normal or damaged brains respond to hypothetical dilemmas revolving around highly artificial scenarios. They may be useful for illustrating some implications of the opposing philosophical traditions of utilitarianism and deontology (which is the purpose for which the dilemmas were originally designed). But academic games about imaginary situations are not sensible proxies for genuine moral commitment and real-life moral choices. To interpret responses to such games as if they tell us something about real-life morality is to distort—and, as we show in this book, degrade—the human moral sense.

There's a historical irony here, one that we've been around long enough to witness. In the 1960s and 1970s, an early landmark program of moral psychology research was Lawrence Kohlberg's efforts to describe stages in the development of moral reasoning. Both of us were close to the effort: Bill as a sympathetic but often skeptical student and observer, Anne as a sympathetic although sometimes critical collaborator with Kohlberg. The Kohlberg stage system, we believed, was valuable as a description of important modes of moral judgment. But, in the end, it was inadequate for predicting moral conduct, since it didn't take adequate account of the many other cultural, relational, and affective forces that drive moral conduct.

At the time, however, the major criticism leveled at Kohlberg's research program, especially from those who claimed the mantle of hard science methods, was that the Kohlberg methodology relied on *hypothetical dilemmas*. This observation was true: For example, the "Heinz dilemma" asks subjects whether a man should steal a drug if that is the only way to save his wife's life. Kohlberg borrowed this dilemma from the situation that Victor Hugo had placed Jean Valjean in at the outset of *Les Misérables* (Jean Valjean had stolen a loaf of bread to feed his sister's hungry children, leading to his arrest and imprisonment). It is the stuff of great fiction but not a circumstance that most are likely to encounter (although more likely, certainly, than stopping a runaway trolley car with a body[2]).

The scientific objection to the hypothetical method as invalid proved devastating to Kohlberg's research program, resulting not only in a series of critical journal reviews but also in the rejection of his funding requests to NIMH and similar agencies. As far as we know, no one ever managed to mount a successful defense of this method as an adequate or ecologically valid representation of human morality. Yet the discredited hypothetical dilemma approach has now reappeared in more extreme form as the basis of the "new" science of moral psychology.

Our own method of choice in this book, "exemplar methodology," cannot be faulted for its lack of authenticity, since it examines the words and deeds of people who already have engaged in life events with indisputably moral dimensions and who have responded in ways that reflect moral awareness and intentions. We shall sing this and other praises of exemplar methodology when we describe it more fully later in this book. But now is the time to caution that exemplar methods such as the ones we use also have serious limitations. For one thing, exemplar methods are based on subjective, usually retrospective accounts of highly charged events. At its best, human memory is replete with inaccuracy and even outright invention. Memories of the dramatic personal crises and adventures that flow from moral actions are especially at risk of distortion. Beyond this fundamental shortcoming, there are limits in the scientific design of studies that examine exemplary figures. Such studies inevitably have tiny samples, since case studies of exemplars require time-consuming, in-depth analyses. Proper comparison groups are difficult, if not impossible, to assemble.

For all these reasons, we believe that to obtain the comprehensive account that the immensely rich and complex area of human functioning of morality deserves, a full range of scientific methods is required, with the exemplar methodology just one part of an experimental, observational, neuroscientific, interview, survey, case study, and big-data mix.

Even so, we have found that there is nothing like case studies of exemplary figures to yield insights on the inner workings of human development in any area of adult life. We found this method to be productive in our study of living moral exemplars reported in *Some Do Care*. Now that, in the present book, we turn to historical cases rather than living ones, and to analyses of established records rather than in-person interviews, we hope readers will agree that exemplars' lives offer profound and moving insights into moral commitment that can be uniquely valuable for the rest of us.

We use this last phrase, *the rest of us*, intentionally, and we wish to emphasize it. It's true that exemplars are, by definition, extraordinary, but they are not of a different species. They all have their share of human frailties, they make mistakes, and in some areas of their lives they may act in far less than venerable ways. Exemplars are by no means perfect, as they would be the first to admit. Indeed, one of the hazards of this kind of research is that inevitably a reader will object that such-and-such a figure has demonstrated feet of clay. (Entire treatises have been produced about why Mother Teresa does not deserve esteem for various reasons, including, for example, that she treated her secretaries harshly.) During all of our forays into exemplar research, as we have become familiar with these people whom we admire so greatly, we have been struck by how thoroughly human they are, in every sense of the word, weaknesses and all.

This realization brings with it an important implication regarding the significance of exemplars' lives "for the rest of us." *It means that we can learn from them.* We share with them all the challenges and opportunities of human life and human development. We acquire skills and strengths in much the same way, we are susceptible to the same illusions and misguidance, and we build our intelligence and character through the same psychological processes. Although they have reached farther than most in their developmental journeys, the nature of the journey is similar in essential ways. Most importantly, this means that an understanding of exemplary lives can offer great educational benefits to ordinary people of all ages. As we note below, this is our foremost hope for the uses of this book.

This book follows *Some Do Care*, but we do not consider it a sequel in the sense of "here's another look at..." or "here's more about..." In *Some Do Care*, we reported findings that, to varying degrees, had taken us by surprise during our case studies of twenty-three living exemplars. For example, we had not expected that every one of these highly dedicated, risk-taking people would deny that he or she displayed courage while pursuing moral aims. Without exception, they told us, basically, that they had not needed to draw on courage because, with respect to the actions called for, "there was no choice in the matter." In retrospect, we realized that similar sentiments had been expressed by intrepid Europeans who rescued Jewish families during the Holocaust—but we still felt astonished when we heard, for example, a civil rights leader whose children had been threatened, or an antiwar campaigner who had been subjected to vicious attacks, deny that they had been brave. Other surprises for us included the disproportionately high percentage of exemplars who were people of religious faith (in a study with strictly secular selection criteria); the positivity expressed by those who readily admitted that their life's mission to, say, diminish the overall state of poverty, had failed; the life-long capacities of the exemplars to revisit and transform their goals to align increasingly with their moral purposes; and the almost sublime unity of self and morality demonstrated throughout their everyday and long-term activities.

These findings constitute part of the launching pad for the present book, but they are not the subject of it. Rather, our driving question here is no longer what morally committed people are like (intrepid, faithful, positive, unified, and so on) but rather on *how they manage to do it*. We assume that, for example, acting bravely without feeling the need for courage is easier said than done, as is staying on the right side of the line between passion and fanaticism, or remaining positive in the face of failure. So how is it that some people manage to accomplish these feats?

To get a handle on this question as we worked through the cases of six extraordinary twentieth-century world leaders, we turned to considerations of virtue. That is, we began an examination of the character strengths that enable people to achieve difficult moral goals. To understand how people manage to sustain and achieve moral commitment, we have found three virtues to be especially noteworthy: truthfulness (importantly including *inner* truthfulness); humility (including open-mindedness); and faithfulness (including spiritual and religious sentiments of the kind that we discovered but did not have a chance to explore in *Some Do Care* as well as secular variants of faith). Our main mission in the present study was to see how these and other associated virtues work to make possible the pinnacles of moral commitment.

Beyond this main mission, we have a topical agenda as well. We began this introduction with our complaints about currently influential directions (or *mis*directions) in the field of moral psychology. One cultural result of these misdirections has been a popular derogation of the power of moral beliefs and ideals (and even reason) to shape human affairs. In our intellectual climate, we are seeing a return to the law of the jungle in the guise of scientific realism. Now if the science were valid, we might need to accept the result and find a way to live with or compensate for it. But, as we have already noted (and go into more seriously in the following chapter), these scientific claims are based on limited samples of immature subjects, on experimental situations that depart radically from authentic lived experience, and on generalizations of odd behaviors to vast realms of moral conduct that have little to do with those behaviors. This is hardly the formula for a valid scientific account.

We are not only critical of the science that has produced such findings but also of the wild interpretations that have been made of them, particularly in the popular media. Thus we have taken on, as a secondary purpose of this book, an attempt to address and correct this culturally trendy misdirection. It is one thing to have hard life experience drive out a community's belief in noble ideals; it is another thing entirely to have this done by an invalid, spurious, and overstated set of "scientific" findings.

We write of the power of ideals, but we don't wish to float on clouds of naïve idealism. We are aware that there is a heavy dose of immorality in human affairs, and we have no good guess as to the balance of good versus evil now or in times past. As for moral choice, we agree that biological, cultural, and situational forces play significant roles. We welcome studies in the social, behavioral, and brain sciences that illuminate the workings of such forces.

In this book, though, we try to show the particular role of ideals within the context of other psychological influences on moral choice. Our chapter integrating all the disparate psychological influences is called "Toward a Moral Psychology in Full." The word "Toward" in the title is meant to indicate our own very real humility regarding how much is still unknown about the workings of moral choice and commitment.

A word about authorship: For this book, we decided to reverse the authorship order from that of *Some Do Care*, to distinguish the two books for the sake of reference. In all other respects, the ordering of names bears no significance. Although we both worked on all of the chapters, Bill took the lead on the critique and the universal morality sections, and Anne took the lead on the book's treatment of virtues and the ways people form and sustain their moral commitments.

Our ultimate hope with this book is that it will validate efforts to improve moral choice and encourage moral commitment. Of course, such efforts are worth making only if choice and commitment can indeed be fostered. Apart from Orwellian modes of behavior change, the only way to foster choice and commitment is through education that engages the conscious mind. Views of the moral sense that reduce moral responding to biological impulses or social pressures—views that remove agency from the individual—cannot encourage attempts to educate people for improved moral choices or their characters for deeper moral commitment. This is the reason we believe it's worthwhile, even necessary, to take to heart the messages offered by the exemplars we examine in this book.

NOTES

1. Joshua David Greene, *Moral Tribes: Emotion, Reason, and the Gap between Us and Them* (New York: The Penguin Press, 2013).
2. It's also worth noting that some of Kohlberg's scenarios drew on some familiar problems, such as a father trying to decide whether he was obligated to keep a promise to a son after the promise turned out to be inconvenient.

CHAPTER ONE

WRONG TURNS IN THE NEW SCIENCE OF MORALITY

Morality has always been the subject of passionate dispute. For all of recorded history, people have fought about what's right and wrong and who should be the judge. From the dawning of philosophy and science, scholars have argued whether human nature is moral or immoral at its core, about how people learn to be morally good, about whether there ever can be any agreement across cultures about what's right, and about what determines moral conduct and misconduct. This perennial questioning suggests that moral concerns are fundamental to human experience and that recognizing and dealing with such concerns are essential parts of adapting to civilized life.

Morality makes civilized life possible. Its hold on people is powerful, but its power is perplexing when viewed through the lenses of our personal self-interest and survival instincts. As a rule, people try to behave morally most the time. In fact, despite counter-examples large and small, human behavior more often than not turns out to be civilized, law-abiding, caring, and downright decent. Most people usually resist their antisocial urges. Why is that? Why don't people do whatever it takes to advance their own interests, whatever the cost to others? Why don't people constantly prey on one another and turn a deaf ear to the needs of anyone beyond themselves? Most people, for some reason, don't act this way. Why not?

Layered on this question is another, even more perplexing question: Why do so many people go well beyond resisting antisocial urges and actively devote themselves to moral purposes such as justice, liberty, peace, and the welfare of others? Some people achieve amaz-ingly noble things and set inspiring examples for others, in some cases even risking their lives to do so. Often their efforts on behalf of moral causes are creative as well as generous and brave. They may even defy conventional public approval in pursuit of a lofty moral end. How does this happen? What can explain this apparently selfless, often counter-conventional, behavior?

Morality also can have a familiar, friendly face, in the everyday transactions that bind society together. Many people care for their families and work hard to ensure their welfare. They value friend-ships, treating their friends with generosity, honesty, and respect, and maintaining loyalty or doing favors they know can't be recipro-cated. Many people dedicate themselves to their work and try to do it responsibly. Many people care about their communities and help those in trouble.

Commitment, compassion, integrity, inspiration, sacrifice, honesty, loyalty, social responsibility—this is the stuff of the robust moral sense that has held societies together and enhanced personal well-being in every civilized society the world has ever known. It is also the stuff of the moral sense that philosophers, theologians, scientists, and other scholars have sought to understand through millennia of private reflection and public discourse.

But this lively, multifaceted human moral sense is far from the stuff of a self-named "new science of morality" that has come to domi-nate today's social science of moral behavior. Nor is it the subject of the numerous recent treatments of morality in major media outlets such as *The New York Times, The Wall Street Journal*, and National Public Radio. Many journalists have become captivated by the "new science" view, a view that is narrow, reductionist, and bleakly cynical in its implications. Popular media representations of this view have suggested that people at their core are cruel, uncaring, hypocritical, and dishonest—and that perhaps they *should* be this way, in order to get ahead in this dog-eat-dog world.[1] This has degraded public discourse about morality and added to the overall sense of cultural decline that many social critics have observed in recent years. In this way, the vision that characterizes current academic studies of morality has produced a cultural effect that is far from academic.

The phrase *new science of morality* was introduced by psychologist Jonathan Haidt in a 2007 *Science* essay announcing this "new synthesis in moral psychology."[2] In his essay, Haidt emphasized two founding assumptions of this "new science" school: "the importance of inborn moral intuitions" and "the socially functional nature of moral thinking." These assumptions place the new science school in opposition to the vision of morality's truth, virtue, and justice-seeking nature, as emphasized by philosophers from Plato and Aristotle to Kant, John Rawls, Alasdair MacIntyre, and most recently, Kristján Kristjánsson.

Along with Haidt's writings on the matter, there is a loose association of complementary writings emanating from parallel research programs that also aim to demonstrate the nonconscious, unreflective, and irrational nature of human behavior. These research programs share the assumption that people make their most important decisions quickly and automatically. Such "blink"-like judgments[3] are made with reference to emotional and other natural intuitions rather than carefully considered principles. If conscious principles are at some point invoked, according to this view, they are used *after the fact*, only to rationalize the automatically intuitive choices, rather than to drive or shape them. Haidt refers to "the emotional dog and its rational tail,"[4] and he is clear about his belief that it is the emotions wagging the reasoning, rather than the reverse.

Not surprisingly, the new science school's emphasis on emotionality and irrationality in decision making means that it takes a jaundiced view of the quality of moral thinking. In *The Righteous* Mind, Haidt questions the sincerity of moral thinking: "...the take-home message of the book is...that we are all self-righteous hypocrites." Others in this vein, such as experimenters who use economic or philosophical games to assess moral judgments, question the logic, rationality, and intellectual soundness of the human moral response. One dissenting scientist has labeled this the "people are stupid" school of psychology, noting how ironic it is that this claim about the non-rational character of morality is made by intellectuals through laboriously reasoned argumentation.[5]

One might expect this line of argument to be questioned by journalists who work to inform and persuade the public with their own writing. Yet, as one commentator noted, "Researchers making these assertions and generalizations derive a great deal of public exposure from the media (especially the Op-Ed section of *The New York Times* and its Science Section, whose reporters seem enamored with all manner of biological and evolutionary explanation), as well as from popular books written by journalists...with catchy titles like *Blink* and *The Hidden Brain*."[6]

Much of the so-called new science of morality is based on a series of studies that have adapted for experimental use the far-fetched hypothetical problem taken from academic philosophy that we described briefly in our Introduction. As we noted, these studies ask subjects about variants of the following imaginary dilemma: A runaway trolley car, which has lost its brakes, is heading toward five people walking on the tracks. If the conductor lets the train stay on course, these people will be run down. But if, instead, he steers the train in another direction, or if someone throws a large man off the bridge in front of the car, it will run down only one hapless person who has found himself in the wrong place at the wrong time.

Most people have no problem concluding that the right thing to do is to switch the train to the side track in order to save four lives, even though that would require the conductor to actively choose to kill a person rather than allowing the train to wreak havoc on its own. But when saving the five hikers would require actually pushing a man off a bridge onto the train track (in order to throw the trolley off course), most people say that would be wrong, even though the logic of this problem is—the researchers claim—essentially the same as that of the switch dilemma. These different responses to dilemmas that investigators claim to be equivalent (except in their tendency to evoke emotions) is, in the new science view, evidence of the nonrational nature of moral choice.

Of course such dilemmas depict strangely improbable situations. They are distant from the things most people confront and care about

4

in their moral lives—concerns such as caring for their families, resisting temptations to act badly, or pursuing positive moral goals. The purely hypothetical trolley-car dilemma was originally devised by philosophers as a thought experiment. It was used to demonstrate the limitations of one particular moral theory (utilitarianism, also known as consequentialism). The dilemma was not designed to represent the actual moral experience of ordinary people. Nevertheless, new science and similar writings have treated responses to this scenario as proxies for morality in general. In this way, they base their claims about the intuitive, unthinking nature of the human moral sense on an exotic species of behavior elicited only in strange experimental situations.

Writings emanating from the new science school do make concessions to what they see as certain occasional (but usually feeble) contributions of higher-level intellectual processes to judgment and behavior. We discuss these more nuanced positions later. But, for the most part, the new science studies have been designed (and widely interpreted) to show that our species is wired to act primarily in an involuntary, automatic manner ruled by biological forces beyond our conscious control.

A *New York Times* review of recent books in this vein concluded, "These books possess a unifying theme: The choices we make in day-to-day life are prompted by impulses lodged deep within the nervous system."[7] The review was charmingly headlined *"The amygdala made me do it!"* At least the headline writer had a sense of irony—or, more to the point, a sense of the absurd.

One proponent of this view that "morality is grounded in our biology" is former Harvard professor Marc Hauser (2006), whose influential book *Moral Minds* drew heavily on responses to hypothetical trolley-car dilemmas. The book promoted the view that the fundamental bases for moral judgments are instinctual, nonconscious, and programmed into our genome. Hauser's central idea was that "we evolved a moral instinct . . . designed to generate rapid judgments about what is morally right or wrong based on an unconscious grammar of action."[8] That "grammar" is essentially a set of computations, inaccessible to the conscious mind, that automatically generate judgments of right and wrong without the need for conscious deliberation.

The invention of a widely available technical tool, functional magnetic resonance imaging (fMRI), has abetted this biological reductionism. In one study using this tool, philosopher Joshua Greene teamed up with neuroscientist Jonathan Cohen and others to observe brain processes that accompany responses to trolley-car dilemmas.[9] When confronted with the variant of the trolley-car dilemma in which saving lives requires pushing a man off a bridge, most subjects decide quickly which choice (active or passive killing) they are most comfortable with: Most judge throwing the man from the bridge as "inappropriate" (which we find an odd choice of word for a judgment about whether to kill an innocent person). While the subjects think about this problem, magnetic images of their neural processes reveal patterns of activity in areas of their brains that have been identified with emotion.

When responding to the version of the trolley-car dilemma in which most subjects decided that flipping a switch to save more people would be "appropriate," the emotion-connected areas of their brains were not activated, unlike in the version that required the "inappropriate" act of throwing a man off a bridge. These findings were said to demonstrate that, even through rational analysis would treat these two solutions as equivalent, their differential engagement of emotions leads to different judgments. The authors' point is that nonrational, emotionally based factors based in brain activity are more powerful in shaping people's moral judgments than deliberative thinking about right and wrong. In another article citing the same research, coauthored by Greene and Haidt, the conclusion was that "moral judgment is more a matter of emotion and affective intuition than deliberate reasoning."[10] In the new science camp, this biological determinism relegates the role of judgment and other forms of conscious choice to what is known in psychology as "epiphenomena": that is, after-the-fact rationalization that plays no part in actually determining the behavioral choice.

Although the scientific evidence cited in support of this conclusion is far from convincing (given the arcane, hypothetical nature of the experimental situation), these kinds of studies and their dubious interpretations have been extensively covered by the mass media. Any neuroscience research, no matter how conceptually misguided, tends to have a certain prestige today. In an examination of this cachet, Deena Weisberg and her colleagues[11] have shown that when given neuroscience information that experts have determined to be entirely irrelevant, people feel more satisfied with explanations that the reports offer. Weisberg concludes that irrelevant neuroscience information in any explanation of a psychological phenomenon actually *interferes* with people's abilities to critically weigh the underlying logic of the explanation.

We believe that there is a great deal of promise in neuroscience explorations of moral judgment, and we have gained valuable insights from a number of recent fMRI studies, as we discuss in Chapter 2. But not every fMRI study reveals something new or interesting. Analyses of fMRI studies overall have concluded that only a minority of the studies contributes anything new to understanding the phenomena under investigation.[12] Brain activity picked up by fMRI images may be no more than a physical correlate of a psychological process offering no explanatory value, but this lack of significance is rarely discussed. Yet for some consumers, fMRI studies have a hard science aura that can cover up a lack of informative new findings.

In addition to hypothetical trolley cars careening out of control, there is another implausible paradigm that has fueled the "new science" of morality and the biological determinism it promotes. The key method of study in this related paradigm is to trigger feelings of disgust by asking subjects to think about abhorrent activities, such as incest between a brother and a sister, or sex with dead chickens (!). Obviously such activities are rather deviant in human affairs. The experimenter tries to rule out any possible nonemotional basis for objecting to such behavior by asking respondents to assume, for example, that the amorous siblings in the incest case will use birth control, that they will not experience any psychological ill effects, and that they will keep their activities entirely private. As for the chicken, it is, after all, dead—in fact, it already has been chopped up into parts (another! is in order). When, despite such qualifications, subjects in these experiments instantaneously recoil from such imaginings (as most do), their reactions are taken as evidence that morality is ruled by automatic, nonrational, inborn emotions, rather than by moral reflection or reasoned judgment.

In its crudest form, this emphasis on biological determinism leads not only to a view that morality is shaped mostly by instinct, but also to an equally nonrational moral relativism. The logic takes the following course: Even though moral reactions are seen as "grounded in biology," it is impossible for any serious scientist to deny the clear variation in moral practices and beliefs across cultures. Thus, environmental experience must also be given some credit for determining people's behavior.

Now keep in mind that the new science school considers conscious reasoning to be irrelevant and ineffectual, and thus it sees little or no role for human judgment in deciding how to interpret or value environmental experience. The only environmental factor that need be considered, in the new science view, is the particular cultural information that people (who are nothing more than passive, nonpurposeful response machines) happen to be exposed to. Moral values thus are arbitrary relics of the cultures they spring from, not beliefs that people weigh or choose for themselves. To the extent, therefore, that we are not enslaved by our preprogrammed biological impulses, we are helplessly ruled by arbitrary cultural values also beyond our control. Whatever its scientific merit—which we dispute—this is certainly a dispiriting view of the human moral sense.

The new science paradigm joins a set of social psychology studies that also has discounted human powers of intentional moral choice—although one of the founders of this research tradition (Philip Zimbardo) has taken his work in a far less bleak direction in recent years. The social psychology studies, conducted in the latter half of the twentieth century, also conveyed a deterministic message, but the deterministic forces they envisioned were situational or economic rather than biological. For example, in a famous experiment on obedience to authority, Yale professor Stanley Milgram demonstrated that experimental subjects will administer what they believe are excruciating levels of electric shock to others when instructed to do so by men in white coats.[13] Fellow social psychologist Philip Zimbardo assigned college students to guard over other students in a mock prison. After six days of what had been planned as a two-week study, the student guards' behavior became so cruel that Zimbardo decided to stop the experiment.[14] The message from these studies was that our moral sense is so externally driven—and so fragile—that we have the potential for unlimited cruelty if placed in the wrong situations. In the worldview created by such experimentation, only self-interest is sturdy enough to endure the vicissitudes of situational pressures.

The highly influential discipline of economics has also contributed to the view that human behavior is determined by forces beyond our control. Economic models interpret most altruistic behavior as mere reflections of instrumental desires and self-oriented goals.[15] In the economic view, behavioral choices are determined by calculations of risk and gain or the maximization of "utilities" that represent various aspects of the individual's self-interest. Experimental studies of behavior in economic games sometimes grant the existence of altruism and preferences for solutions that can be considered fair. But such preferences are understood to be anomalies that only minimally affect the overall picture of the human condition as a collection of self-interested actors pursuing their own preferences, or "utilities."[16]

In this manner, the views from converging fields of recent behavioral study—the "new science" of moral psychology, experimental social psychology, and behavioral economics—have pitted an array of powerful forces (biological, cultural, social-situational, and economic) against our facility for moral reasoning and judgment—what has been called over the ages the voice of conscience. In the new science view, that voice is not just still and small, it is mostly ineffectual, even illusory.

It does not seem to bother purveyors of these deterministic views that the posited forces come from opposite directions and are therefore theoretically incompatible with one another. After all, how can the same behavior be determined both by irrational internal impulses and external social situations at the same time? No matter: Any and all findings that discount the power of moral ideals to guide human behavior have been welcomed into today's social-science grab-bags, and the findings have been accepted in the name of scientific realism and tough-minded methodological rigor.

To what extent, in fact, is the dispiriting view of human nature advanced by these lines of research based in genuine scientific validity and well-grounded methodological rigor? Let's now examine this question in some detail.

THE SCIENTIFIC VALIDITY OF THE NEW SCIENCE OF MORALITY

One primary indicator of any study's validity is the sample of subjects it uses—that is, who participates in the study. A biased or unrepresentative sample can skew the findings of a study so dramatically that the conclusions may turn reality on its head. Election pollsters, for example, who have not paid proper attention to the representativeness of their samples have made famous mistakes. During the 1948 presidential election, only people who had telephones were surveyed. Since these tended to be the well-off people of the time, this sample skew led to predictions of an easy win for Republican Thomas Dewey over Democrat Harry Truman. The upshot was a morning-after photo of a smiling Harry Truman waving an erroneous newspaper headline stating "Dewey defeats Truman."

Studies that claim to examine the nature of human functioning in any area must have broad samples with a range of lower- and higher-functioning participants if they are to provide valid accounts of people's capacities to function in that area. As one example, no study of human intelligence would be complete without a look at people who operate at the highest levels of genius as well as more ordinary performers. Thinking patterns of high-level experts or creative geniuses may have different characteristics than ordinary mental processes, so experts must be included in the sample.

In addition, for a sensible research design, sample selection and measurement must be coordinated. If a study is to capture what is special about how expert cognitive ability works, the study may need to use different instruments than those designed to capture routine mental functioning. To provide a complete view of human intelligence, a study's sample must include people who perform at a wide range of levels, and its instruments must be designed to capture the special features of all points in that range.

Studies that have made broad and disparaging claims about the nature of moral behavior have been based on restrictive samples of ordinary people drawn from the general population. Frequently, this has meant samples of typical college students, whose main distinguishing quality is their availability as study participants (since they are conveniently enrolled in the courses taught by the professors conducting the experiments). Now we do not in any way mean to imply that typical college students are particularly immoral (lurid pop exposés to the contrary). Yet few college students have encountered the challenging and complex life experiences that can lead to full moral maturity. Also, typical people of *any* age are, by definition, unexceptional. For these reasons, the behavior of typical groups of college students in experimental settings cannot represent the entire spectrum of human moral potential.

One of the new science's mistakes is to conclude that when some typical, less-than-fully-mature people act in ways that are confused, irrational, thoughtless, uncaring, pliable, or profit-maximizing, this means that *people in general* are (and thus that the human moral sense itself is) irrational, blindly obedient to authority, readily corruptible, and fundamentally self-interested. We have yet to see a new science study in which investigators conclude that, even though typical respondents may be confused or biased in their own favor, such shortcomings may not be shared by those whose moral understanding and character are more fully developed.

New science researchers not only fail to acknowledge that their findings may reflect nothing more than the moral limitations of the particular samples they use, they also neglect to consider that these limitations could be overcome by further development—or, related to this point, that they could be addressed educationally. The new science's lack of attention to variations of response among different people, and to people's potential to improve through education and other developmental experiences, throw into serious question interpretations of findings from this line of research.

We also note that some findings even from studies with restrictive samples reveal a more complex pattern than is usually reported. For example, in every implementation of the Milgram situation that ordered subjects to shock another person, there were always a few people who refused to shock. Moreover, some of the subjects who succumbed to the experimenter's commands later came to regret their actions, triggering changes in their moral judgments that long outlasted their behavior in the experimental situation. What were *those* people like? Whatever their characteristics, they are certainly part of the human population.

Some, it seems, are more resistant than others to pressure from authorities; some are more open to learning. Any claims about the nature of morality must take such people into account. Inferences based only on samples limited to typical people lead to a distorted view of human morality.

Beyond the limited nature of the samples in today's experimental studies of morality, the experiments themselves do not validly represent the full moral sense that people display in their everyday lives. We have already commented on the improbability of the trolley-car situation that has been used in so much of the brain-scan research on "the moral mind." The improbability of the situation makes it entirely an exercise in hypothetical reasoning, an "as if" thought game with little resemblance to the actual moral problems (involving our responsibilities to family, friends, and communities) that commonly stir our emotions. We noted in the Introduction the irony that, over forty years ago, Kohlberg's pioneering research was roundly criticized by the scientific community of that time for relying on a methodology of hypothetical word problems. The hard science argument at the time was that no hypothetical word problem can gain access to the real gist of morality, which resides in conduct and the emotions that drive it. This critique, made at the time in the name of scientific validity and methodological rigor, applies even more strongly to the wholly hypothetical trolley-car and moral disgust paradigms used in new science research.

Finally, there is also a developmental point here. To say that people do not always make conscious choices before they act doesn't mean that conscious choices never were made, nor that those earlier choices are irrelevant to present behavior. Most of the routine habits we rely on to guide us honorably through daily life have been worked out during childhood and do not need to be thought about once they've been solidly acquired. Mature people don't need to make a conscious choice about whether or not to grab some candy they might like from a store shelf if no one is looking. They pay for it without thinking twice about it. But at age four this basic rule of conduct may have been less obvious. For the young child, taking candy without paying for it may be a tempting option.[17] The choice to pay for the candy needs to be learned, perhaps in the course of stern inputs from nearby adults. If learned well, the choice eventually becomes habitual and non-conscious. In general, choices that become habitual and automatic later in life often begin as decisions requiring learning and reflection. This is a basic principle of development: Once a skill is learned, we can perform it quickly; but the process of learning can be laboriously reflective and far from instantaneous. We do not "blink" and immediately drive a car through the streets of Brooklyn, although such behavior may become routine after a while for the stout of heart.

Research on expertise in many different areas makes essentially this same point about quick and slow mental processes, intuition and reflection. Studies on capacities as different as chess, physics, and law have shown that, with a great deal of guided practice and experience, individuals develop expertise in the skills of their domain.[18] At that point, their approach to problems and tasks differs from that of novices. Experts have developed richly elaborated, highly organized systems of understanding, and they can draw on this quickly to solve problems. Once expertise is established, however, the application of deep, well-organized understanding usually takes place very quickly.

An expert chess player, for example, can look at a board and instantly, seemingly intuitively, identify the most important alternative next moves and their implications. These experts no longer need to reason through each decision in a laborious way, but their perceptions and intuitions are not without cognitive foundations. Quick, apparently intuitive, perceptions and decisions are grounded in deep understanding of and knowledge about the game. Similarly, in the moral domain, behavior that becomes habitual and automatic later in life needs time and experience, accompanied by reflection and ideational guidance, to fully develop. Adult intuitions about fairness and other moral issues are no more biologically given than are our intuitions about chess. They need to be learned over time.

Moreover, even after adults have achieved relative maturity in their moral thinking, some situations may still require explicit reflection, deliberation, and often consultation with others before they can be understood and resolved. In such situations, people may be morally confused or react in a way that they later come to question. Moral education can facilitate the process of stepping back to think more carefully about the nature and significance of morally charged situations and one's own responses to them.

In fact, Philip Zimbardo relied on a conscience-driven judgment of his own (spurred by feedback from his partner) by stopping his prison guard experiment when it became apparent that it provoked startlingly cruel behavior in his students. Years later, reflecting on the implications of his earlier work, Zimbardo launched a "Heroic Imagination Project" dedicated to building the cognitive capacity of people to think about, recognize, and resist the demands of situations that pressure them to act immorally.

Zimbardo's name has been almost synonymous with the view that moral power lies in situational contingencies. Yet his new work emerges from the belief that, through education that supports moral understanding, people can learn to notice illegitimate situational demands and take action to resist them. Rather than being forever victims of their contexts, people can push back against and even sometimes succeed in changing those contexts. Zimbardo's recent work acknowledges the promise of human development—that people can transcend their biological inheritance through education, understanding, and conscious choice.

Something like this same optimism characterizes *Thinking Fast and Slow*, a book by Nobel Prize–winning psychologist Daniel Kahneman. Kahneman's groundbreaking research with Amos Tversky originated the distinction between fast, automatic, sometimes misleading thought processes and processes that are slower, more effortful and reflective, and more accurate in the end. In *Thinking Fast and Slow*, Kahneman describes System 1 thinking (fast, automatic, intuitive) and System 2 thinking (slow, effortful, deliberative). Kahneman asserts that System 1 is typically in control most of the time and that, in many cases, what people believe to be their chosen opinions are simply judgments that are borrowed uncritically from System 1: "System 1 is the secret author of many of the choices and judgments you make."[19] System 1 is said to be evolutionarily based and constitutes a set of heuristics that make possible timely and useful responses to challenges most of the time. But, because these heuristics developed to cover many but not all situations, their broad application by System 1 leads to an extensive set of biases that often generate invalid judgments. The large body of work by Kahneman and Tversky documented these biases in elaborate detail.

Why do we consider this a less cynical view than the new science approach to morality? Because Kahneman's litany of biases and mistakes does not lead him to conclude that rationality itself is an illusion. Instead, he argues that people *can* and *should* be wary of System 1's intuitive biases and that people should strive to override these irrational biases in their daily judgments. In fact, Kahneman's book seems to be, in part, an effort to give the reader a greater capacity to avoid falling into the cognitive traps set by System 1. Toward this end, each chapter concludes with suggestions for how to guard against the biases described therein, showing how the reader can develop habits of mind that regularly (and eventually habitually) bring System 2 to bear.

Kahneman also shows much greater recognition of variability in the quality of people's thinking than does the "new science" view: "[S]ome people are more like their System 2; others are closer to their System 1."[20] Kahneman points out that people who are more knowledgeable or expert in a given area are much less likely to exhibit the familiar cognitive biases. An admirer of true expertise, Kahneman stresses that some of the complex mental activities that originate in System 2 become fast and automatic—and more accurate—through prolonged practice, accompanied by informative feedback. Thus, what comes to seem intuitive in experts has been built up over time through the operation of System 2. In this way, System 1 can be shaped by System 2 as well as the reverse. And it is this experience-enriched version of System 1 intuition that is trustworthy, not intuitive judgments more generally. Summarizing Kahneman's perspective on the popular claim that quick, unreflective responses are more trustworthy than considered assessments, philosopher Jim Holt quipped, "If you've had 10,000 hours of training in a predictable, rapid-feedback environment—chess, firefighting, anesthesiology—blink. In all other cases, think."[21]

Kahneman also points out that people make the predictable mistakes he describes largely because they aren't *motivated* to stop and think more carefully. When they are so motivated, they do see the fallacies and the misleading ways the problems are framed. As he puts it, "Those who avoid the sin of intellectual sloth could be called 'engaged.' They are more alert, intellectually active, less willing to be satisfied with wrong or easy answers."[22] In Kahneman's view, promoting this kind of engaged, active mind is an important goal of education. Such a perspective is in sharp contrast to the new science view, which accepts moral irrationality as inevitable and suggests no basis for moral growth through education or character development.

Psychologist Jonathan Baron and others have done extensive research on high-quality thinking of the sort that Kahneman has identified as "thinking slow." Baron calls this capacity for and disposition toward careful, high-quality reasoning *actively open-minded thinking.*[23] Research in this area shows that people vary a great deal in the quality of their thinking, that many undesirable outcomes result from poor-quality thinking about important issues, and that education focused on teaching people to think more carefully does work.[24] Baron and his colleagues are not afraid to be prescriptive about the value of actively open-minded thinking, arguing that poor-quality, biased, often overconfident thinking is widespread but need not be, and that educators have a responsibility to help students develop not only the ability to think clearly but also the personal disposition to hold themselves to high standards in this area. From our point of view, a sustained tendency to guard against and avoid self-serving biases, to take seriously perspectives different from one's own, and to avoid unwarranted confidence in views that rest on shaky grounds is an aspect of character.

THE CHECKERED TRADITION OF SCIENTIFIC RESEARCH ON MORAL FORMATION

The recent turn toward a deterministic, nonrational view of human moral capacities is a shift away from the cognitivist tradition that dominated research on moral development during the middle to late twentieth century. Cognitive-developmental psychologists such as Piaget, Kohlberg, and Turiel took people's moral ideas and thinking processes seriously, and they assumed that moral understanding affects people's behavior, although not necessarily in a strict one-to-one correspondence. This cognitive approach was a reaction against prior psychological theories that dismissed moral thinking as epiphenomenal—or materially beside the point—in much the same way that the new science views do.

One of these prior theories, behaviorism, dismissed the "black box" of judgment (which was assumed to be inaccessible to scientific study) in favor of methods that track observable behavior and analyze the environmental contingencies—rewards and punishments—that supposedly shape it. The other main nonrational theory, preceding the behaviorist approach but surviving to coexist along with it, was Freud's psychoanalytic theory, which envisioned plenty of internal activity but gave most of the action to biologically based subconscious desires. Freud did posit a conscience-like superego, informed by a reality-sensitive ego, and he wrote of a weak intellect that, with persistence, could make a difference in the long run. But no one reading

through the annals of psychoanalysis could come away with anything but an image of individuals without any real access to their own
motivations, dragged here and there by inner urges that threaten to
slip entirely out of control. If not completely deterministic (there was
always the possibility of learning through therapy), the psychoanalytic
perspective was generally pessimistic about most people's ability to
guide their lives through conscious moral choice. Nor did it assume
that the rationales that people put forward to explain their own behavior really had much to do with the often neurotic or libido-driven
motives that "actually" determined their choices.

By contrast, Kohlberg spoke of "the child as moral philosopher,"
by which he meant that children are not puppets ruled by their urges
or passive recipients of socialization but, instead, are actively trying to
make sense of their social experiences, usually in communication with
others. In the process of grappling with their daily experiences, children come to better understand moral concepts like fairness, rights,
equality, and human welfare. Unlike behaviorist and psychoanalytic
theories, this formulation refused to view morality as externally
imposed on people in order to subdue inevitable conflicts between
their wants and needs and the interests of society.

Nor is morality based solely on avoiding negative sanctions or emotions such as guilt and anxiety. Kohlberg and others working within
the cognitive-developmental tradition believed that individuals develop
increasingly mature ways of thinking about moral questions through
their active participation in relationships with various dimensions of
the social world, including adults, peers, cultural practices, and social
institutions.

As the major defender of intentional moral behavior guided by
principles and ideals, this cognitive-developmental approach brought
an Enlightenment-like spirit of liberation to views of human nature
and its moral sense. Ideas matter, it professed, and through deliberation, discourse, and determination, people could work their way
toward a more functionally adequate and subtle grasp of moral truths.
Leaders of this approach, most prominently Lawrence Kohlberg, posited developmental stage sequences that describe progressively more

sophisticated modes of thinking about challenging moral issues.[25] Extensive research documented these regular developmental transformations in individuals' patterns of thinking about difficult-to-resolve hypothetical dilemmas for both males and females in many different countries and social circumstances. And progress through the sequence was shown to be related to education and other forms of intellectual achievement, adding an uplifting sense of possibility to this enterprise.

Despite this appeal, cognitive-developmental theory came up short as a full scientific portrait of moral development. Most problematic was the inability of its moral judgment stage assessments to accomplish the foremost goal that the field holds for any psychological indexes: the reliable prediction of behavior. Greater degrees of moral sophistication as captured by Kohlberg's stages could predict moral choices in some kinds of situations, for example those that involve consideration of civil liberties or due process. But other choices, such as decisions to take part in a blood drive or help the poor, do not require especially sophisticated moral understanding and, not surprisingly, were not associated with moral judgment stage. Behaviors such as donating blood and helping the poor reflect morally important choices, so if the stages of moral judgment had little to say about them, the reach and explanatory power of this theory were clearly limited. Many adherents of the cognitive-developmental approach have concluded that Kohlberg's theory provided a compelling account of certain important dimensions of moral psychology but neglected other essential dimensions, especially the motivation to act.

In a domain of human life as multifaceted as morality, no single psychological process, such as moral judgment, can account for all the behavioral action. Any attempts to explain moral choices in the real world (as opposed, for example, to choices triggered by hypothetical dilemmas) must account for the key roles played by moral goals, habits, emotions, and other motivations.

This brings us to revisit the new science view, this time with an eye to what can be learned from it—despite the missteps we've noted. One important insight from this body of work is that much of everyday moral decision making is indeed experienced as immediate or intuitive.[26] It's true that when we resist doing harm to people who offend us, or when we rush to the aid of a loved one in peril, these moral responses often come quickly, seemingly automatically, with little conscious reflection.[27]

It's also true that an understanding of these common behaviors must take into account our biological and emotional dispositions. Evolutionary science and research in both animal and human behavior has yielded a consensus view that moral concerns such as fairness, empathy, and altruism are part of the biological makeup of our species. Although the specific implications of this consensus are subjects of intense debate and disagreement, acknowledgment of the degree to which moral concerns are deeply rooted in human nature constitutes an advance over earlier views in which people were understood to be primarily self-interested by nature, or, even more incorrectly, intrinsic blank slates.

What's more, the new science school makes a useful point by taking a broader view of the moral domain than did cognitive-developmental theory, which focused exclusively on problems in justice, human rights, and harm avoidance. These are central moral issues, to be sure, but they do not exhaust the entire moral universe. Writings by new science scholars build on the work of anthropologist Richard Shweder[28] to bring in moral concerns such as purity, loyalty, sanctity, community, and respect for authority, which are emphasized in many cultures around the world, as well as in significant parts of our own. This inclusive view is an important corrective to the too-narrow uses of the term *morality* in much prior scientific research, which focused solely on justice and individual rights rather than the full array of values represented in a comprehensive account of moral concerns.

Too often, scholars have examined issues that are important to them personally and written about those issues as if they stood for the entire human moral sense. In his most noted work, *The Righteous Mind,* Haidt makes the case that both progressive and conservative political positions have solid, although distinct, claims to moral legitimacy that grow out of different ways of framing morality's central issues (which are individual rights and the avoidance of harm for progressives, as opposed to authority, divinity, and community for conservatives).[29] In this view, the difference of moral perspective makes it difficult for people from the two political camps to connect, but Haidt urges that both groups give it a try. This message advances comprehensive moral science as well as mutual understanding among conflicting groups. It also introduced a welcome breadth, and a humane diversity, to the scientific purview of the moral sense.

But despite the work's breadth and humanistic intent, its core message is a relativistic one that leads nowhere in the end. In the new science view, because the definition of what counts as morality (and what's considered right or wrong) differs widely around the world, there is no way to adjudicate between conflicting perspectives. This, once again, leaves no possibility for rational moral choice. Yet people are called upon all the time to make good choices in their pursuit of an honorable life. In any society, we are beset by conflicting perspectives on the good and right thing to do. Is it pointless to think hard about what we believe and to make the best choices we can between the options presented to us (or even perhaps to come up with our own new options)?

Haidt's stated enemy is what he calls "moral monism," by which he means a morality with a single moral foundation—that is, one based on just one of the multiple moral worldviews he has described. Haidt writes, "Beware of anyone who insists that there is one true morality for all people, times, and places..."[30] Agreed, a monistic morality that excludes the concerns of any culture is limited and narrow-minded. But it is a serious mistake to conflate this kind of monism with an attempt to choose among conflicting perspectives through rational thought processes that reflect moral concerns shared among virtually all cultures—as in, for example, the universalistic perspective that created the celebrated United Nations Declaration of Universal Rights, which we discuss in Chapter 7 as a landmark achievement in moral choice. The vision of the Declaration's drafters—who themselves represented multiple diverse cultures—was pluralistic and inclusive. At the same time, the Declaration's drafters searched for and enshrined a set of ideals that cultures have in common as they focused on moral concerns that people everywhere consider essential.

Such universal moral concerns clearly exist; Haidt himself acknowledges this in his writings. For example, he approvingly quotes Isaiah Berlin's rejection of moral relativism. Berlin ridiculed relativistic sentiments such as "I am in favor of kindness, and you prefer concentration camps."[31] When Haidt himself advocates mutual understanding among conflicting persons, he promotes a universal standard of tolerance (the one moral value that relativists never seem to question).

But it's hard to find within Haidt's framework a means to resolve conflicts when the values of different cultural perspectives clash, as they often do internationally or even within a single multicultural nation. To resolve differences, we need reference points that establish universal moral priorities, as was the Declaration's brilliant accomplishment.

Many new science scholars, embedded in a relativistic worldview that denies the existence of universal moral truths, devise laboratory experiments that purport to show that human behavior is determined by forces other than individuals' moral beliefs, convictions, or ideals. Some of these studies locate the uncontrollable forces within the person (as in biology and emotions), and others locate them externally (as in situational pressures or cultural norms). But the deterministic message is the same, removing moral agency from the individual. The notion that people can be moved to action by ideals has no place in these brands of moral science.

In recent years, this perspective has come to dominate both scholarly and public perceptions of human nature. We believe that this debased view of human behavior not only has produced an incomplete and distorted science but has also contributed to the cynical tenor of our times. Social trust is eroded when we habitually assume the worst about people's motives, that their beliefs are only rationalizations, that they are not seeking truth but rather influence, control, and self-promotion.

Assuming that other people are driven by only irrational emotions, blind conformity, and personal self-interest seems to excuse our own passivity and selfishness. Moral psychologies that try only to demonstrate the limitations of everyday morality but ignore people's authentic search for truth and goodness capture only the weakest elements in our nature. If moral limitations and confusions are understood as essential features of our permanent moral selves instead of as potential areas for future growth, where is the basis for personal and educational aspiration?

In a recent incisive treatment of these matters, the psychologist John Gibbs[32] has written that the new science of morality is marred by a negative skew that is not only unwarranted but also defeatist and deleterious. A balanced and complete portrait of moral possibility, one that "encourages us to be and do better,"[33] requires an account of moral goodness as well as moral mediocrity. We turn in the next chapter to the consideration of humanity's better nature.

NOTES

1. See, for example, Sue Shellenbarger, "The Case for Lying to Yourself," *Wall Street Journal*, Aug. 2, 2012.
2. Jonathan Haidt, "The New Synthesis in Moral Psychology," *Science* 316 (2007): 998–1002.
3. Malcolm Gladwell, *Blink: The Power of Thinking Without Thinking* (New York: Back Bay Books/Little, Brown and Co., 2007).
4. Jonathan Haidt, "The Emotional Dog and its Rational Tail: A Social Intuitionist Approach to Moral Judgment," *Psychological Review* 108, no. 4 (October, 2001): 814–834.
5. John F. Kihlstrom, "Is there a "People are Stupid" School in Social Psychology? [Commentary on "Towards a Balanced Social Psychology: Causes, Consequences, and Cures for the Problem-Seeking Approach to Social Behavior and Cognition" by J. I. Krueger and D. C. Funder]," *Behavioral & Brain Sciences* 27, no. 3 (June, 2004): 348.
6. Shankar Vedantam, *The Hidden Brain: How our Unconscious Minds Elect Presidents, Control Markets, Wage Wars, and Save our Lives*, 1st ed. (New York: Spiegel & Grau, 2010), 4.
7. James Atlas, "The Amygdala Made Me Do It!" *New York Times*, sec. Sunday Review, The Opinion Pages, May 12, 2012.
8. Marc D. Hauser, *Moral Minds: The Nature of Right and Wrong*, 1st ed. (New York: Ecco, 2006), xvii.

9. Joshua Greene et al., "An fMRI Investigation of Emotional Engagement in Moral Judgment," *Science* 293 (September 14, 2001): 2105–2108.

10. Joshua Greene and Jonathan Haidt, "How (and Where) Does Moral Judgment Work?" *Trends in Cognitive Sciences* 6, no. 12 (December 1, 2002): 517–523.

11. Deena S. Weisberg et al., "The Seductive Allure of Neuroscience Explanations." *Journal of Cognitive Neuroscience* 20, no. 3 (March, 2008): 470–477.

12. Tyler Burge, "A Real Science of Mind," *New York Times*, sec. The Stone: Opinionator, December 19, 2010.

13. Stanley Milgram and Philip G. Zimbardo, *Obedience to Authority: An Experimental View* (London: Pinter & Martin, 2010).

14. Thomas Blass, "Obedience to Authority: Current Perspectives on the Milgram Paradigm," in *Reflections on the Stanford Prison Experiment: Genesis, Transformations, Consequences,* eds. Philip G. Zimbardo, Christina Maslach and Craig Haney (Mahwah, NJ: Lawrence Erlbaum Associates, 1999), 193–237.

15. Charles R. Plott and Vernon L. Smith, eds., *Handbook of Experimental Economics Results,* 1st ed., Vol. 1, 2008.

16. Serge-Christophe Kolm and J. Mercier Ythier, *Handbook of the Economics of Giving, Altruism and Reciprocity,* 1st ed., Vol. 23 (Amsterdam & London: Elsevier, 2006).

17. William Damon, "The Moral Development of Children," *Scientific American* 281, no. 2 (August, 1999): 72–88.

18. K. Anders Ericsson et al., eds., *Cambridge Handbook of Expertise and Expert Performance* (Cambridge, UK: Cambridge University Press, 2006).

19. Daniel Kahneman, *Thinking, Fast and Slow,* 1st ed. (New York: Farrar, Straus and Giroux, 2011).

20. Kahneman, *Thinking, Fast and Slow,* 48.

21. Jim Holt, "Two Brains Running," *The New York Times,* sec. Sunday Book Review, November 25, 2011.

22. Kahneman, *Thinking, Fast and Slow,* 46.

23. Jonathan Baron, *Thinking and Deciding,* 3rd ed. (Cambridge, UK, & New York: Cambridge University Press, 2000).

24. Thomas Gilovich, *How We Know What Isn't So: The Fallibility of Human Reason in Everyday Life* (New York: Free Press, 1991); Irving Lester Janis, *Groupthink: Psychological Studies of Policy Decisions and Fiascoes,* 2nd ed. (Boston: Houghton Mifflin, 1982); Jonathan Baron and Rex V. Brown, *Teaching Decision Making to Adolescents* (Hillsdale, NJ: L. Erlbaum Associates, 1991); Jonathan Baron, "Beliefs about Thinking," in *Informal Reasoning and Education,* eds. James F. Voss, David N. Perkins and Judith W. Segal (Hillsdale, NJ: L. Erlbaum Associates, 1991), 169–186.

25. Lawrence Kohlberg, "Stage and Sequence: The Cognitive-Developmental Approach to Socialization," in *Handbook of Socialization Theory and Research*, ed. David A. Goslin (Chicago, IL: Rand McNally, 1969).

26. Jonathan Haidt and Craig Joseph, "The Moral Mind: How 5 Sets of Innate Moral Intuitions Guide the Development of Many Culture-Specific Virtues, and Perhaps Even Modules," in *The Innate Mind*, eds. Peter Carruthers, Stephen Laurence and Stephen P. Stich, Vol. 3 (Oxford & New York: Oxford University Press, 2005), 367–391.

27. Philip Davidson and James Youniss, "Which Comes First, Morality Or Identity?" in *Handbook of Moral Behavior and Development, Volume 1: Theory*, ed. W. M. Kurtines & J. L. Gewirtz (Hillsdale, NJ: Lawrence Erlbaum Associates, 1991), 105–122.

28. Richard Shweder et al., "The "Big Three" of Morality (Autonomy, Community, and Divinity), and the "Big Three" Explanations of Suffering," in *Morality and Health*, eds. A. Brandt and P. Rozin (New York: Routledge, 1997), 119–169.

29. Jonathan Haidt, *The Righteous Mind: Why Good People Are Divided by Politics and Religion*, 1st ed. (New York: Pantheon Books, 2012).

30. Shweder et al., "The "Big Three" of Morality," 316.

31. Shweder et al., "The "Big Three" of Morality," 368.

32. John C. Gibbs, *Moral Development & Reality: Beyond the Theories of Kohlberg, Hoffman, and Haidt*, 3rd ed. (New York: Oxford University Press, 2014).

33. Gibbs, *Moral Development & Reality*, 34.

CHAPTER TWO

THE ACTIVE, IDEAL-SEEKING, MOTIVATED MORAL SELF

What moves us to make the important choices that shape our behavior and, ultimately, the directions of our lives? The answer will not be exactly the same for any two people. Every life takes its own direction, influenced by a unique pattern of decisions and circumstances. Yet we all share this characteristic: We are driven by many different kinds of motives, some self-serving and some aimed at purposes beyond the self. Mixed motives are a standard condition of human life.

It is often easiest to recognize the self-interested drives. Personal ambition, self-promotion, and self-protection are always highly visible. When financial markets tumble and soar, we can see fear and greed in the foreground. When a group of people feels attacked, we see the naked anger of a mob. Self-serving and self-protective motives are conspicuous parts of our everyday mental states, reflecting our common tendencies to experience the world through our own perspectives and "look out for number one."

Motives that are oriented toward self-protection or self-promotion do not engender a pretty picture of human nature. The ignoble tendencies evoked by the experiments we discussed in Chapter 1 revealed the subjects' self-protective or self-serving desires. We know from these studies—as well as from any glance at the daily news—that at times many people will succumb to dishonorable situational pressures, obey the dictates of brutal authorities, give in to antisocial temptations, behave in accord with unjust cultural norms, grasp greedily for personal advantage, and act dishonestly, all in order to protect themselves or advance their own interests. What's more, people some-times allow their choices to be dictated by irrational feelings or forces, even when they know better. The present-day skepticism about moral motives that we discussed in Chapter 1 has many grains of truth behind it: The self-serving and nonrational aspects of human nature exist, and they should not be denied. It's understandable that scientists and media commentators who want to be tough-minded in their work make a point to emphasize the dark side of human behavior.

The research we described in Chapter 1 describes these common-place, lower-quality types of moral functioning. In attempting to do this, new science investigators claim that they are simply reporting what *is*, not prescribing what *should* be. Yet a descriptive account is misleading if it's one-sided. Claiming that people are driven *only* by selfish motives and forces beyond their conscious control mischarac-terizes the greater part of the human moral sense.

In addition to selfish, venal, and mindless desires, people also can be moved by a concern for others, a wish to be good, and a desire to contribute something positive to the world beyond the self. Just as people can be self-serving and uncaring, they also can feel empathy, a desire for fairness, loyalty to others, and unforced respect for rules and authority. In light of the complex reality of mixed motives, the "new science" view does not do a credible job of describing what *is*, as straightforward as that goal may seem to be. An exclusive focus on moral responses that are mediocre, confused, and self-serving does not include the full range of what *is*, even if, in its exaggerated way, it may illuminate one segment of that range.

Also, there's another point here—an essential philosophy-of-science point—regarding what's required for a valid scientific account of human morality. A moral psychology cannot entirely avoid questions of what *should* be (questions that philosophers call *prescriptive* or *nor-mative*). Prescriptive statements always sneak in to descriptions of the moral sense, even if authors fail to recognize them. Most social scien-tists, especially those who study human development, realize this and acknowledge the impossibility of completely value-neutral social sci-ence. Any study of development must attempt to describe progressively more mature or advanced, not just different, approaches to a domain of functioning. This is because observed shifts in behavior over time may represent growth or they may simply represent changes with no implication of developmental advance—such as shifts in one's food or clothing tastes. Indeed, changes that take place over time may even represent a regression from more to less advanced functioning.

The question of whether a given change represents an advance, a nondevelopmental change, or a regression must be addressed conceptually, by analyzing behavior according to its functionality and adaptiveness within the domain being studied. This kind of analysis brings in *values* to determine what is most functional and most adaptive, and it will be an analysis that relies on philosophical argumentation rather than empirical validation. In this way, any analysis of moral development must go beyond a descriptive account of what *is*: it cannot avoid the evaluative question of the relative *quality* (adaptiveness or functionality) of the observed behavioral patterns.

For these and other reasons, research on moral psychology can't avoid prescriptive or normative questions—questions about what it means to be more morally mature, and questions about what kinds of moral responses are of higher quality and ought to be supported and nurtured. After all, why is the field of moral psychology important? One reason certainly is because we want to understand what contributes to positive morality—honesty, fairness, compassion, respect, integrity, and the like—in order to encourage it. Another is that we wish to understand negative moral behavior—cruelty, injustice, corruption—in order to discourage it. Both goals require distinguishing the positive from the negative and the immature from the mature, distinctions that require values.[1]

Another issue that bears on the soundness of a moral psychology is the concept of *moral agency*. The new science's vision of people dragged around by internal or external forces beyond their control removes agency from the individual. It assumes that people are passive players in the moral universe. In this sense, the new science vision throws into doubt the entire concept of moral responsibility. How can people be responsible for their actions if they have no conscious control over them? How can people be held accountable for something they're preprogrammed (by biology or culture) to do?

These overarching conceptual points are central to our reasons for writing this book. Our aim is to present a fuller and more accurate view of the nature of human moral functioning. Three assumptions are foundational for this aim:

(1) A comprehensive moral psychology must include the full range of moral possibilities—not just the human frailties that are all too familiar, but ordinary and exceptional moral goodness as well.
(2) The study of moral development requires an evaluative stance.
(3) People are active in the choices they make, and the notion of moral responsibility necessarily implies moral agency.

One direct implication of these assumptions is that a moral psychology must examine moral *virtue*, not just problematic moral responses such as those documented by the new science school, experimental social psychologists, and behavioral economists. This means studying a wider range of people than college students and other similar populations. It means including people who have demonstrated genuine moral commitment over time and who, as a result, have performed admirable actions often in their lives. Of course, selecting such people for a study itself requires a prescriptive stance, the assumption that some people can be chosen to represent high degrees of moral virtue. And to be considered especially admirable, the actions of such people must demonstrate agency: What may seem to be virtuous acts would still not be especially admirable if caused entirely by factors beyond the control of the persons carrying them out.

This chapter introduces the people who were the subjects of the case studies that inform this book. We use case studies because we believe they are essential for capturing the moral sense as it plays out in the context of complex, whole lives. Case studies contrast sharply with experimental studies, in which very narrow slices of people's behavior are observed in artificial settings, uninformed by knowledge of the broader contexts of their lives. In selecting subjects for our case studies, we have looked for people whose lives illustrate a manner of behaving that is impossible to reconcile with a cynical, reductionist view in which people are understood as pawns of unconscious impulses or situational contingencies.

Why study people like this? The lives of people who are generally recognized as morally exceptional show what morality can be, what educators can aspire to for their students, and what individuals can work toward in their own aspirations toward morally fulfilled lives. The qualities evident in moral leaders and other moral exemplars are present to some degree in almost everyone. A moral psychology that recognizes this is essential for inspiring and supporting people's efforts to strengthen those qualities. Observing positive moral qualities acted out in the dramatic form of an exemplary life can help define the more modest variants of these same qualities as they occur in all of our lives.

For these reasons, we have found it helpful to examine the lives of people who have gone farther than most in developing the capacity to guide their important choices through their moral ideals. This kind of examination is known as *exemplar research* because it refers to the stories of extraordinary people as examples of what's possible in human development.

In this book, we provide a detailed account of how moral choices can be shaped through conviction, based on our analyses of the words, deeds, and life histories of six men and women widely known for moral leadership during the twentieth century. We believe that the insights generated by a close look at the lives of these leaders apply in numerous ways to anyone's quest for a moral life. We hope the stories we tell here will help convince readers that such a quest is worth pursuing.

JANE ADDAMS

When Jane Addams won the Nobel Peace Prize in 1931, she was known the world over for her pioneering social reform efforts at a time when the United States was undergoing massive industrialization and struggling to incorporate huge numbers of immigrants. She was a leader in campaigns to improve conditions for workers, protect free speech and other civil liberties, secure the rights of women, and foster world peace.

Addams was a central figure in the great wave of social reforms that transformed American life during the first decades of the twentieth century, a period that became known as the Progressive Era. She was co-founder of the most influential settlement house in American history, Hull House, and was also involved in the founding of the National Association for the Advancement of Colored People, the American Civil Liberties Union, and the Women's International League for Peace and Freedom. Addams was a prolific writer, especially in the emerging field of applied sociology, and her work influenced many prominent intellectuals of her time, including John Dewey, the great educational philosopher.

In the absence of the social reforms that Addams campaigned for, modern life would be unrecognizable (and in many ways unbearable). Addams' efforts helped establish voting rights for women, safe building codes, high standards of public health, anticorruption measures for municipal governments, and laws eliminating child-labor. Although she was unable to prevent U.S. involvement in World War I (despite her prominent international efforts), she worked to protect the rights of conscientious objectors in that war, and she was centrally involved in programs to supply American troops overseas with food and feed the starving civilian populations in Allied and neutral countries. After the war, she continued her work to prevent hunger and extended it to include civilians in Germany, her country's defeated enemy. During all this activity, Addams articulated original and compelling visions of democracy, visions which remain vital for our twenty-first-century society.

No one can deny that Jane Addams was one of modern history's powerful moral leaders, yet early in life she did not seem a likely candidate for such a role. In 1885, at age twenty-five, she was a wealthy but unhappy young woman battling severe depression, morally earnest but overcome by crippling self-criticism and doubt. Long plagued with curvature of the spine and other health problems, she felt both physically and emotionally inadequate. Adding to her deep-seated insecurity, her beloved father, her main source of support since the early death of her mother, suddenly died. A man of strong religious and moral convictions, John Addams had taken part in the Underground Railroad and was friends with Abraham Lincoln. His social status, wealth, and moral seriousness made a huge impression on everyone he knew, not least his young daughter. He was an outsized figure in Jane Addams' life.

After her irreplaceable father died, Jane saw no way out of her malaise. The restrictive culture of her day offered no help, discouraging women of her class from pursuing careers or social causes beyond simple charity work. She was always a deeply serious girl, longing to do something worthwhile with her life. But now, overcome with grief, Jane despaired of ever finding something to which she could really commit herself. "How purposeless and without ambition I am!" she complained to a close friend at the time.[2]

In light of these discouraging beginnings, what happened next in Addams' life is nothing short of astonishing. Within five years, Addams had founded Hull House, which quickly became an internationally-recognized model for a new and more enlightened way to address the needs of the economically disadvantaged. Founded in one of Chicago's poorest neighborhoods, Hull House established a setting where middle-class volunteers lived alongside low-income immigrants and shared knowledge and culture with one another. Hull House offered a revolutionary mode of delivering social services, based on the creation of a democratic community that broke through class, gender, and ethnic boundaries to build a culture of universal humanity. Addams understood these efforts at community building as an experiment in developing an essential aspect of a flourishing democracy. The many organizations that she later helped create and lead also were most centrally means for pursuing a new vision of democratic ideals.

How did a young woman with a dreary litany of physical and mental ailments turn into a forceful national and international moral leader in an era when few women were taken seriously outside the home?

One thing that the young Jane Addams had going for her was a love of ideas. While a student, she devoured books about moral heroism, women's history, religion, and moral philosophy, as well as Charles Dickens' vividly humane portrayals of society's outcasts. She acquired from Dickens her lasting desire to live among the poor and find ways to relieve their suffering. As a young adult, Addams cast about for ways to overcome her sense of failure by finding some way to live her ideals. After a trip to Europe in which she was shocked by the wretchedness of urban poverty and inspired by records of early Christians' joyous message of love and human fellowship, she read two books by the Russian aristocrat Leo Tolstoy, who had recently renounced his material possessions and worldly life as a famous novelist to become a devout Christian. In his books *My Religion* and *What to Do*, the middle-aged Tolstoy wrote that he now considered his prior existence to have been a moral failure and described how he had completely reshaped his life to live by the Christian aspiration to relieve the suffering of the poor. Addams wrote that these books changed her life forever, showing that it was possible to make a radical change, since Tolstoy had set aside the privileges of class and the social conventions and roles that had defined his previous life to organize instead around his most deeply held ideals. This is exactly what she longed to do.

Soon after, when Jane read a magazine article describing a new approach to urban poverty in a settlement house in London called Toynbee Hall, she knew she had found her purpose and direction. This democratic Christian community, in which well-educated people lived among the poor and worked to enhance the lives of the poor and privileged alike, was the master idea that would lead her to the fruitful pathway that had thus far eluded her.

Addams had already been planning another trip to Europe with two friends, and she added Toynbee Hall to their itinerary. A budding "social Christian" movement in Britain had spawned the idea of the settlement house, in which the privileged would live with the poor as social equals, for the mutual learning and benefit of both. The institution embodying this radical new idea was named for the rambling, Gothic-style London building in which it had taken shape.

Addams was enthralled, describing Toynbee Hall as "a community of University men who...have their recreation clubs and society all among the poor people, yet in the same style in which they would live in their own circle. It is so free of 'professional doing-good', so unaffectedly sincere and so productive of good results in its classes and libraries that it seems perfectly ideal."[3] She saw in Toynbee Hall a modern realization of the early Christians' dream of people from all walks of life working together for the good of all.

Addams confessed her dream of starting a settlement house at home to her friend and traveling companion, Ellen Gates Starr, who was enthusiastic about joining Jane in this unusual and ambitious project. Less than a year later, Jane moved to Chicago to join Ellen, and the two of them founded Hull House. The Nobel Prize statement in honor of Addams' life's work described this remarkable initiative:

> Miss Addams and Miss Starr made speeches about the needs of the neighborhood, raised money, convinced young women of well-to-do families to help, took care of children, nursed the sick, listened to outpourings from troubled people. By its second year of existence, Hull-House was host to two thousand people every week. There were kindergarten classes in the morning, club meetings for older children in the afternoon, and for adults in the evening more clubs or courses in what became virtually a night school. The first facility added to Hull-House was an art gallery, the second a public kitchen; then came a coffee house, a gymnasium, a swimming pool, a cooperative boarding club for girls, a book bindery, an art studio, a music school, a drama group, a circulating library, an employment bureau, a labor museum.[4]

How can we understand the passion, commitment, creativity, and resourcefulness that made such an achievement possible? There is no simple answer to what motivated Addams to turn her life to this and other social causes, or that can account for her brilliant success. No doubt she was strongly influenced by growing up in a family in which moral righteousness and social contribution were central values. The traumatic loss of both parents when Jane was still young likely left its mark on her as well. Perhaps due to these influences, perhaps due to some genetically based temperamental disposition, or perhaps due to a combination of the two in addition to other factors such as her own growing social understanding, Jane was intensely empathic, suffering along with those around her and relieved from that suffering only by the hope that she could make a difference.

Yet these characteristics and factors did not by themselves determine the course that Jane Addams' life took. If one had tried to predict where Jane would end up, a better bet would have been a life of affluent religiosity and charity work, within the conventional patterns for women's lives at the time (and probably accompanied by the kind of moral self-righteousness that was so evident in her father). But Jane's strong desire for a life of meaning was accompanied by a need for freedom and a belief in the importance of independent thinking. She questioned and eventually freed herself from conventional expectations just as she questioned and transcended some of her family's moral teachings and ideals.

Jane's empathy was lifelong, but the form it took evolved in response to ideas she encountered and ideas she and her collaborators created. She came to question the ideals of charity and benevolence she had learned at home, replacing them with a more democratic conception of social progress. In this and other ways, her empathy was informed and changed by her reflection and conceptual sophistication yet remained authentically emotional in nature. Similarly, Jane questioned her family's tradition of moral self-righteousness, rethought its significance, and then fought her own tendency toward it for the rest of her life.

Jane Addams' life illustrates the ways that individuals can choose the social contexts in which they live and develop. Imagine how different her life would have been if she had given in to the pressure to marry one of her suitors and settle into the life of a well-to-do matron. But instead, Addams chose to live and work in settings that daily pushed the boundaries of social change and the meaning of democracy and citizenship at every level. Addams was herself aware of the implications of this active selection of life contexts: "We are under a moral obligation in choosing our experiences, since the result of those experiences must ultimately determine our understanding of life. We determine our ideals by our daily actions and decisions."[5] And, as her life illustrates so well, those ideals then shape decisions, emotions, impulses, and the meaning and nature of the self.

For Addams, ideas and action were inseparable and mutually influential. Her ideas informed and motivated her work and then developed more fully as she and her colleagues reflected together about how their initial ideas had played out in action. In this way, their work in the world, including the creation and leadership of organizations, was part and parcel of the ideals themselves.

Indeed, the articulation of this process was one of Addams' original contributions to the development of American democracy. Through the breadth, originality, and visibility of her work, and through the many papers and books she wrote reflecting on that work and drawing out its lessons, Jane Addams did more than break free of the cultures of her family and her time and place: She changed the nature of modern life, including the conditions of work, urban living, gender roles, international relations, civil rights, and civil liberties—and in so doing, she transformed the values, expectations, and practices of the culture.

NELSON MANDELA

At the other end of the twentieth century, Nelson Mandela dedicated most of his adult life to the fight against the brutal regime of apartheid in South Africa. As a result of his activism in this cause, Mandela spent twenty-seven years in prison. Amazingly, he managed to use this decades-long stretch in prison to educate himself and other inmates, sharpen his capacities as a moral and political leader, and work successfully toward the overthrow of the apartheid regime.

When Mandela was eventually released, he already had a well-developed political power base that allowed him to step into the leadership of the dominant black African party, the African National Congress (ANC). He also emerged from prison with an astonishing lack of bitterness and a scrupulously constructive approach to dealing with South African whites, both of which were essential to his capacity to bring unity to the country. Mandela was the one person who could deal with the country's deeply, and violently, divided factions, and he was elected the first black president of South Africa. His steady leadership brought the country into the postapartheid era as one of Africa's leading nations.

Although Mandela was adored at home and abroad, he refused a second term, believing more in the power of democracy than in one man's charismatic leadership. After he stepped down, Mandela continued to work on important issues facing his country and continent, most notably racial unity and harmony and the fight against AIDS, which had begun ravaging all of Africa. Mandela radiated warmth and humility as well as strength; long after he retired from the presidency, he remained one of the most admired and beloved men in the world. He received the Nobel Peace Prize and countless other awards. Mandela is celebrated worldwide as one of history's great moral leaders.

Based on Mandela's almost saintly embrace of forgiveness and reconciliation, his deep wisdom, charming humor, and radiant smile, many people imagine him as a person of sweet and peaceful temperament, unaware of the fiery toughness and overpowering strength that were also characteristic of the man. As a teenager and young man, Nelson was a proud, fearless, often angry rebel. His courage crossed over into recklessness on many occasions. He was impulsive and willing to risk everything. Many times the young Mandela's fiery nature got him and others into serious trouble.

As a child, Nelson progressed well through mission schooling and, at the age of nineteen, was given the privilege of beginning college-level studies at the South African Native College at Fort Hare. Graduation from this elite institution would ensure success in any career open to black Africans.

After an academically successful start at Fort Hare, Nelson joined in a protest over a relatively trivial issue and refused to back down, even when his classmates did. He was threatened with permanent expulsion and still stubbornly resisted. Nelson was given the summer to think over the matter. But during that summer, a fight with his guardian combined with his troubles at Fort Hare to spur him to run away to Johannesburg, abandoning forever the privilege he would have enjoyed if he had stayed to graduate from Fort Hare.

Without money or credentials, Mandela took a job as a night watchman in a mine. But he was resourceful despite his recklessness, and he managed to get support to enter a law practice as a clerk and study through correspondence courses to finish his university degree and training in law. Later, as Mandela built his own law practice, he was known for his elegant dress, his way with women, his love of boxing, and his self-confidence, even arrogance, in court. Although a skilled litigator, Mandela was much more interested in politics than in responsibly building a business, and his legal practice never flourished financially. He was acutely attuned to and completely intolerant of injustice and was willing to throw over his livelihood, his safety, and eventually his life to pursue that purpose.

Over time, Mandela was drawn more fully into the political struggle against white domination. He quickly assumed leadership positions in the ANC, advocating confrontation, and even the use of violence, against the ruthless tactics used by the increasingly oppressive regime. This stance, along with his visibility as a powerful leader of the resistance to white rule, led to harassment, banning, arrests, and charges of treason against Mandela. He responded defiantly, and, at the age of forty-three, was convicted of conspiracy and began a life prison sentence. He remained in prison until international pressure led to his release at the age of seventy. Most of his twenty-seven years in prison were spent at hard labor under harsh conditions at the notorious Robben Island prison camp.

Mandela's support for sabotage and, as a last resort, armed resistance was—and still is—controversial, but it was clearly based on principle. At the time of his sentencing, Mandela made the following famous statement:

During my lifetime I have dedicated myself to the struggle of the African people. I have fought against white domination, and I have fought against black domination. I have cherished the ideal of a democratic and free society in which all persons live together in harmony and with equal opportunities. It is an ideal which I hope to live for and to achieve. But if need be, it is an ideal for which I am prepared to die.[6]

Despite some of the most extreme situational pressures imaginable, Mandela found ways at every period of his imprisonment, often at the risk of his life, to continue working toward greater justice for the African people. Through his fearless and relentless determination, he even managed to gain significant national and international political power while still in prison. In the last several years of imprisonment, Mandela was offered release, but only under conditions that he believed would undermine his ability to achieve his democratic goals. Time and again, he refused release under those conditions, remaining in prison with no assurance that he would ever be freed. Throughout this long ordeal, Mandela controlled his anger and resisted the warders' efforts at manipulation in order to keep advancing his humanitarian and political goals.

Mandela thus survived unbowed, with will and purpose intact, decades of hostile and unjust confinement. But once released, he made a determination to forgive those responsible in order to help create greater harmony in a deeply divided country. After his release from prison, Mandela showed an astonishing, almost miraculous, generosity of spirit and absence of bitterness, which infused his presidency and shaped his responses to the country's warring constituencies.

Early in his presidency, that spirit of hope and conciliation was the source of truly exceptional moral creativity. In the face of horrific offenses against his people, Mandela and his collaborator Bishop Desmond Tutu instituted a strategy for national healing that was original, counterintuitive, risky, and controversial—the Truth and Reconciliation Commission (TRC). The TRC departed radically from the Nuremburg model that the Allies used to prosecute Nazi war crimes after World War II. Its purpose was to discover and reveal past wrongdoing on all sides. To this end, the forum was opened to accused and accusers alike, and amnesty was liberally used to elicit frank confessions.

Although its de-emphasis on criminal prosecutions was under-standably controversial among apartheid's victims and their fami-lies, the TRC was universally given credit for bringing out the full scope of human rights violations that had occurred under previous regimes. It led to confessions, apologies, and statements of regret by perpetrators that made possible the beginnings of productive dia-logues among previous opponents, a large step toward national heal-ing and the eventual national unity that many thought impossible in South Africa.

Another telling illustration of the way Mandela was able to draw creatively on his ideal of forgiveness was his avid but unlikely enthusi-asm for the country's rugby team. In the face of opposition and cries of betrayal from his own supporters, Mandela threw the blessings of his government behind South Africa's national rugby team, long a hated symbol of white privilege among the black and colored com-munities. He invested his own time and political capital to build the team's morale and tried to mobilize the country to root for the team's victory in the Rugby World Cup. Few understood what Mandela was doing: His own bewildered staff counseled him against it. But it worked. As time passed, everyone could see that he had created a strategy for uniting a society that had seemed hopelessly fractured. On a moral level, his leadership inspired the country to rise above its still-deep enmities; on a practical and political level, Mandela strengthened his own mandate and stabilized his society. His actions had effectively made the point that he was not the president of black South Africa; rather, he was president of the whole country, black and white alike.

Once again, there are many psychological theories, from the cul-tural to the biological, that could be used to explain Mandela's achievements. It is clear that Mandela's complicated cultural history and distinctive temperament are part of the mix that made possible his exceptional moral leadership. But such psychological theories leave off the table the most decisive factors that shape the moral choices of people like Nelson Mandela: the ideals and convictions that these people find worthy of their commitment.

Mandela drew some of these ideals from his upbringing in tribal Africa: "Sometimes my aunt [would tell] us stories, legends, myths, fables which have come down from countless generations, and all of which tended to stimulate the imagination and contained some valuable moral lesson."[7] He loved stories about native freedom fighters of earlier times, and these tales fed his growing sense that he would not let whites or anyone else in power undermine his dignity or freedom.

Other memorable stories came from respected teachers and clergymen. He used the lesson from this one as a guide throughout his life:

> He once gave a sermon about a man whose house was haunted by evil spirits. He did everything to drive them out, but he failed. Then he decided to leave his *kraal* [a rural settlement of huts and houses], packed all his things on a wagon and started driving away to settle elsewhere. Along the way, he met a friend and the friend asked, "*Where* are you going?" Before he answered, a voice came out of the wagon, "We are trekking, we are leaving our *kraal*." It was one of the evil spirits! He thought he was leaving them behind, but he actually came along with them. And he says, the moral was "*Don't* run away from your problems; *face* them! Because *if you don't deal with them*, they will *always* be with you. *Deal* with a problem which arises; face it courageously." That was the moral. I never forgot that.[8]

Clearly, Mandela incorporated images and themes from cultural teachings into his developing ideals. But he also actively questioned many of the dominant assumptions he encountered. This habit of questioning the status quo and his genius in imagining creative alternatives were at least as important as the lessons his eager receptiveness led him to absorb. Mandela questioned the inevitability of white subjugation of his race. He questioned and defied prevailing assumptions of black African inferiority. He questioned his people's powerlessness under the apartheid regime and even his own powerlessness as an inmate in the country's most brutal prison. Most surprisingly, he questioned the prevailing anger and desire for revenge coming from his own community after his release from prison and the fall of apartheid.

Likewise, Mandela's dominant, commanding demeanor and his impulse of resistance to authority also played important roles in making him the successful freedom fighter and leader he became. But Mandela chose to control and carefully channel these impulses in the service of his ideals of universal human dignity, freedom, and democracy. If he hadn't done that, he probably still would have resisted apartheid, but he would have been unable to negotiate successfully with more reasonable prison warders, and later with apartheid's leaders, as he did so successfully. And surely he would not have been able to lead the country toward unity and relative harmony.

In addition to culture and biology, many psychologists writing about morality attribute almost irresistible power to situational incentives and pressures. Unlike Jane Addams, Mandela could not choose the settings he lived in or the people who surrounded him for a large part of his life. But Mandela's laser focus on his political and moral goals and his fierce commitment to ideals of freedom, dignity, and justice allowed him to gain an astonishing degree of control over even the strongest imaginable situational pressures.

Jane Addams ushered in the twentieth century with her influential new ideas about democracy and her progressive zeal. Nelson Mandela drew its closing curtains with his powerful insistence on justice and his great-hearted spirit of forgiveness. In the years between these two, other moral leaders fought against the powerful tyrannies that had captured much of the world, campaigned for world peace and social justice, worked to alleviate poverty and promote public health, and built institutions that advanced all of these moral causes. Adding to our examinations of Jane Addams and Nelson Mandela, we selected four midtwentieth century leaders to represent a variety of influential moral approaches to major societal problems.

DAG HAMMARSKJÖLD

As the second secretary-general of the United Nations, Dag Hammarskjöld was the moving force behind the UN during its formative years. He interpreted the groundbreaking organization's charter to staff, volunteers, and constituents and created mechanisms for pursuing the goals articulated in the charter: creating a firmer foundation of international order and promoting peace, freedom, equality and justice among nations. Hammarskjöld created the UN Emergency Force, gave new significance to the UN's role in helping economically underdeveloped and newly independent countries, organized scientific conferences on environmental issues and the peaceful uses of atomic energy, and gained the release of American pilots imprisoned by China. He negotiated crises in hot spots around the world, including Palestine, the Suez Canal, Lebanon and Jordan, Hungary, Cambodia, Thailand, and Laos.

Hammarskjöld died in the crash of a small plane while trying to negotiate a ceasefire among warring factions in the Congo. Despite his early death, Hammarskjöld's influence on the culture, structure, and operation of the UN and on the way international conflicts are settled lives on. U. S. President John F. Kennedy called this Swedish civil servant and diplomat the greatest statesman of the century. He was posthumously awarded the Nobel Peace Prize, one of only four persons ever to receive that honor.

Like several of the leaders in our study—indeed, like many self-reflective people in the modern world—Hammarskjöld struggled with a personal search for meaning during his early adulthood. He was a brilliant student who became a successful banking executive and advisor on economic and foreign policy to the Swedish government. His government work was nonpartisan, marked by objectivity and technical expertise. During this period, he often despaired of finding a greater purpose in the work that he did so competently. He wrote in a diary, "Never let success hide its emptiness from you..."[9] and he reported feeling strongly tempted to remove himself from anything productive in the world.

The opportunity for Hammarskjöld to lead the United Nations during its formative early years arose unexpectedly. It was said that he was selected because he was one of the only diplomats that the United States and the Soviet Union could agree on—but this was the case only because he had done so little publicly that his worldview was largely unknown. This opportunity opened a new path to purpose for Hammarskjöld. His self-ruminations began to take a more positive direction. As he later recalled (in a way that reflected his sense that there were transcendent influences at work), "I don't know Who— or what—put the question, I don't know when it was put. I don't even remember answering. But at some moment I did answer Yes to Someone—or Something—and from that hour I was certain that existence is meaningful and that, therefore, my life, in self-surrender, had a goal."[10]

Once Dag Hammarskjöld found his purpose leading the pioneering organization in its mission to advance world peace and human welfare, his despair about the meaninglessness of life gave way, and his constant and debilitating self-criticism was reduced. The experience as secretary-general of the UN had a tremendous influence on his development. But the reciprocal was also true: Hammarskjöld created the shape of the UN and the direction it has taken ever since. His life illustrates a comment attributed to the sociologist Robert Merton— that institutions powerfully affect the individuals who live or work within them, but it is just as important to recognize that institutions are themselves created by individuals, whose choices determine the institutional conditions that then shape the people they touch.

Through a deep belief in the possibilities of international cooperation, Hammarskjöld imagined and implemented an ambitious vision of what the UN could accomplish. But he was no dreamer. People who knew him said that he was as disappointed by shallow optimism as by cynicism. He brought to his leadership role an abiding but nondoctrinal spirituality, a deep moral sense, and exceptional sophistication about the realities the UN had to negotiate. All of this was grounded in and driven by ideals of world peace, freedom, and equality.

Among Hammarskjöld's many achievements was a sustained and explicit effort to create a culture of integrity and meaning within the organization he led. He spoke often to the staff and other constituents about the values the institution stands for and how the behavior of all, including its leader, could best be informed by those values. Chief among these values was truth as both a public and private virtue: He believed that good ideas depended on a commitment to rigorous frankness with oneself and others. To change the world, Hammarskjöld said, a person needs to look squarely, clearly, and honestly at what *is*, with full awareness of the limits of human understanding. He sought absolute honesty about his own limitations, errors, and failings, aligning his personal quest with the value of impartiality in negotiating among nations' competing interests and claims. He conveyed to everyone involved with the UN the essential place of impartiality in its credibility and effectiveness. He also wrote and spoke frequently about how important impartiality and truthfulness are for the functioning of any democratic society.

Hammarskjöld was widely known for his ability to be open-minded and consider many perspectives on issues, through many different cultural lenses, without losing hold on overriding principles. And he reinforced his commitment to inner truthfulness with a conscious sense of the transcendent. In this, he was a devotee of Christian mysticism and spiritual principles that cut across the many religions of the world. These beliefs led him to create a beautiful meditation room at the UN, with all its materials and symbols carefully designed to represent the institution's ideals and aspirations. The meditation room remains a place where the world's most powerful men and women can examine their crucial decisions in a spirit of repose and contemplation.

ABRAHAM JOSHUA HESCHEL

Abraham Heschel was born in 1907, descended from a line of famous rabbis. He grew up in Poland and was an extremely devout child, assiduously studying Jewish texts and trying to live in perfect conformity with Jewish law. Heschel was studying and teaching in Germany when Hitler came to power. Like other Polish Jews, he was deported from Germany back to Poland and, seeing the horrors that Hitler was already perpetrating, he escaped from Poland just six weeks before the Nazi invasion of his country. Heschel made his way to the United States and eventually to a faculty position at the Jewish Theological Seminary in New York.

During his long career at JTS, a Conservative seminary, Heschel became one of the leading Jewish theologians of the twentieth century. His work drew from several traditions, cultures, and scholarly fields, including German-Jewish thought, Hasidism, and American Jewish life. Building on these rich traditions, Heschel developed an approach to Jewish spirituality that was creative, fresh, and compelling. Much of his life was centered on articulating his evolving understanding of the nature of God and humanity's relationship with God or the sacred.

Heschel viewed the teachings of the Hebrew prophets as clarion calls for social action in the world, and he threw himself into the major issues of his time. He mobilized the world Jewish community against the Soviet Union's mistreatment of Jews and was active for years in the movement to end the U.S. war in Vietnam. Heschel also fought for black civil rights in the United States, marching with Martin Luther King Jr. in Selma and other landmark civil rights demonstrations. Lobbying fellow religious leaders for their support of the civil rights cause, Heschel made the following public statement, later encapsulated in a famous and compelling telegram to President John F. Kennedy: "We forfeit the right to worship God as long as we continue to humiliate Negroes. Our churches and synagogues have failed; they must repent. I ask religious leaders to call for national repentance and personal sacrifice...I propose that you, Mr. President, declare a state of moral emergency... *The hour calls for moral grandeur and spiritual audacity.*"[11]

Heschel's approach to Conservative Judaism and Jewish education brought together in a new way a belief in a transcendent sense of the divine or sacred, realized through direct connections with God; religious experiences of awe, which he referred to as *radical amazement*; and a call to social action, the unrelenting pursuit of justice. For the Conservative Jewish academic context that Heschel was operating in at the time—a context defined by highly analytical and abstract approaches to religious life—this understanding of God and spirituality was far outside the mainstream and alienated powerful colleagues at JTS and beyond. Heschel's political activity was also unusual within

Conservative Judaism, and he was severely criticized for it by his colleagues and by national Jewish organizations.

Heschel was a constant critic of the status quo in Judaism and in other religions and in societies ranging from the United States to the Soviet Union. He was constantly seeing how things could and should be different and calling people to account. As his daughter Susannah Heschel noted, "Sometimes organizations mistakenly thought they were inviting a gentle, meek rabbi to speak to them and then heard a powerful and charismatic challenge to their complacency."[12] But Heschel's message was not a negative one. Through his original perspective, expressed in his prolific writing, his highly visible speaking engagements, his dramatic political action, and his life as a devout practitioner of a vibrant although traditional Judaism, Heschel presented creative and inspiring alternatives to the status quo.

Heschel's critiques of contemporary Jewish practice and education were often eloquent, almost poetic, expressions of the need to keep religious ritual fresh and vital and reflections on how humanity can best live in the light of God. As Susannah Heschel remarked, "My father's genius was to say the unusual and unexpected and yet to have what he said resonate deeply with his listeners."[13] This resonance reached many Protestants and Catholics as well as Jews, and his close friends included the celebrated Christian theologians Reinhold Niebuhr and Thomas Merton.

In the Vatican, where Heschel served as an official spokesperson for American Jewish organizations, he worked with others to persuade the Catholic Church to eliminate passages in its liturgy that demeaned the Jews and to stop trying to convert Jews to Christianity. Despite the criticism he received and the evident lack of appreciation for his work by the JTS leadership, Heschel remained steadfast in his support for spiritual truth as he saw it, the universal sacredness of life, and human rights. He felt very intensely the suffering and injustice of the troubled world and spoke of his deep anxiety about "the madness that has taken over so-called normal society" as it massacred innocent women and children in Vietnam and Cambodia. But he believed it

was possible to find "meaning beyond absurdity"[14] and worked hard
to convey this hope for meaning to others, especially to young people.

DIETRICH BONHOEFFER

Dietrich Bonhoeffer began his adult life as a brilliant, charismatic
Lutheran pastor in pre-World War II Germany. He was entirely
immersed in his life's mission—deepening his own understanding of
Christian theology and teachings, writing to articulate his own (ultimately very influential) perspective on theological questions, leading
religious congregations, providing religious education for children and
for young men training for the ministry, and above all, trying to live in
"imitation of Christ." Bonhoeffer was a natural leader and, like Jane
Addams, exceptionally talented at creating communities of people
working together to realize their shared ideals.

In ordinary times, this pastoral and theological work in devotion
to Christian ideals would probably have fully defined Bonhoeffer's life
mission. But the times were anything but ordinary, and before long
Bonhoeffer's sense of Christian purpose expanded to include resistance to Nazism. That resistance and its results for him came to define
his place in history.

Bonhoeffer saw immediately the evil in Hitler's horrifying agenda,
even before Hitler came to power in a formal sense. As a German
clergyman, Bonhoeffer felt a responsibility to mobilize the churches to
resist Hitler's continued rise to power and the Nazis' genocidal campaign against Jews, the mentally retarded, and others. He was horrified
to see both Protestant and Catholic Churches in Germany capitulate
and become complicit in Hitler's plans, and he worked with others
to establish a bulwark of churches, called collectively the Confessing
Church, that would oppose the compromises the church establishment
had made.

Seeing over time that this resistance could not stop Hitler, and after
much agonizing inner appraisal, Bonhoeffer began to cooperate with
conspiracies to remove Hitler from power by any means necessary,
including taking his life. For a devout Christian pacifist, this was a

choice that could be made only through intense prayer and highly conscious reflection. Although he chose to support the conspirators, Bonhoeffer did not claim to know for certain whether the taking of any human life, even Hitler's, could be justified—only that he had done his best to meet the dictates of his own conscience. In a letter at the time, he described his feelings about his decision this way: "When a man takes guilt upon himself in responsibility, he imputes his guilt to himself and no one else. He answers for it. Before other men he is justified by dire necessity; before himself he is acquitted by his conscience; but before God he hopes only for grace."[15]

Eventually, the conspiracies came to light, and Bonhoeffer was implicated. He was arrested and confined in an SS prison for two years and was executed in April 1945, just one month before the Nazi surrender. Like Mandela, Dietrich Bonhoeffer was handsome, magnetic, charming, and lovable, with a warm sense of humor and rock-solid faith and courage. He endured his imprisonment and went to his death with an almost otherworldly serenity and good cheer, attributing this astonishing equanimity to his trust in God's will. He made his decisions according to conscience, then entrusted the outcomes to God. This faith enabled him to approach life with gratitude and hope, even when this seemed impossible, and to confront the most extreme difficulties with quiet courage. He was loved and admired by everyone, including all of his fellow prisoners and even many of the guards. The image of Bonhoeffer going to his death with such peace and grace has inspired people throughout the world ever since.

Both before and during his months in prison, Bonhoeffer wrote theological expositions that have remained among the world's most influential readings in Protestant seminaries and churches. His beautiful *Letters and Papers from Prison* are widely regarded as among the most moving letters ever published. Bonhoeffer's writing influenced the anticommunist democratic movement in Eastern Europe during the Cold War, Martin Luther King, Jr. and the civil rights movement, and the antiapartheid movement in South Africa. It's easy to see why people from both faith and secular traditions today hold Bonhoeffer as a model for conscientious moral choices in trying times.

ELEANOR ROOSEVELT

Eleanor Roosevelt may be best known as the wife of a U.S. president, but in her own right she was one of the most consequential public figures of the twentieth century. She transformed the role of First Lady into a true partnership of ideas, in particular speaking out for the unprotected and disadvantaged in the circles of power to which she had access. And she also assumed her own leadership roles in organizations dedicated to workers' rights and racial and gender equality. After her husband's death, Eleanor continued to work for peace and social justice, forging an exceptionally creative approach to human rights internationally through her seminal work on the UN's Universal Declaration of Human Rights.

Although born to a privileged and powerful family, Eleanor Roosevelt did not take easily to a life of political influence and leadership. Both parents died when she was young. Her mother had been highly critical of her, and her father, whom she adored, was an alcoholic who was rarely present. Left without either parent by the age of ten, she struggled with feelings of abandonment, shyness, and lack of confidence. She also felt constrained by the traditional roles for women of her class at the time, much as Jane Addams had. Even when her husband decided to run for president—long after she had become active in a number of social and political causes and had served as First Lady of the state of New York—she tried to avoid the limelight whenever possible. When FDR won the presidency, she confided, "I never wanted it....I never wanted to be a president's wife, and I don't want it now."[16]

Yet, together with her husband, Eleanor Roosevelt changed the way people thought about the role of government and its potential to support the well-being of all citizens. She questioned and reshaped cultural assumptions that took for granted the almost total dominance of whites and men. Like Jane Addams, she questioned the concept of *noblesse oblige* in favor of a truly respectful and democratic attitude toward people with less privilege and wealth. She defied received wisdom that it would be impossible to get countries with radically different cultures, religions, ideologies, and vested interests to agree on a set of universal rights.

What drove Eleanor Roosevelt in her unceasing work for the common good were a firm belief that a life of private privilege and luxury was unsatisfying as well as illegitimate, a passionate desire to "be useful," authentic personal connections with people in great need, and the appeal of the particular social causes that she believed in and engaged with first-hand. Roosevelt was drawn to the early feminist movement, no doubt because of her own experience with the limited horizons faced by women at that time. In addition, her passion for social equality drew her into campaigns for the rights of workers, farmers, African-Americans, and others who lacked privilege and political power.

Late in her life, Roosevelt's concerns for human rights expanded to an international level. Her crowning achievement was the crafting and ultimate passage of the UN's Universal Declaration of Human Rights. As we discuss in Chapter 7, her highly improbable success in this matter did more over the long run to promote the cause of social justice globally than any other legislative act. For this achievement, President Harry Truman called her the First Lady of the world.

Eleanor Roosevelt's effectiveness as a moral leader stemmed directly from her enduring commitment to the ideal of social equality and the evident humility with which she pursued this ideal. In a practical sense, Roosevelt's humility went a long way toward disarming the strong egos of the world leaders she needed to line up behind the value-laden document for which she was trying to gain worldwide acceptance. In a personal sense, her humility granted her the open-mindedness she needed to amend and adjust the document in ways that would make it truly universal. In a spiritual sense, her humility was a central element in her religious faith—a faith that she encapsulated in a prayer that she wrote and repeated nightly during the challenging later years of her life. The prayer is remarkable not just for what it says but for who was saying it:

Our Father, who has set a restlessness in our hearts and made us all seekers after that which we can never fully find, forbid us to be satisfied with what we make of life. Draw us from base content and set our eyes on far-off goals. Keep us at tasks too hard for us, that we may be driven to thee for strength. Deliver us from fretfulness and self-pity. Make us sure of the good that we cannot see and of all the hidden good in the world...Save us from ourselves and show us a vision of a world made new.[17]

Roosevelt's nightly prayer could stand by itself as a statement of the themes of this book. The "base content" of our moral lives certainly does drive its share of human behavior. But so do the "far-off goals," if we choose to follow them. In academic psychology and the popular press, too much has been made of the base content and not enough of the far-off goals. Not only does this distort the full story of our nature, but it also can bend our lives in the wrong direction, toward the base and the cynical and away from the elevated and inspiring.

IDEALS AND THE MORAL LIFE, EXEMPLARY AND IMPERFECT, EXTRAORDINARY AND ORDINARY

This chapter introduces six men and women whose choices and actions were clearly informed, and in many ways driven, by their ideals and beliefs. Like all human beings, these six made mistakes and sometimes conducted themselves in ways that were not admirable. None of them would be hard to debunk, at least in part, by focusing on their mistakes and limitations. Often these mistakes represent aspects of human frailty that we all experience—struggles against vanity and ego that don't always succeed, periods of despair and loss of hope, or moments when facing the truth is too difficult to bear. In other cases, deeply-held values conflict, and the right choices are clear only in retrospect. The case material we examined provided examples of all these frailties and more. But we don't need a study to tell us that all human beings, even the most inspiring moral leaders, at times have feet, or at least a few toes, of clay.

Even so, with remarkable consistency, the case material is even clearer about the ways these six leaders searched sincerely for moral truth and acted on what they found. They left legacies of good work that benefited millions of people. Their lives, justifiably, still are cited as models for people living today. In the following chapters, we refer to these and others who have tried to live according to their carefully considered ideals, as we sketch out a more complete account of moral psychology than those we reviewed in Chapter 1.

This account applies not only to people who are shining examples of moral virtue and leadership like those we profile in this book, but also to the full range of humanity. Ordinary people, too, make sacrifices and show similarly admirable qualities, even if in less dramatic and celebrated ways. Ordinary people love and care for others, both within their own families and beyond; they dedicate themselves to their work and aim to do it in ways that are socially responsible; they help people in need, often without expecting recognition or reward. Some risk their lives to rescue strangers. This kind of vital moral commitment, which uplifts the lives of ordinary as well as extraordinary people, can't be explained by a science that reduces morality to biological impulses, situational pressures, or economic self-interest. All these forces may come into play, but in the end, a moral life is guided by the nature and power of a person's ideals.

NOTES

1. For useful discussions of the unavoidability of prescriptive judgments in the study of moral psychology, see Kristján Kristjánsson, "Virtue Development and Psychology's Fear of Normativity," *Journal of Theoretical and Philosophical Psychology* 32, no. 2 (© 2011 American Psychological Association, 2012): 103–118, and John C. Gibbs, *Moral Development & Reality: Beyond the Theories of Kohlberg, Hoffman, and Haidt,* 3rd ed. (New York: Oxford University Press, 2014).
2. As noted by Louise Knight, *Jane Addams: Spirit in Action,* 1st ed. (New York: W. W. Norton & Co., 2010), 40.
3. Knight, *Jane Addams: Spirit in Action,* 63.
4. Frederick W. Haberman, ed., *Nobel Lectures, Peace 1926–1950* (Amsterdam: Elsevier Publishing Company, 1972).
5. Jane Addams, *Democracy and Social Ethics* (Cambridge, MA: Harvard University Press, 1964), 256.

6. Nelson Mandela, S. K. Hatang, and Sahm Venter, *Nelson Mandela by Himself: The Authorised Book of Quotations* (Johannesburg: Pan Macmillan South Africa, 2011), IX.

7. Nelson Mandela, *Conversations with Myself*, 1st ed. (New York: Farrar, Straus and Giroux, 2010), 10.

8. Mandela, *Conversations with Myself*, 24.

9. Dag Hammarskjöld and W. H. Auden, *Markings* (New York: Knopf, 1966), 55.

10. Hammarskjöld and Auden, *Markings*, 205.

11. Susannah Heschel, "Theological Affinities in the Writings of Abraham Joshua Heschel and Martin Luther King, Jr." *Conservative Judaism* 50, no. 2-3 (Copyright 1998 by the Rabbinical Assembly, 1998): 126–143.

12. Abraham Joshua Heschel, Jacob Neusner, and Noam M. M. Neusner, *To Grow in Wisdom: An Anthology of Abraham Joshua Heschel* (Lanham, MD: Madison Books, 1990), 196.

13. Heschel, Neusner and Neusner, *To Grow in Wisdom*, 206.

14. Heschel, Neusner and Neusner, *To Grow in Wisdom*, 358.

15. Dietrich Bonhoeffer et al., *Ethics* [Ethik. English], 1st English-language ed., Vol. 6 (Minneapolis: Fortress Press, 2005), 14.

16. Allida M. Black, "The Eleanor Roosevelt Papers Project," http://www.gwu.edu/~erpapers/abouteleanor/erbiography.cfm (accessed January 14, 2013).

17. Mary Ann Glendon, *A World Made New: Eleanor Roosevelt and the Universal Declaration of Human Rights*, 1st ed. (New York: Random House, 2001), unnumbered page after title page.

CHAPTER THREE

TOWARD A MORAL PSYCHOLOGY IN FULL

In Chapter 2 we introduced six exceptional moral leaders. Their lives throw into relief some processes in moral development that can be harder to see in more ordinary lives, even though these processes are present in everyone. The six cases show the influence of culture on individuals, but they also show the active nature of individuals' engagements with their cultures. What's more, they show people's capacity for creative moral imagination, which enables them to influence the future directions of their cultures. The leaders' lives illustrate the role of emotional states, including affective dispositions that are present very early in life, but these lives also illustrate the ways that emotional states can be shaped through evolving understanding: People can reflect on their own emotional states and work toward aligning their emotions with their ideals. Perhaps most importantly, the leaders' stories reveal the essential role that virtues play in keeping changes across life moving in a positive direction.

The views of morality that are most popular these days—the "new science" of moral psychology, much of behavioral economics, and the brand of experimental social psychology that stresses situational control—are not well aligned with the lives of these moral leaders. These popular theories are also at odds with the rich moral lives of ordinary people. Most disappointingly, these views readily dismiss the crucial roles played by moral understanding and moral agency. A comprehensive account of moral psychology must capture these and other undeniable features of morality that are left out of the views that are currently fashionable. It must include the full range of moral responses that people perform in real life, from the everyday and mundane to the heroic and sublime. Capturing this full range requires going beyond single-process explanations that make broad claims based on narrow experiments—especially untenable claims that our moral choices are determined by inherited instincts, situational pressures and incentives, authoritarian demands, or whatever factor of the moment a particular experiment is investigating.

An adequate account of morality must not only include the entire range of mental, emotional, and behavioral processes that contribute to moral choice, but it must also *connect* them, showing how they interact with each another during our human experience. For in actuality there is one person and one mind, not a host of distinct constructs devised by scientists attempting to analyze and understand what's going on. The various elements inform each other. This means that sometimes they support each other, while at other times they conflict. Each element can influence others over time. The strength and effectiveness of our moral sense derive from the way these elements combine as people anticipate and respond to social situations with moral implications.

A comprehensive account of moral psychology must also represent both the *constraining* and the *aspirational* functions of morality. The chief question in moral psychology to date has been how people try (or don't try) to resist temptation. Legions of studies have tried to examine what happens when people are offered a chance to cheat, lie, steal, eat marshmallows when they shouldn't,[1] and so on. To the extent that such studies inform us about the morality of constraint, there is a certain value in this focus. But morality also has an aspirational dimension—such as, for example, when people use their moral imaginations to create finer, more ethical ways of conducting themselves in the world, or when they discover and pursue noble aims. The cultivation of character virtues often has this aspirational quality, whenever it is motivated by an attempt to acquire personal excellence.

As recent research within the positive psychology movement has convincingly shown, people are more than walking bundles of neuroses and weaknesses.[2] In their better moments, people can be generous, caring, honest, courageous, even heroic. Although this certainly is not the case all the time, or even most of the time for some, it is unquestionably a real part of the human story, and it must be addressed by any complete account of moral development.

In this chapter, we present a framework for understanding moral behavior that stands in contrast to those currently in vogue in the popular media. It is a framework that highlights how positive moral habits develop and how reflection and judgment contribute to a moral life. It emphasizes the truth-seeking, ideal-guided nature of moral action, at least when it takes its most elevated and highly developed forms. This framework does include some worthwhile insights that recent work in the "new science" of moral psychology has contributed, but it aims for a more balanced view that incorporates the finer aspects of human potential as well.

We would never claim that truth-seeking, ideal-guided, reflective moral responses are always present: We agree with the new science school that much everyday behavior is automatic and reflexive. But even the most routine, seemingly automatic habits and intuitions owe a debt to conscious learning. The developmental theory that we present shows how ingrained habits and deliberate reflection are interconnected parts of the dynamic process of learning and growth.

Biological Endowment—The Seeds of Moral Growth

Advances in evolutionary science in recent years have revealed the great extent to which humans come into the world prepared to lead a moral life. Most evolutionary scientists agree, at least in broad outline, that empathy and attachment, social reciprocity, cooperation, and generosity (even toward those from outside "tribes") are all natural to our species. Although a good deal of learning is necessary for these natural dispositions to develop into the kinds of moral character that produce reliable prosocial behavior, the seeds of morality are present in all of us at birth.

Research that has contributed to this understanding of the human biological endowment in the moral domain includes studies of infants and young children as well as observations of the social behavior of primates and other animals (even including insects such as ants and bees). The advent of video recording during the late twentieth century, enhanced by computer analysis methods, made possible revealing looks into the social world of human newborns. Most astonishing has been the discovery, now widely confirmed by over three decades of replication studies, that newborns and infants in the early months of life have the capacities to share the emotional state of others—in other words, to experience a rudimentary form of empathy.

Other researchers have documented empathic, altruistic, and fairness-oriented behavior in animals. For example, De Waal[3] found that chimpanzees and bonobos are sensitive to the pain of others. More recently, Dunbar[4] found that monkeys who groom their peers show greater increases in biological markers of well-being than do those who are being groomed. Animals such as chimpanzees and other primates show evidence of aversion to unequal divisions of goods, an aversion that goes beyond a simple desire for a larger quantity of the goods.[5]

Evolutionary science has identified genetic and other biological mechanisms that begin to explain these revealing findings. These mechanisms suggest that evolutionary fitness is enhanced when animals become integrated into cooperative social structures. Animals interact with others in ways that are good for their species in the long run, even if these ways may be nonoptimal for individual survival.[6] This is because, at the species level, an inclination toward communication and cooperation is important in allowing it to gain dominance over other species.

Of course not all people behave in prosocial ways for all (or even much) of the time: Achieving the positive potential that evolutionary science has revealed is not inevitable. In addition to our innate dispositions toward prosocial behavior, we are also prone to self-serving desires, self-deception, fierce competition, and the imposition of power through force. Clearly, human beings are capable of both good and bad. But the recognition that *both* capacities are built into the species at birth represents an important shift in scientific understanding. Views of moral development that assume humans are fundamentally self-serving and need to be socialized into getting along, a task that such views consider to be a never-ending struggle, are clearly imbalanced and outdated.[7]

Any focus on humanity's moral potential must recognize that our evolutionary legacy is only the beginning, a sapling from which a tree of mature morality can grow. No evolutionary heritage can guarantee full moral development: Learning is necessary. With learning, people's moral sense can become more mature over the years in systematic and predictable ways. But there is also great room for variability, and not all people reach their full potential in this or any other area.

THE ENCOMPASSING MORAL CULTURE

Moral character must be developed through experience before it becomes a steady and effective guide to moral action. Much of this learning comes by way of face-to-face interactions with parents, peers, teachers, and other members of the community, but some of it is less direct. These indirect experiences, although encompassing, tend to be less visible, deeply embedded in a society's backdrops of values, codes, and practices—that is, rooted in culture.

Participation in cultural routines and practices is generally known to be one of the most powerful influences on the moral sense as it develops beyond our initial biological endowment. In every culture, the moral sense is fashioned and reinforced by cultural traditions, routines, and norms that have evolved over many generations. These traditions and norms often are embodied in formal religious and legal doctrines, as well as in countless customs and rituals. This cultural legacy of moral norms and standards builds on humans' biological legacy of moral impulses. Culture adds a societal dimension to our psychological experience, establishing particular ways of thinking and feeling about the self and the social world. Cultural norms, often accompanied by sanctions, provide moral motivation as well as guidance. Among other things, these cultural norms and sanctions help constrain people's egoistic motives, reducing the conflict that would otherwise make it impossible for groups of people to live together.

Once learned, culturally shaped behaviors tend to become so ingrained that they operate habitually, influencing emotional responses without reference to conscious reflection. So, for example, mature Hindu Brahmins, long immersed in a culture that prohibits the killing of cows, will likely feel disgust rather than temptation when offered a hamburger. Habits that are built in in this way can give certain social responses an automatic quality, so that they are experienced simply as "proper" behavior that all civilized people perform as a matter of course.

Engagement in cultural routines influences moral understanding as well as moral emotion and habit. As anthropologist Richard Shweder has pointed out, an immersion in cultural practices over time can make those practices seem morally right, intellectually as well as emotionally.[8] Shweder describes three clusters of values that are differentially important in different cultures. The first of these is what he calls *the ethic of divinity*, which is a central theme in Hindu Brahmin India, where Shweder did much of his fieldwork. In this divinity worldview, godliness is seen as permeating the social order. This is reflected in sacred traditions that are part of daily life, which is governed by rules of purity and contamination. Those rules are a familiar part of life as early as childhood. Through participation in these practices, children develop deeply embodied intuitions about purity and contamination, sacred spaces, and essential rituals. When later they learn about the ideational rationale for these customs—for example, ideas such as asceticism, transcendence, and immanent sacredness—they are already prepared to accept these ideas, which now seem intuitively right or even self-evident to them.

In these and other ways, cultures influence people by engaging them in routine practices and familiar ideas that create habits of mind and behavior. Among the most common vessels for ideas are widely shared metaphors of the sort that cultures use to represent strategic features of the natural and social worlds. Often these metaphors are so ubiquitous that those who use them fail to see that they are metaphors at all, taking them for literal representations of reality. Such metaphors can shape people's worldviews without their awareness, and worldviews and values represented in metaphors can carry implicit moral implications. For example, young women's moral worth and desirability as marriage partners in most times and places have depended upon their chastity as represented by images of spotless purity, the absence of sully or stain, and, in many places, the obligatory color white for women's wedding gowns.

Over time, people who participate in a culture also come to share some iconic narratives or stories that teach moral lessons and values. Many of these are stories about people whose lives illustrate the virtues that are prized by that culture. In the United States, for example, it would be hard to grow up without knowing that George Washington had demonstrated exceptional honesty as a child by confessing that he had chopped down his father's favorite cherry tree. Today, over 300 years later, cherry pie is a traditional treat for celebrations of Washington's birthday. Other well-known stories (Pinocchio, for example) describe dishonest behavior, serving to warn about negative consequences that follow from the violation of important moral norms such as honesty. Both kinds of stories invite listeners to identify with the main character, thereby incorporating into their own identities the aspirational and cautionary lessons featured in the stories.

ACTIVE ENGAGEMENT WITH CULTURE

The new science of morality, in an effort to explain moral conduct with the least possible reliance on moral thinking or agency while at the same time bowing to the obvious role of non-biological factors such as culture, emphasizes the ways that key narratives—the oft-repeated stories of one's family, tribe, or community—shape moral sensibilities. But in so doing, the new science account misses the degree to which people actively *select* the narratives they identify with and use those narratives in their own ways. Cultural narratives are not incorporated wholesale into an individual's moral perspective or moral identity. All people understand the iconic stories of their families and communities in their own unique ways, making their own sense of the stories, considering and examining their implications, adapting them to their own personal meanings, and sometimes even creating new narratives to communicate their own visions of what's important and good.

This kind of individual engagement with the shared narratives of a culture illustrates a more general point. People are active, not passive, when they engage with the world. They don't just sit and let social experience wash over them from the outside. They choose what to notice and what to make of it. They select and interpret their experience. Although many people share the same culture, they each pay attention to different aspects of it, and they may even argue about it. People understand the same cultural symbols and rituals differently. Some people look critically at their cultures, raising questions about beliefs that others take for granted. Such people may try to change the unexamined assumptions of others. People do not pass through life like unthinking cultural sheep.

It is also important to recognize that no culture is a single homogeneous whole. Every culture includes multiple subcultures. To some degree, people actively seek out the subcultural settings they wish to participate in, thereby choosing the influences that subsequently shape their development. Many American teenagers, for example, actively choose whether or not to become part of their school's jock crowd, its artsy theater group, its techies, its competitive good-student group, the rebels, the nerds, and so on. Such choices immerse them in settings that further influence the way they talk, the clothes they wear, or the substances they ingest. The influence of such settings is real but not irresistible. When people choose a particular subculture, they still can resist its norms, try to change them, or eventually depart that subculture for another.

People also can change their minds about their cultural beliefs: Judgments are not frozen in place. Conversion from one culture-based ideology to another is a common occurrence within religious and other ideologically based communities. Indeed, many times religious or ideological rebels come from the ranks of the community's most loyal followers. Often the creators of new cultural beliefs were once fierce devotees of the cultural traditions they later worked to replace.

In our study, we observed many instances of such breaks with cultural tradition. Several of the moral leaders, for example, grew up in highly privileged families that espoused the culture of *noblesse oblige*, in which people of financial means are expected to help the poor with money and other acts of charity. But some of the leaders we studied came to see this charitable approach as less desirable than drives for greater justice, professing in writings and public statements that the wrong kinds of charity actually interfere with the realization of justice for the less privileged.

Jane Addams arrived at this conclusion early in her quest to find new ways to boost the lot of the disadvantaged. Her biographer Louise Knight has written that Addams questioned the value of the charitable ethic for achieving "the necessary end of benevolence" for some time before she adopted the settlement house approach that was to be her great legacy. "It seems that everywhere she looked," Knight wrote, "she saw the dangers that ethic posed to society....she began to see it in relationships between the household employer and the servant; between the charity worker and the beneficiary; between the prosperous citizen and struggling union member..."[9] Addams's settlement house approach substituted a more equal relationship for the asymmetrical dealings between donor and recipient that often characterize charitable giving. Eleanor Roosevelt was influenced by Addams's thinking on this matter and adopted a comparable approach in her political campaigns for laborers, women's equality, and civil rights.

In these and other cases, ideas take shape in a person's mind not just because the person is influenced by the surrounding culture but also because the person reflects on that culture. People also look to others as models of what they admire and want to be like (or as models of what they hope they won't become). But, here again, identification with figures they admire and look up to is an active process, something to be thought through, often in interaction with peers, and subject to change over time. Through conversations with others and reflections within themselves, people clarify, articulate, and communicate their own ideas about the beliefs, narratives, and models they encounter in their cultures. They argue about differences of perspective, often changing their understandings and beliefs as a result. In this truth-seeking process, individuals develop, and cultures evolve.

The impact of the engaged individual on cultural evolution is especially clear when moral leaders, such as those we studied, create new social and institutional cultures. A dramatic feature of the extraordinary lives that we described in Chapter 2 is the extent to which they sought to create or change important cultural institutions: Jane Addams created Hull House, Nelson Mandela created the Truth and Reconciliation Commission, Dag Hammarskjöld created the institutional culture of the UN. And all six leaders influenced the broader cultures of their countries, the world, and their religious faiths. Abraham Heschel provided rich new images of Jewish practice and education; Jane Addams created models of a new kind of social solidarity in the United States; Dietrich Bonhoeffer worked to rally Christian churches in Germany to resist Hitler. While cultures can to a certain degree shape individuals, cultures themselves are shaped by individual actions.

The crucial moral importance of institution and culture building is often left out of the social psychological, brain-based, and economic models of human moral functioning. Also missing is any attention to moral creativity, or what might be called moral imagination. It is undeniable that some people critique their own cultures and consciously resist the demands they disagree with. And some people go beyond such opposition to imagine alternatives that are better aligned with the cultures' own best statements of aspirations and ideals. Successful social movements such as the independence movement in India and U.S. movements toward civil rights and gender equality are shining examples of this. These are instructive examples, because they reveal the breadth of involvement of ordinary people along with highly committed and creative leaders.

This view of individuals actively engaging, choosing, and even creating or dramatically changing their cultural and institutional contexts illustrates another point of contrast between the new science vision and the view we're outlining here. We believe it's essential to understand that people are moral agents with their own mental lives, with the capacities to interpret events and to understand the world on their own terms, to engage actively with it, and to exert some control over their choices. Moral agency, an idea essential for most philosophical accounts of morality, is entirely missing from the reductionistic views that have become dominant in today's media accounts—in fact, those views' failures to appreciate the importance of moral agency is at the heart of what we mean when we say that they are reductionistic. The view that morality is nothing more than enculturation into the norms and values of one's own culture[10] makes little sense when considered against the realities of individuals' active engagement with their cultural contexts, the multiplicity of subcultures within any given society, and the ongoing evolution of culture through individual action.

MORAL UNDERSTANDING

One of the salient features of the new science view is its claim that moral choices are generally irrational, rarely (if ever) guided by moral understanding. In dismissing the importance of moral understanding, the new science conflates it with conscious, analytical deliberation *in the moment of choice*. This mistaken, straw-man assumption makes it easy to conclude that thinking is not an important part of everyday morality, since it's obviously true that analytical deliberation is seldom evident when moral behavior is observed from the outside. The conclusion that morality is not guided by understanding reflects a serious misconception about the way that understanding operates.

Moral understanding should not be equated with analytical deliberation in the moment of choice. Although people sometimes do grapple with moral questions in the process of developing their mature understanding, once they acquire new moral insights, even provisionally, these become background assumptions that influence their moral perceptions, their interpretations, and their choices without the need to deliberate about them anew in each instance.[11] This works in much the same way as when, without conscious deliberation, a basic understanding of arithmetic stops an adult from accepting three pennies in exchange for a dime, despite the apparent gain in size and number of coins, which might give a young child pause. As with mathematical knowledge, by the time people reach adulthood, basic moral understanding is baked into the habits of thought and action that govern much of their everyday behavior.

Once established, habitual ways of thinking and behaving take over in routine situations: hence the automatic quality of moral responding that the new science school has correctly noted. But the new science view misattributes the source of this automaticity. It's not because our moral responses are determined by evolutionarily based biological impulses that they often appear automatic; nor is it because we mindlessly act out culturally induced customs. Rather, we act quickly because we've already worked through much of our functional moral understanding, at least with regard to familiar situations. In the course of development, conscious reflection is the leading edge of moral understanding. Once reflection has done its developmental work, moral understanding and the habits it shapes can operate quickly and effortlessly.

In his summary of research on the relationship between moral reflection and intuition, psychologist John Gibbs[12] points to extensive evidence supporting our claim that moral intuitions are strongly shaped by prior deliberative moral reasoning. The research that Gibbs cites makes it clear that once a person has thought through a moral issue, subsequent responses to situations that involve this issue are likely to be fast and seemingly automatic. As Gibbs puts it, complex cognitions are said to "migrate" over time into automaticity. This key developmental principle has been supported by a strong foundation of scientific theory and data in recent years.[13]

In an early but less-known statement of this key developmental principle, Davidson and Youniss[14] distinguished between two quite different kinds of moral process, which they called *reflective* morality and *habitual* (or *spontaneous*) morality. Reflective morality, which involves careful evaluation and justification, comes into play relatively infrequently—usually only when the right course of action is not obvious or when one's initial moral response is challenged and there is time to reflect. In contrast, most moral actions—the many unnoted moral acts that permeate civilized daily life—have become habitual and therefore are no longer preceded by conscious reflection. Ideas that we acquire through the development of our moral understanding become so readily accessible over time that they are taken for granted; in this way, they evolve into spontaneous intuitions that influence our actions immediately, often under the radar of our conscious awareness.

In a report of her research on moral interpretation, Janet Walker[15] mentioned that she automatically has a reaction of anger at her husband when she sees his dirty socks lying on the floor. As she put it, this emotional reaction results from the habitual interpretive scheme that is triggered by the sight of the socks, something like "he leaves his dirty stuff around and I have to pick it up."[16] But what Walker didn't point out was that this interpretive scheme is based in a particular view of fairness in domestic (or gender) roles. Only women or men with that view would consider the need to constantly pick up after their spouses to be unfair. That is, Walker's understanding of gender roles and justice within the family played a key, although perhaps invisible, role in her emotional reaction to the sight of laundry scattered on the floor. More generally, the way people understand concepts central to morality, such as justice, moral authority, trust, and accountability, influence their decisions as they respond to moral situations they face in daily life.

Research on children's working conceptions of distributive justice shows how this works. In his extensive research on how children develop an increasingly mature grasp of principles of distributive justice, one of us (Damon[17]) studied children's behavior when they were asked to divide up candy bars for work they had each done (making bracelets). The observations revealed systematic age differences in the way children think about the fair way to allocate rewards for work. For the youngest children in the study, the grounds for handing out rewards tended to be arbitrary and self-serving. So, for example, a tall boy might argue that the bigger children should receive more candy, or a girl might argue for more candy for girls because girls "like candy more" than boys. Children who were somewhat older understood that essentially rigging the criteria in order to claim more candy for themselves would not be seen as fair by others in the group and, because they were able to take the others' point of view, they also understood why the others would *legitimately* consider this approach unfair. Having learned this, slightly older children in the study (age six or so) adopted a strategy of *equality*—"let's give everyone exactly the same number of candy bars." This showed an advance in understanding but was still fairly simplistic. In the next older group (age eight or so), most children had moved beyond strict equality to take *merit* into account. These children argued that those who had done more work (made a larger number of bracelets, or nicer ones) should receive a greater reward. In the oldest group of children, a more subtle strategy emerged. For these children, merit was tempered by a sense of equity. If a child's productivity was lower through no fault of his own (let's say he was sick that day, or had never before had a chance to learn how to make bracelets), this factor was taken into account in determining merit, along with productivity.

A follow-up study was able to track what happened to the children as they discussed their decisions about allocating rewards for the work they had done and struggled to make sense of what fairness means in this kind of situation.[18] The very process of engaging in debates with peers about what's fair had a developmental effect on many of the children's moral understanding. This demonstrates that realizing that others may not buy one's mode of thinking, joined with an effort to understand the reasons behind the disagreement, can be a powerful stimulus toward the development of deeper thinking about justice. This kind of experience creates a leading edge for development, marked by debate (inner or outer) and conscious reflection. But once children's understandings of fairness have stabilized, even temporarily, the children don't tend to stop and rethink the fairness of each decision they make—for now, the need for deliberative reflection has passed.

More recent studies by behavioral economists reveal similar age patterns in participants' responses as they engage in what is known in the field as *the ultimatum game*. In this game, two players must divide a sum of money provided by the experimenter. The first player decides how to divide the sum and makes an offer to the other player. The second player can either accept or reject the proposal. If the second player rejects the offer, neither player receives any money. If the second player accepts the offer, the money is split according to the proposal. The game is played only once, so reciprocation is not an issue.

What may have surprised traditional economists is that study participants *cared* about fairness, even to the point of giving up their share if they felt the proposal they were offered was unfair. As in the new science research, the game participants did not stop to reflect on fairness analytically before making their decisions, which tend to be immediate. But age differences in responses to the ultimatum game reveal essentially the same evolving conceptions of fairness that we described decades earlier. In the economic studies, kindergartners were willing to accept very unequal offers (doing so about 70 percent of the time), but less than half of third- and sixth-graders did so. By the time participants became adults, virtually none accepted lopsided offers.[19] These dramatic age differences make it clear that participants' evolving understanding of what constitutes fairness makes a big difference to the actual choices they make. This difference in understanding operates as a background assumption, requiring little or no conscious attention once it's in place.

The new science view of morality portrays moral understanding as simply post hoc rationalization, interpreting the relative infrequency of deliberate analysis in decision making as evidence for an intuitionist theory of morality. Not only does a close look at the experimental research disconfirm this view, but the lives of the moral leaders we described in Chapter 2 also reveal a more central role for moral reflection as it interacts with moral conduct and experience over time.

This is not intellectualizing in a vacuum: It is an active, ongoing process of reflection about one's life and experiences, drawing on ideas, stories, images, and critical capacities, leading to the creation and refinement of the person's moral ideals and understandings. Moral reflection of this kind establishes foundational ideas that strongly influence the actual choices a person makes. Over time, these foundational ideas become so ingrained in the individual's way of seeing the world that they appear to operate automatically, much like intuitive responses, yet they implicitly shape people's choices, even those made quickly and under duress.

Janet Walker has documented the ways in which people reflect on their own moral interpretations and judgments, often in discussions and debates with others. Much as it does in our six moral leaders, this kind of reflection provides the basis for moral growth for ordinary people as well. In the many moments of moral decision they encounter every day, people have the capacity to reflect and the room to choose the interpretation they settle on, over time creating new habits of interpretation that can lead in a different direction. This can mean considering and resolving several conflicting interpretations, or it can mean questioning one's original interpretation after confronting an uneasy feeling that this interpretation may have been self-serving or biased in other ways.

The capacity to override and change one's own habits of interpretation is critical, because by doing so people can actively shape their future moral habits. People grow morally by making an effort to become more aware of their own habits of mind and behavior, by acknowledging and trying to overcome their biases, and by working to understand others' interpretations.[20] In these ways, it's within our power to exercise moral agency by choosing to reconsider our moral ideals and by making choices that reflect these moral beliefs and ideals. Such choices, made repeatedly over time, turn into new, more informed habits that can significantly enhance a person's moral aspirations.

Despite the many explicit and implicit roles that moral understanding plays, it doesn't operate alone in determining moral responses. We fully agree with scholars who point out the important part that moral emotion plays in moral development and functioning. But we don't agree with those who claim that moral emotion's influence on moral

70

behavior implies that morality is fundamentally nonrational. Such a misguided claim reveals another way that currently popular views emanating from the new science school misconstrue moral understanding and fail to appreciate its close and dynamic connections with intuition, habit, and emotion.

MORAL EMOTION

Many distinct emotions energize people's moral convictions and increase the likelihood that people will act on those convictions. The variety of human moral emotions is immense. It includes feelings that negatively evaluate the self (such as shame and guilt), those that negatively assess others (such as righteous anger), feelings that appreciate the moral qualities of self or others (pride, admiration, gratitude, inspiration), feelings that show concern for others' suffering (compassion, empathic distress), and feelings that delight in the others' well-being (empathic joy). Each of these emotions is elicited by a different kind of situation, and each serves a different role in the larger domain of moral functioning.

Moral emotions are built into the human species through evolution, as the new science perspective correctly asserts. Many moral emotions are close to universal. People in all parts of the world recoil from violent events with feelings of horror and disgust, respond with affirmative feelings when they witness generosity or kindness, and experience pain when they see someone hurt. But, like all other built-in moral inclinations, moral emotions need to develop beyond their original immature forms if they are to become fully functional.

As researchers have investigated the growth of moral emotions, it has become clear that development in this area is inseparable from the development of moral understanding. At every step along the way, as emotional patterns grow more mature, the advances take place through the interaction of feeling and understanding.

This principle—that understanding and emotion interact and co-determine each other in the course of moral development—has been confirmed by many decades of solid research. Yet it is either ignored or dismissed (hard to tell which) by the new science school. In writing about the role of moral emotion, Jonathan Haidt takes the following position: "Emotions are *in charge* of the temple of morality... Moral reasoning is really just a servant masquerading as high priest."[21] This comment, like others made by the new science school, separates emotion and understanding into two distinct and supposedly independent domains. Then it goes on to anoint emotion as the prime driver of morality. Regardless of how important emotions are in influencing behavior (and they are indeed important), this is an extreme position, wholly unwarranted by the huge body of careful psychological research on the relations between cognition and emotion.[22]

To see why research on moral emotion doesn't back up the extreme new science views, let's consider in some detail the most extensively studied moral emotion, empathy (see, for example, the work of Martin Hoffman[23]). Empathy research traces the pattern of increasing maturity that characterizes children's growth in compassion, along with its impact on children's caring behavior. Research on the growth of empathy reveals evolving connections between the development of moral emotions and moral understanding. Emotional responses motivate moral concern, and advances in understanding lead to increasingly mature emotional responses. This research illustrates our larger point—that moral emotion and understanding are inextricably intertwined.

In popular discourse, empathy is often confused with sympathy, with acts of compassion, and with moral emotionality in general. These are misuses of the term that can interfere with understanding how empathy and its moral outcomes actually take shape over the course of human development. In its scientific meaning, empathy is the sharing of another's emotional state, no more and no less. As an emotional response, empathy does not in itself come with a program of action. Nor does it provide a wide-ranging sense of identification with those we're unfamiliar with: It takes sympathy, a more fully developed cognitive capacity, to do that (and empathy, a literal sharing of an emotional state, may not even be involved). So, for example, without matching a gambler's emotion in the moment, we may sympathize with him because he is addicted to betting. We may feel sorry for him *even when he's joyfully on a winning streak* if we believe that his gambling habit is beyond his control and that it will eventually bring him to ruin. We may sympathize with and feel compassion for his predicament, but we don't empathize with him (share his emotion) in his moment of joy.

Empathy in its most rudimentary form is present at birth. In subsequent years, at least for most people, the inborn empathic reaction interacts with developing cognitive and interpersonal capacities to become increasingly attuned to the subtleties of social reality. Newborn babies exhibit a simple kind of empathy—for example, crying whenever they hear another baby crying. This behavior reflects a selective responsiveness to the particular sounds that express pain, built into our species: babies don't cry when they hear other noises that are equally loud. In this and other ways, human infants are attuned to react in particular ways to certain sounds and visual patterns but not others.

Yet at this early age children are not able to distinguish between their own distress and that of another. Even later, as toddlers, if they try to help another person, they do so by offering something that would comfort themselves. For example, a little girl trying to be helpful to a distressed child might bring her own mother to comfort the child, even when the other child's mother is available too. When they get a bit older, children realize that others have inner states different from their own. Now if they help, they do it more appropriately, for example bringing to a crying child the other child's mother (or teddy bear), not their own.

At a still more advanced level, made possible by further advances in cognition, the capacity for *sympathetic understanding* of other people's situations emerges. Sympathy enables a person to identify with another even when not sharing an emotional state—in this sense it reaches beyond the limits of empathic responding. With cognitive development, it becomes possible, for example, to experience sympathy for other people's chronic illnesses, economic hardships, or difficult family situations, even when the other person seems happy at the moment of observation, as did the gambler on a winning streak we referred to earlier. Older children also become aware that people who feel bad in some way may try to mask their feelings with a cheerful face and that some don't welcome expressions of sympathy. This more sophisticated grasp of social reality informs and sharpens the developing child's emotional reactions and actions that flow from them.

Cognitive judgments also play a key role in determining whom one will sympathize with. For example, people who are suffering receive less sympathy if they're judged to be responsible for their own plights through carelessness or mischief than if they're seen as innocent victims. In this and other ways, the development of moral understanding shapes the nature and functioning of moral emotion.

Effective parenting builds on this by helping misbehaving children understand how their actions hurt other people. By building in the child the capacity to understand others' experience and perspectives, parents foster the child's emotional capacities. In this way, through support of deeper moral understanding, parents contribute to more mature, adaptive moral emotions in their children.

Over time, empathy and other moral emotions become better attuned to the complexities of life with others than they were in early childhood. But even adult morality includes remnants of its evolutionary roots that don't fully make sense from a rational, analytical point of view. As did Amos Tversky and Daniel Kahneman in the domain of cognitive problem solving,[24] Martin Hoffman identified systematic biases in empathic responsiveness that are built into the species. For example, Hoffman's studies have shown that, although people have the capacity to respond sympathetically to just about anyone in distress, they show biases in favor of family members, close friends, and people they perceive as similar to themselves. This is called the *familiarity bias*: People who are familiar and feel more closely connected to the individual elicit more sympathy and help than those who are more distant. Research on empathic biases also shows that people are more likely to respond sympathetically to people who are right in front of them at the moment than those they know about but who are not present or close at hand. This pattern has been called the *here-and-now bias*.

These patterns make sense in evolutionary terms. Extending help and support to those who are like oneself or present at the moment is more likely to increase one's representation in the gene pool than will helping strangers. Close relatives and others who are most similar to oneself as well as individuals who are close at hand are more likely than strangers to share one's genetic material: hence the evolutionary value of the familiarity and here-and-now biases.

Such well-documented biases in empathic response are adaptive in another way as well. At any one time, countless people all over the world are suffering through no fault of their own. If we were to experience the distress of all these people, the resulting emotions would be overwhelming and unlikely to support constructive efforts to help. Indeed, studies have shown that when people experience an overload of empathic distress, it's immobilizing rather than motivating: When people become overwhelmed in this way, their attention turns to themselves and their own empathic pain rather than toward what they can do for others. One key function of empathic bias is to prevent this kind of overload and the breakdown of constructive reaction it engenders by providing a mechanism through which individuals can regulate the intensity of their empathic arousal.

Although empathic biases are normal and in some important ways adaptive, they don't always rule our moral choices—nor should they. There are times when compassion—or justice—requires us to look beyond the comfort zones of familiar faces and here-and-now experiences. Wise parents will resist the urge to take the part of their own children when they're in the wrong, and good citizenship in any society demands a concern for those who don't share the same ethnicity, social class, family and community ties, or religious and ideological beliefs. In these cases, the circle of compassion can be expanded to include distant acquaintances, strangers, and sometimes even opponents.

This is possible because individuals are not at the mercy of their built-in biases; they're capable of redirecting or overriding their basic emotional inclinations. Here again, there is a striking difference between the new science perspectives and the one we're proposing. Unlike many in the new science school, we don't believe that people's capacity for identification and compassion is rigidly dictated by inherited biases and other impulses that emerged in evolution. In moral emotion, we again see the importance of moral agency and choice.

Extending the boundaries of familiarity and immediacy can be an important component of moral motivation and is part of what we mean when we describe someone as a compassionate person. People vary in how broadly they draw the boundaries of compassion to determine who counts as a member of one's sympathy group. Sometimes a shift of perspective that extends the circle of concern occurs in a quick, intuitive way during a moment of crisis.

A recent news story described a man who saw someone push an older woman onto the subway tracks in New York. After seeing that the woman was all right, the witness chased the perpetrator down and held him until the police arrived. When the witness was asked why he took the risk of going after the assailant, he said he did it because "that could have been my mom, it could have been a friend of mine." In that moment, he substituted "this could be someone close to me" for the more typical "this is a stranger" response. His behavior was dramatically different as a result.

Broadening the circle of familiarity and obligation sometimes goes well beyond this, both in the moment and in a sustained way over time. This is evident, for example, in Sam and Pearl Oliner's study of people who risked their own lives and the lives of their children by hiding Jews from the Nazis during World War II.[25] Although the rescuers the Oliners studied were gentiles, they saw Jews in their community as not really different from themselves, even when they didn't know them personally. With this understanding, the rescuers felt they had no choice but to take the enormous personal risk of sheltering the oppressed families.

This kind of expansive circle of concern is also evident in the moral leaders we described in Chapter 2. Despite her aristocratic background, Eleanor Roosevelt felt close identification and solidarity with working-class people, resulting in tireless efforts to improve the conditions of their lives. Compassion and a strong sense of connection with working people were powerful elements of her emotional experience. These feelings were at least as important in fueling and sustaining her commitment as were her beliefs about what was right to do.

But if we are to understand the origins and particular character of Roosevelt's feelings, we must pay attention to her own understanding of social class and privilege and her conception of the values that make life worth living. In part because of the suffering she experienced in childhood and the vicissitudes of her storied family, young Eleanor Roosevelt came to question the inevitability of the social order that others of her era and class background took for granted as part of the nature of things. She understood that privilege is not always earned and is not in itself a marker of superior character. She also observed at close hand the lives of the rich, and she concluded that the exclusive pursuit of material wealth, pleasure, and comfort is not ultimately satisfying. If these beliefs had been divorced from deep feelings, they could not have sustained her unflagging energy and courage. But woven together as the feelings and beliefs were, the emotional and cognitive strands of her experience made for a resilient, unbreakable cable that supported a lifetime of extraordinary moral accomplishment.

This same moral agency can also be seen in some people's orientations toward their own patterns of emotional response. People can build on their characteristic emotional strengths, as did Nelson Mandela with his inherent fearlessness. They also can take actions to change the less adaptive emotional patterns built into their biologically based dispositions or ingrained early in life. Just as people are not at the mercy of the common empathic biases, neither are they at the mercy of their tendencies toward timidity, rashness, obstinacy, and the like. People can learn to regulate their own emotions; in fact, recent psychological research has found the capacity for self-regulation to be one of the strongest indicators of positive human development across the lifespan.[26]

The idea that it is adaptive for people to intentionally regulate their emotions has a long history. The Stoics of ancient Greece showed long ago that people can actively control their feelings with determined mental discipline. In our time, well-established approaches to mental health, such as cognitive-behavioral therapy, rely on people's capacity to regulate their emotional responses by developing more adaptive thought patterns. Although one's emotional reactions often feel like they have a life of their own, people do have power to govern them. At times this means suppressing or ignoring certain feelings. Other times it means linking them to a purpose one has chosen to pursue, in the way that composers sometimes draw on difficult emotions as a source of material and energy for creating music.

Nelson Mandela's life illustrates how a person's characteristic patterns of emotional response can be reshaped over time with the acquisition of new moral understandings, ideals, and commitments. Mandela as a young man was known for his bold, confident, fearless character. His early emotional profile, especially in the political context of South Africa at that time, might have led him to the life of a revolutionary partisan; instead, he became a moral icon and unifying statesman, leading his country out of apartheid.

In early adulthood, Mandela's emotional life was characterized by anger, pride, even arrogance, and courage that often crossed over into recklessness. But his single-minded devotion to ideals of justice led him to see that he needed to control these emotions if he was to succeed in freeing South Africa from its terrible system of racial injustice. During his many years in prison, Mandela came to understand that advancing his agenda of freedom for his people required him to channel his emotional reactions in a productive direction. He supplanted his anger with a highly focused resolve. He transformed his recklessness into a deliberate kind of courage, a willingness to sacrifice everything for what he believed in, tempered by avoidance of risks that could cause only harm.

This transformation was more than a pragmatic, strategic shift in tactics. It doesn't appear that Mandela's emotional reactions remained the same but were simply kept under wraps. If that had been the case, it would be hard to explain the mature Mandela's astonishing lack of bitterness, or the way that his pride came to represent an insistence on the dignity of each individual rather than arrogance associated with an outsized ego. In Chapter 5, we describe in more detail Mandela's paradoxical combination of strength, pride, and humility. For now, it's enough to note that it was the development of a kind of humility that helped Mandela make the shift from arrogance to a principled insistence on dignity.

Equally important, while in prison, Mandela's commitment to fairness and truth, along with his need to establish alliances, led him to make important distinctions between warders who were simply brutal sadists and those who managed to preserve enough of their humanity to treat the prisoners with some decency and respect. Mandela's appreciation of such differences, and his capacity to understand the perspectives of even his opponents and enemies, had strong and salutary emotional consequences. His generous understanding helped protect him from becoming hardened and embittered during his decades of imprisonment.

This generous spirit of universal humanity was most evident in Mandela's behaviors after his release from prison. Not only did he believe that forgiveness was essential politically if the country was to move ahead, but he seems to have actually *felt* this broad embrace of people from all sides of the long, ugly struggle. Not only did Mandela's judgments, choices, and actions reflect his understanding and convictions, but his *emotional* responses also flowed directly from his moral understanding. One unforgettable example of this generosity of feeling and behavior was when Mandela invited one of his Robben Island prison guards to sit on stage with him when he took his oath of office as South Africa's newly elected president.

The process of exerting a sense of moral agency over one's emotional responses involves self-awareness, reflection, and a desire to put insights and inspiration into practice. The new science of morality points to an immediate, unmediated, largely bodily feeling of warmth and moral elevation in response to stories and models of moral goodness as one of the built-in emotional reactions that make up human morality. But recent research on biological mechanisms that are associated with moral inspiration backs up our claim that reflection and connection of the particular instance with more general moral ideas and principles are critical parts of this process.

Neuroscientist Mary Helen Immordino-Yang[27] presented research participants with carefully crafted representations of true stories about a number of interpersonal situations, some of which described especially generous, selfless acts. Those stories were intended to evoke emotions of inspiration or elevation. Participants were videotaped as they described how the stories made them feel. They later underwent an fMRI, during which they were reminded of each story and asked to indicate how and how strongly it made them feel at that moment. The study reports both videotaped behaviors and fMRI responses.

In the videotaped segment of the study, Immordino-Yang found that people did report feelings of inspiration, and many referred to physical sensations associated with their emotions. In addition, some of the participants stopped, looked up or down, seemed to tune out a bit, and then drew connections between the stories and their own experiences. The participants who exhibited gaze aversion and delays in responding were more likely than others to report feeling inspired. And the more their speech and motor activity slowed, the more likely they were to draw global moral lessons from the stories. Many of these apparently reflective participants also vowed to do something different themselves as a result of having heard and thought about the stories.

The fMRI segment of the study showed that, during the gaze aversion or reflection phase of these participants' responses, brain regions were recruited that serve the functions of self-monitoring, awareness of consciousness, and an internal focus rather than externally directed attention. Based on these records and participant comments during the observations, Immordino-Yang concluded that the engagement of these brain regions tracks the process of reflection in which the mind moves toward more abstract, idealistic concerns. Such reflection is an essential part of people's responses to inspiring stories, yielding insights about moral lessons as well as the determination to incorporate those insights into life decisions and actions.

A final point on moral emotion concerns the issue of prescriptivity, which we introduced in Chapter 2. If one assumes, as we do, that what is typical is not necessarily synonymous with what is morally right, then it makes sense to ask when it *is* right or morally justified to act on the moral emotions that are built into the human organism. The emotion that Jonathan Haidt cites as the quintessential moral response is disgust. The disgust response lies at the heart of the dilemmas Haidt uses to demonstrate "moral dumbfounding"—as in the disgust that experimental subjects feel when presented with the idea of brother–sister incest, even when supposedly no harm will come of it. But demonstrating the presence of moral disgust in such situations does not mean that it is our reigning moral emotion. Nor does it mean that disgust always provides a sound moral compass. Disgust is not always a force for good. Grave harm has been done in the course of history by people's disgust for out-groups, people different from themselves, or those who defy social convention.

As understanding develops, it reshapes and redirects the emotion of disgust—as demonstrated, for example, by our society's changing attitudes toward race and sexual preference. Only moral understanding can serve as the touchstone for deciding whether an emotional response to a person or situation contributes positively to moral good and should therefore be supported and fostered, or whether it reflects prejudice, unfairness, and lack of understanding and therefore should be revised and rechanneled. Here again, reason and emotion are inextricably connected.

MORAL MOTIVATION

Just about everyone's conduct, over the long haul, is some mix of good and bad. The most admirable moral exemplars sometimes make unfortunate choices or succumb to temptations of various kinds. Unscrupulous criminals can be kind or generous at times. Most people at times act selfishly, dishonestly, and hurtfully, at least in small ways. Just about every person occasionally may be driven by a desire for vengeance in response to a real or imagined violation, by a very human wish to get more than one deserves, or by a tendency to make oneself the exception to a rule one hopes others will follow.

Yet, more often than not, people are well-intentioned, trustworthy, responsible, and caring. They want to see themselves as morally good and are honest enough to know that this means actually trying to *act* in moral ways. Most people also think seriously about moral issues. They may be confident in their views and resistant to input, or they may welcome other points of view. Yet in many cases, people are confused about moral questions, not as clear-thinking as they may feel, and sometimes self-serving in justifying unfair acts that make their own lives easier. In all these ways, most people are works in progress, not as fully developed as they might be, never perfect in a moral sense, but capable of improving themselves under the right circumstances.

The mix in people's conduct reflects an underlying mix of moral and nonmoral in their motives. Moral motives include goals of restraint (staying within the bounds of law and moral norms) and aspirational goals that include longer-term moral purposes (going above and beyond to help others, or committing to a broader noble cause).[28] And of course people are driven not only by a variety of moral goals but also by self-oriented goals such as prudential concerns and desires to protect and advance their own interests.

Evidence of the mixed motives people bring to their daily lives sometimes fosters cynicism—as if the presence of self-oriented motives negates the value of the more idealistic aims. We don't believe such cynicism is warranted. In some ways, evidence of mixed motives is a sign of robustness in the human moral sense: It shows that cultural norms, social and legal sanctions, moral understanding, moral emotions, and moral sense of self generally come together to support and stabilize an orderly world, where people can count on others not to exempt themselves from that moral order.

Mixed motives may be understood as redundancies in the moral system, much as modern airplanes are designed with redundant components to keep them aloft in case an engine dies or a wing is damaged. The presence of mixed motives is what gives the moral system the redundancy it needs to be generally reliable. We follow social rules for multiple reasons: because breaking them could trigger social disapproval or worse; because we have learned *habits* of moral response; because we buy into the rules and find them fair; because we abhor disorder and chaos; because we would feel guilty or ashamed to be (or be seen as) a miscreant; and because we have respect and affection for our society's traditions. And we care for others for multiple reasons: because we love and sympathize with them; because we believe they would care for us, and we value reciprocity; because we believe in the Golden Rule and other principles of fairness and compassion; because we don't want to feel or be seen as heartless; and because we accept the obligations of membership in a social group. Some of these reasons may not apply in any particular case, yet the moral acts still occur, because the other reasons kick in. This is why, although bloody wars and appalling crimes make the news, the vast majority of human behavior is civil, caring, and responsible.

Of course, people's various moral, cultural, and personal goals don't always line up in a moral direction, and people's moral motivations are not always strong enough to overcome their self-serving desires, fears, or other frailties. The most finely crafted redundant systems sometimes fail: Airplanes, unfortunately, do crash on occasion. This raises the most basic questions about moral motivation: What makes some people likely to do the right thing with regularity, while others consistently fail to do so?

Important as mature moral understanding is, it's well known that, taken alone, it doesn't reliably predict or determine behavior. Clearly, moral motivation involves more than knowing the good and therefore doing it. One of the factors that's most powerful in explaining the well-documented discrepancies between moral judgments and moral actions is *moral identity*. To reliably act in accord with their own best judgments about morally challenging situations, people need to believe that not only is a particular course of action morally good or right in general but also that they have a *personal responsibility* to take that course of action. This sense of personal responsibility is closely related to how important the moral issue or goal is to them, how central it is to their sense of who they are.[29] It is what leads to moral commitment, a sustained dedication to do the right thing.

In our earlier study of people who are highly morally committed, we found that their moral goals and concerns were so central to their sense of who they were that they experienced almost no conflict between moral goals and self-interest.[30] For these moral exemplars, what they wanted to do and what they felt they should do were so fully integrated that this commonly experienced conflict was essentially absent. As a result, they felt that actions they took that seemed highly risky and courageous to others hadn't required courage at all. When talking about what we understood as their exceptional generosity in helping the poor or their dramatic bravery in fighting racial segregation in the southern United States, the exemplars simply said, "How could I have lived with myself if I had just stood by in the face of that injustice (or need)?"

That and subsequent studies have made it clear that one of the most compelling moral motivations is the sense that failing to live up to one's moral ideals would be a deep, even intolerable, violation of one's own sense of self. When an issue is less central to one's identity, it's possible to feel, for example, "I really should do more to help those in need, but it's just too hard" or "I just can't find the time." But when the issue lies at the very heart of who one is, it becomes unthinkable to turn away from it.

A full account of moral motivation must also recognize that there's more than one way to maintain consistency between one's sense of self and one's strongly held moral beliefs. The first is straightforward—do what you believe is right, and you'll have no problem maintaining a sense of yourself as honest, caring, responsible, generous, or fair. The other approach, well documented by research, is rationalizing. Albert Bandura has documented in great detail the widespread practice of rationalizing, justifying one's behavior in all kinds of creative ways, so as to maintain a moral self-image while acting in apparent contradiction with moral precepts. He calls this *moral disengagement*.[31] Bandura's research has described a number of rationalization strategies such as *euphemistic labeling*, in which, for example, innocent civilians killed in military strikes are called "collateral damage;" *advantageous comparison*, in which one's violations are compared with others that are worse; *diffusion of responsibility*, the excuse that "everyone was doing it;" or *dehumanization*, in which one's victims are disparaged as "savages," "degenerates," "animals," and the like.

84

It's hard to imagine that anyone fully avoids rationalization, but people do differ in the extent to which they try sincerely to live their beliefs, ideals, and principles. When individuals are described as persons of integrity, this generally means that moral values and goals are central to who they are and, at least as important, it means that they don't often rationalize their violations of those values in order to let themselves off the hook. The avoidance of rationalization (which we call inner truthfulness) is widely recognized as a central feature of strong moral character.

In addition to variations among people, researchers have also documented situational variation *within* persons. This has been a major goal of the social psychologists who explore and articulate the power of situational contexts to influence, often to degrade, the behaviors of otherwise upstanding people. Because motives are virtually always mixed, situations with strong pressures to conform, act dishonestly, or hurt others are often successful in strengthening self-serving motives, fear of challenging authorities or social conventions, and the desire to avoid the embarrassment that could result from refusing to go along with others in the situation. When self-serving motives press against motives of moral concern and integrity rather than aligning with them, many people will succumb, often through self-deception in which rationalization covers up the violations. But, as we discussed earlier, not everyone gives in to temptation or situational pressure, so an investigation of morality requires that we understand not only why so many do succumb but also why some do not.

Fleeting emotional states and longer-term emotional tendencies are another source of variability within and among people. Again, this phenomenon is best understood from a baseline recognition of mixed motives. When people are feeling rushed, irritable, depleted, or beleaguered, they're much less likely to be generous and helpful, more likely to put their own interests ahead of others' welfare. Social psychologists have documented this in many experimental studies. But, even in these studies, people are not entirely led around by momentary emotional and physical states. These conditions or their opposites (situationally induced feelings of warmth, inspiration, and well-being) often shift the salience and strength of the various motivational factors that are always in some sense present but may or may not win the day. With self-awareness, these influences can be resisted. So, for example, research has shown that judges assign more lenient penalties in cases they hear after lunch, when presumably they feel more physically comfortable. Once judges become aware of biases like this, however, it's not terribly difficult to take them into account by giving those cases extra scrutiny. Understanding, as always, shapes the emotional response and its consequences for action.

MORAL CHARACTER AND VIRTUES

Not just for moral leaders and exemplars but for all people, one other factor is critical for maintaining the strength of positive moral motives and diminishing the power of moral vulnerabilities and destructive motives: the willingness to be honest with oneself. We spoke earlier in this chapter about the capacity shown by moral leaders and also many ordinary people to reflect on and even change their own emotional reactions when those reactions don't allow them to be their best selves or when they fail to serve their moral purposes. We also described the tendency of some people to take the qualities of inspiring models into themselves, seeing the ways their own behaviors fall short of those they admire and working to become more like them. These capacities for continued moral growth, like the tendency to avoid rationalizations that excuse immoral behavior, require that people are honest with themselves and able to learn from others in an open-minded way. Similarly, when people have come to see that they're not the center of the universe, but rather one among many, when they're able sometimes to take their attention off their own welfare and put it onto the welfare of others, the most prevalent competing motives—protection and advancement of self—are diminished. When their commitment to their ideals and moral goals run deep enough, when it is sustained by a moral faith, competing concerns lose their power. These three qualities—inner truthfulness, humility, and faith—are all *virtues* that help guide moral growth in a positive direction.

Over the years, many philosophers, social scientists, and educators have treated principled reasoning and moral virtue as opposing, almost mutually exclusive drivers of moral goodness. But we believe it's a mistake to place them in opposition to each other. In fact, one way to think about virtues is that they represent the dynamic intersection or culmination of the many distinct moral processes we've outlined here. Those processes include moral habit, emotion, perception, understanding, commitment, identity, integrity, and sense of purpose. When all these moral dimensions come together, we speak of moral character.

For many years in the middle to late twentieth century, people's demonstrated lack of behavioral consistency across situations led psychologists to deny that moral virtues exist. More recent research has been informative in identifying systematic patterns of "domain specificity," in which people demonstrate greater consistency within than across different areas of life.[32] This is an illuminating contribution, but it leaves in place the conception of virtues as traits, in a sense fixed quantities of a moral good that a person either has or doesn't have.

In the end, it may be more helpful to see in virtues the evolving interaction of the multiple processes represented in this overview of the multifaceted nature of moral functioning, along with others we may have neglected to mention. Habit, identity, commitment, foundational moral concepts and assumptions, and sometimes conscious reflection are all involved. The results are virtues, which are elements of moral character. Although it isn't realistic to expect complete consistency even *within* domains of life, strong moral character is revealed by virtues in action as they powerfully influence a person's capacity for moral growth.

Our study of the six moral leaders introduced in Chapter 2 takes a close look at the three virtues we just described, all of which are important for keeping moral growth on track across life. Those three—truthfulness, humility, and faith—are not the only important moral virtues—far from it. But we hope our discussions of these three virtues will shed light on the operation of moral virtues in a more general sense as they play out in the lives of more ordinary people as well as the place of these particular virtues in lives of exceptional moral commitment and influence.

In the aspirational view of morality explicated in our studies of inspiring and admirable people, we may appear to be neglecting the real limitations in their behavior and in the moral behavior of most ordinary people, not to mention those who do real evil in the world. But in saying that inner truthfulness, humility, and faith facilitate positive moral growth, we also wish to indicate that the absence of these virtues severely limits this potential for development. When people fail to look honestly at themselves, when they are arrogant, dogmatic, and closed-minded, when they are unwilling to consider the critical feedback of others. they will be unlikely to continue learning and evolving morally over time. Beyond the lack of inner truthfulness, a thoroughgoing cynicism that prevents some people from finding anything to believe in or commit to also limits their capacity to reach their full moral potential. In the following chapters, we explore the developmental answer to these potentially limiting qualities, the three virtues of truth, humility, and faith.

NOTES

1. Children in Walter Mischel's pioneering studies of self-control were told they would receive more marshmallows to eat if they could wait until later. The children who delayed gratification in this study had positive developmental outcomes years later. Mischel W., Shoda, Y., and M. L. Rodriguez, "Delay of Gratification in Children," *Science* 244, no. 4907 (May 26, 1989): 933–938.

2. Martin E. P. Seligman, *Flourish: A Visionary New Understanding of Happiness and Well-Being* (New York: Free Press, 2011).

3. F. B. M. de Waal, *Good Natured: The Origins of Right and Wrong in Humans and Other Animals* (Cambridge, MA: Harvard University Press, 1996), 296.

4. R. I. M. Dunbar, "The Social Role of Touch in Humans and Primates: Behavioural Function and Neurobiological Mechanisms," *Neuroscience and Biobehavioral Reviews* 34 (2010): 260–268.

5. Sarah F. Brosnan and Frans B. M. de Waal, "Monkeys Reject Unequal Pay," *Nature* 425, no. 6955 (2003): 297–299; Sarah F. Brosnan and Frans B. M. de Waal, "Animal Behaviour: Fair Refusal by Capuchin Monkeys," *Nature* 428, no. 6979 (March 11, 2004): 140.

6. Elliott Sober and David Sloan Wilson, *Unto Others: The Evolution and Psychology of Unselfish Behavior* (Cambridge, MA: Harvard University Press, 1998).

7. One famous example was Sigmund Freud, *Civilization and its Discontents* [Unbehagen in der Kultur. English], trans. Joan Riviere (New York: J. Cape & H. Smith, 1930).

8. Richard A. Shweder, *Why Do Men Barbecue?: Recipes for Cultural Psychology* (Cambridge, MA: Harvard University Press, 2003).

9. Louise Knight, *Jane Addams: Spirit in Action*, 1st ed. (New York: W. W. Norton & Co., 2010), 105.

10. Jonathan Haidt and Frederik Bjorklund, "Social Intuitionists Answer Six Questions about Moral Psychology," in *Moral Psychology: Vol. 2. The Cognitive Science of Morality: Intuition and Diversity*, ed. W. Sinnott-Armstrong (Cambridge, MA: MIT Press, 2008), 181–218.

11. Eliot Turiel, "Thought, Emotions, and Social Interactional Processes in Moral Development." in *Handbook of Moral Development*, eds. M. Killen and J. G. Smetana (Mahwah, NJ: Erlbaum, 2006), 7–35; Anne Colby, "The Place of Moral Interpretation and Habit in Moral Development," *Human Development* 43, no. 3 (2000), 161–164.

12. John C. Gibbs, *Moral Development & Reality: Beyond the Theories of Kohlberg, Hoffman, and Haidt*, 3rd ed. (New York: Oxford University Press, 2014).

13. David A. Pizarro and Paul Bloom, "The Intelligence of the Moral Intuitions; Comment on Haidt," *Psychological Review* 110 (2003): 193–196; Gordon B. Moskowitz et al., "Preconscious Control of Stereotype Activation through Chronic Egalitarian Goals," *Journal of Personality and Social Psychology* 77 (1999): 167–184; Turiel, *Thought, Emotions, and Social Interactional Processes in Moral Development*, 7–35; Ran R. Hassin, "Yes It Can: On the Functional Abilities of the Human Unconscious," *Perspectives on Psychological Science* 8 (2013): 195–207; Steven Pinker, *The Better Angels of our Nature: Why Violence Has Declined* (New York: Viking, 2011).

14. Philip Davidson and James Youniss, "Which Comes First, Morality or Identity?" in *Handbook of Moral Behavior and Development, Volume 1: Theory*, ed. W. M. Kurtines & J. L. Gewirtz (Hillsdale, NJ: Lawrence Erlbaum Associates, 1991), 105–122.

15. Janet Walker, "Choosing Biases, Using Power and Practicing Resistance: Moral Development in a World Without Certainty," *Human Development* 43 (2000): 135–156.

16. Walker, "Choosing Biases, Using Power," 138.

17. William Damon, *The Moral Child: Nurturing Children's Natural Moral Growth* (New York: Free Press, 1988), 166.

18. William Damon and Melanie Killen, "Peer Interaction and the Process of Change in Children's Moral Reasoning," *Merrill-Palmer Quarterly* 28, no. 3 (1982): 347–367.

19. Colin Camerer and Richard H. Thaler, "Anomalies: Ultimatums, Dictators and Manners," *The Journal of Economic Perspectives* 9, no. 2 (Spring, 1995): 209–219.

20. Walker, "Choosing Biases, Using Power," 135–156.

21. Jonathan Haidt, "The Moral Emotions," in *Handbook of Affective Sciences, Series in Affective Science*, eds. Richard J. Davidson, Klaus R. Scherer, and H. Hill Goldsmith (New York: Oxford University Press, 2003), 852.

22. As one classic and widely respected statement on the cognition/affect relation that gives due credit, but not sole primacy, to the importance of emotions, see Robert B. Zajonc, "Feeling and Thinking: Preferences Need No Inferences," *American Psychologist* 35, no. 2 (1980): 151–175.

23. Martin L. Hoffman, *Empathy and Moral Development: Implications for Caring and Justice* (Cambridge, UK, & New York: Cambridge University Press, 2000).

24. Daniel Kahneman, Paul Slovic, and Amos Tversky, *Judgment Under Uncertainty: Heuristics and Biases* (Cambridge, UK, & New York: Cambridge University Press, 1982).

25. Samuel P. Oliner and Pearl M. Oliner, *The Altruistic Personality: Rescuers of Jews in Nazi Europe* (New York: Free Press, 1988).

26. Roy F. Baumeister and John Tierney, *Willpower: Rediscovering the Greatest Human Strength* (New York: Penguin Press, 2011).

27. Mary Helen Immordino-Yang et al., "Neural Correlates of Admiration and Compassion," *Proceedings of the National Academy of Sciences, U.S.A.* 106, no. 19 (May 12, 2009): 8021–8026.

28. William Damon, *The Path to Purpose: Helping Our Children Find Their Calling in Life* (New York: Free Press, 2008).

29. Augusto Blasi, "Moral Understanding and the Moral Personality," in *Moral Development: An Introduction*, eds. William M. Kurtines and Jacob L. Gewirtz (Boston: Allyn & Bacon, 1995), 229–253; William Damon and Daniel Hart, *Self-Understanding in Childhood and Adolescence*, Vol. 7 (New York: Cambridge University Press, 1991); Jeremy A. Frimer and Lawrence J. Walker, "Reconciling the Self and Morality: An Empirical Model of Moral Centrality Development." *Developmental Psychology* 45, no. 6 (November, 2009): 1669–1681; D. Hart, R. Atkins, and T. M. Donnelly, "Community Service and Moral Development." in *Handbook of Moral Development*, eds. M. Killen and J. G. Smetana (Hillsdale, NJ: Lawrence Erlbaum Associates, 2006), 633–656; Hoffman, *Empathy and Moral Development: Implications for Caring and Justice*; David Moshman,

Adolescent Rationality and Development: Cognition, Morality, and Identity (New York: Psychology Press, Taylor & Francis Group, 2011).

30. Anne Colby and William Damon, *Some Do Care: Contemporary Lives of Moral Commitment* (New York: Free Press; 1992).

31. Albert Bandura et al., "Mechanisms of Moral Disengagement in the Exercise of Moral Agency," *Journal of Personality and Social Psychology* 71, no. 2 (1996): 364–374.

32. Christian B. Miller, *Character and Moral Psychology* (Oxford: Oxford University Press, 2014).

CHAPTER FOUR

TRUTHFULNESS

How important is it to be truthful? And how truthful should we be with ourselves and with others? In line with the cynicism of the so-called new science of morality, contemporary social science, especially as represented in the popular media, has cast a skeptical light on the value of being rigorously truthful. A recent *Wall Street Journal* story covering recent social science research is headlined "The Case for Lying to Yourself."[1] The article goes on to assert that some kinds of dishonesty can "boost your power and influence." A recent *US News* story stating "We're All Lying Liars"[2] suggests that "sometimes that may be a good thing" because "people who deceive themselves...tend to be happier than people who do not." It cites a study that shows most people lying at least once a day and some people telling lies every five minutes. Such accounts generally do warn that too much or the wrong kind of lying may impede success, but these warnings are almost always set in the context of an overall skepticism about the value of too much truth telling. These accounts condone small acts of self-deception and they go easy on occasional bigger lies to others. "Admit it. You lied," the *US News* article concludes. "Don't feel bad. You're in good, dishonest company."

Indeed, it does seem to be the case that most people do lie and cheat frequently. In *The (Honest) Truth about Dishonesty,*[3] Dan Ariely explains that this widespread dishonesty is stimulated in part by a perception that everyone else is doing it—a perception that makes each person's own dishonesty easy to justify. In this way, a culture of dishonesty perpetuates itself.

The contagion of dishonesty is to be expected in societies where corruption has begun to take root, and it helps explain why corruption is so hard to turn around without strong leadership and measures explicitly designed to suppress it. What's disturbing in our present-day society is that opinion leaders from the intellectual elite are actually trumpeting the benefits of self-deception and justifying other common forms of dishonesty. Rather than speaking out against the encroaching corruption of a growing culture of dishonesty, they have been trying to make a virtue out of a vice by claiming that the right types and amount of deception serve our self-interest. Such claims from esteemed scientists, and the numerous popular accounts these claims have engendered, have raised doubts throughout society today about whether a commitment to truthfulness is achievable, necessary, or even desirable in many instances.

It is now time to ask: Are we missing something today concerning the personal and moral risks of even minor acts of deceit? Are we overlooking the moral advantages of sticking to the truth even when it's inconvenient?

Traditionally, honesty has had a secure place in the pantheon of moral virtues. To the ancient Romans, who believed that the illuminating sunshine of truthfulness engendered honorable behavior of every kind, the goddess Veritas (Latin for truth) was considered "the mother of virtue." The Romans had lots of company in this view. Confucius considered honesty to be the primary source of love, communication, and fairness in human relationships. In the Western tradition, the Bible prohibits bearing false witness as one of its Ten Commandments. In the United States, the two most heralded presidents (George Washington, who "could not tell a lie," and Abraham Lincoln, known as Honest Abe) were widely known for their truth telling. The world's literature is so packed with tributes to honesty that literally thousands of immortal quotations on the matter can be gathered by a quick online search.

These public celebrations of honesty stem from a universal recognition: A basic assumption that most people can usually be taken at their word is required for all sustained civilized dealings. No civilization could tolerate for long a general expectation of untrustworthy communications. Human relations require the trust that people will, as a rule, try to tell the truth. This provides both a practical and a moral demand for truth telling.

All societies recognize this demand, but few consider it absolute. Tact and other humane concerns can mitigate the need to be completely honest on every occasion. Reassuring an ungainly teenager that she conveys her own special beauty can be a sensitive and responsible expression of a less literal truth. In a more consequential instance, people who lied to storm troopers about the whereabouts of hidden Jewish families during the Nazi occupation of Europe were performing honorable and courageous deceptions. Most moral philosophers don't consider honesty a moral absolute that demands strict allegiance at all times. Compassion, diplomacy, and life-threatening circumstances sometimes require a departure from the full, literal truth.

Seen in this light, the recent turn in social science in favor of self-deception and "minor" lies to other people may seem harmless enough. *WSJ*'s "The Case for Lying to Yourself" focuses almost entirely on self-deception around nonmoral issues such as body image or intelligence. Is there really any problem with convincing yourself, even if not accurately, that your high score on the Body Mass Index is due to dense muscle mass and large bones rather than to unhealthy amounts of fat (especially if you're not going to do anything about it anyway)? Or what about the familiar phenomenon of public speakers who talk themselves into believing they're great when they're actually mediocre or worse? Does that matter? The *WSJ* article quotes a Rutgers professor who claims that the ill-founded confidence of such speakers increases their chances of fooling their audiences into sharing their delusion—presumably a good thing, at least for the speakers. Well, after suffering through interminable lectures by blustering speakers with nothing interesting to say, we're doubtful that many listeners are fooled. Still, are the self-deluded speakers any worse than those with equally boring lectures who begin and end with apologies?

Yes, they are worse—or, to put it more precisely, they are in worse shape regarding their own future prospects. Ill-founded confidence and swagger are not favorable to growth. Self-deception is a particularly toxic form of swagger, because it closes the door to the inner criticism that spurs learning. Public pretense alone may discourage helpful feedback, but it leaves open a crack through which the truth might be seen, especially if the public pretense is accompanied by at least a modicum of private doubt. But self-deception lets nothing in. This is why psychology's "Dunning-Kruger effect" shows that the people who are the least skilled in a domain are the ones who overestimate their competence the most. People who truly understand the area of competence being assessed and are working to advance tend to be aware of their limitations. Their accurate self-awareness sets them up to become more expert through openness to feedback and targeted learning.

As a rule, a focus on learning is far more adaptive in life than unfounded reassurance. One of us (Damon) showed in *Greater Expectations*[4] how showering children with false praise diminishes their capacity for acquiring important skills and the secure, authentic self-confidence that accompanies them. The irony is that well-meaning adults will often use false praise to boost children's self-esteem, whereas the only sure way to do this is to help children develop genuine competencies by offering them, gently but honestly, feedback about what they still need to learn.

Unfortunately this sound approach flies in the face of some popular views on the matter. The self-esteem-at-all-costs approach, although shown to be invalid by decades of research, still looms large in contemporary childrearing and early education. And the recent self-deception movement (if we may call it that) has added ammunition to this misguided approach.

Self-deception advocates argue that children thrive on believing that they're smarter than they really are. They assume that self-deception is a natural and emotionally comforting response to life's challenges. Does this mean that it's cruel to set children straight? Where attainable skills are concerned, developmental research has shown that the wisest approach is to neither indulge nor denigrate such illusions, but rather to draw children's attention away from themselves and toward the benefits of learning. Studies by Stanford psychologist Carol Dweck have shown that children who believe they're really smart and care mostly about showing it (as well as children who think they're not smart and care mostly about hiding it) are at a serious disadvantage compared with children who value learning and have what Dweck calls a *growth theory of intelligence*.[5] The "growth theory" children understand that success depends on their motivation to learn and their willingness to work hard, not on a fixed amount of intelligence they may or may not already have. This kind of growth mindset brings many benefits, including optimism, persistence, and intrinsic motivation to learn. Well-established findings like Dweck's cast a harsh light on well-intentioned but misguided attempts to reassure children about abilities they could improve. False assurances can encourage self-deception rather than learning, not a happy outcome.

If honest self-assessment is important for developing competence, it's essential for moral growth. Philosopher Sissela Bok[6] writes that Iris Murdoch got to the heart of the matter when she commented that self-deception attacks morality at its roots. Self-deception undermines morality because it interferes with the ability to refine (or, if necessary, reform) one's character. Serious mistakes can arise from the slippery slope that begins with small lies to oneself or others.

The twelve-step program of Alcoholics Anonymous reflects this insight. A passage from the "Big Book," read at the beginning of each meeting, refers to "the capacity to be honest" as a requirement for recovery. Many of the twelve steps are organized around recognizing, acknowledging, making restitution for, and monitoring one's moral transgressions, especially the ways that one's behavior has harmed others. This process of reshaping one's character toward integrity and trustworthiness is seen as necessary if the recovering alcoholic is to regain the self-respect that out-of-control drinking has destroyed, thus establishing a solid foundation for long-term sobriety. AA's emphasis on honesty with oneself as a necessity for moral growth applies equally to nonalcoholics. If you deny your dishonest, self-seeking, or callous behaviors, there's no hope of avoiding dishonesty, selfishness, or callousness in the future. In this way, honesty within oneself is vitally connected with honesty toward others.

Now, we have no qualms about approaches that promote positive thinking and optimism as healthy ways of orienting to life, as long as these approaches do not substitute illusions for reality. Hoping for the best and taking an optimistic view of one's chances for success have little in common with an unwillingness to examine objectively one's real competence. There's a big difference between telling yourself "I can do it!" and telling yourself "I'm the smartest guy in the room and don't need to know anything more." Approaching challenges with confidence, even if success seems improbable, and blocking out negative thoughts to focus on the positive are adaptive mental patterns. They are not self-deceptive in any significant way. It is entrenched denial—the habitual distortion of reality—that is dysfunctional, not attempts to think about reality in affirmative ways.

Actually, it may be that some of the recommendations made by today's self-deception advocates are indeed simply suggestions that we not dwell on negative thoughts and that we try to adopt optimistic attitudes—in effect, that we accentuate the positive. This isn't really self-deception at all but rather an exercise in healthy mental discipline. Other behaviors that have been tossed into the "deception" category by popular accounts seem even further from being dishonest in a harmful sense; for example, one study includes wearing false eyelashes in its list of present-day deceptions. Whatever one may think of the aesthetics of false eyelashes, it would be quite a stretch to say that the people wearing them are "lying" about their looks. If you felt that way, you would have a hard time finding a fashionably adorned person anywhere in the world who would seem genuine. Transparent manipulations of reality that are not conducted in the spirit of deception will not produce the harms of dishonesty.

The problem with the breezy discussions of deception in the popular press is that they conflate inner pep talks and social conventions such as "It's lovely to see you" with serious and habitual denial of reality. Distinguishing between these forms of untruthfulness is crucial for understanding what truthfulness is and how it works to foster growth and adaptation.

Philosophers throughout the ages have taken such distinctions very seriously. A classic work on this topic, *Lying* by Sissela Bok,[7] defines lying as an intentional effort to mislead. With this definition in mind, she points out that courtesies such as greeting people by saying, "How nice to see you" fool no one and are not intended to. These social conventions aren't even white lies—they're simply good manners. In the case of actual lies, Bok puts forward a "Principle of Veracity," which states that "in any situation where a lie is being considered, one must first seek truthful alternatives. A lie, though sometimes justified, should be a last resort."[8] This principle applies even to small lies or well-intentioned deceptions. Some lies, including white lies that are harmless and lies to prevent harm to an innocent person, are justifiable, but all too often lies are told out of convenience rather than necessity and thus don't meet the "last resort" condition.

Bok calls attention to three kinds of harm that result from dishonesty: harm to the person lied to, harm to the liar, and harm to the general level of trust and social cooperation. Lies rob the victim of trust and the information needed to make rational choices; they put the receiver of the lie in an unfairly disadvantaged position; and they violate the principle behind the golden rule by treating another person deceitfully, not as one would wish to be treated. Furthermore, each act of lying erodes the teller's psychological barriers to dishonesty, making future lies easier to tell and establishing habits that can become automatic, without any consideration or awareness of consequences. Bok quotes an anonymous wit in saying that the first lie "must be thatched by another or it will rain through" and "it takes an excellent memory to keep one's untruths in good repair and disentangled."[9] Needless to say, liars can also be unmasked, and the credibility and regard they lose are very hard to regain. Still, the more people lie, the more oblivious they become to the risk of this grave loss.

Liars are also likely to ignore the larger social consequences of their behavior. As Bok points out, "The veneer of social trust is often thin. As lies spread...trust is damaged. Yet trust is a social good to be protected just as much as the air we breathe or the water we drink."[10]

In contemporary life, the veneer of social trust has worn exceedingly thin in many places. In the educational world, cheating and misrepresentation of credentials are rife. In professional and business circles, a now-familiar complaint is, "It used to be your word was good, but those days are gone." Contemporary journalism has lost credibility with much of the public for its perceived biases and its sacrifice of truth to profit. Most troubling for a democratic republic, political discourse is no longer considered a truthful source of information; rather, it's assumed that political leaders make statements merely to posture for effect or win political advantage, not to engage in honest discussion and fact-driven debates. In this kind of climate, facts may be readily manipulated (or made up) in the service of a predetermined interest, not presented accurately and then examined in good faith. The main victim of this absence of credible discourse is the public trust.

Entrenched dishonesty can destroy a democratic system. It takes away freedom of choice, because free choices require accurate information. It destroys the trust needed for civic devotion on the part of the citizens. Distrust, like the dishonesty that engenders it, reproduces itself: When one member of society gives up on the possibility of dealing honestly with others, that person joins the ranks of the distrustful and dishonest, influencing yet others to abandon their own commitment to the truth.

Of course, humane considerations sometimes call for a mistruth as a last resort. Very few moral philosophers (a notable exception is Immanuel Kant) insist on rigid adherence to the truth no matter what the circumstances. But in the more flexible sense outlined by Bok and other contemporary philosophers, a reliable commitment to truth is indispensable for individuals' own development; for their relations with family, friends, neighbors, coworkers, and society; for institutions such as schools, courts, and corporations; and for the community, the culture, and the nation.

WHY PEOPLE STRUGGLE WITH HONESTY

Considering honesty's importance for individual and social well-being, why is it such an unreliable feature of human behavior? It might seem that people would estimate the likely costs of deceiving someone, weigh these costs against the deception's expected benefits, and (rightly or wrongly) decide that the benefits outweigh the costs, at least to themselves. This would follow from the basic economic principle that people will rationally pursue their own self-interest. But author Dan Ariely (a professor of behavioral economics) dismisses this model, believing it to be a poor explanation for the results of his experimental studies of cheating. If cost–benefit principles were driving the behavior, the amount that people cheat would depend on three things: the amount they stand to gain from cheating, the probability of being caught, and the size of the penalty if they are caught. Over and over in these studies, manipulating the size of incentives and the probability and severity of penalties failed to drive changes in the likelihood that subjects would cheat.

Ariely does believe that people often cheat because they want the extra money or other rewards that cheating brings; at the same time, people want to see themselves as honest and good people. Ariely argues that his studies show that most people are able to cheat a little bit and still see themselves as basically honest. If people cheat for larger sums, it becomes harder to see themselves as good people. That's why raising the amount of the potential gains will discourage cheating instead of increasing it. A small amount of cheating (or stealing) allows people to come away with a clean moral slate, because they can deny that it represents real dishonesty.

At the heart of this explanation is the influence of self-deception—that is, denying the nature of your behavior by minimizing and rationalizing it. We agree that this is the process at work in the lion's share of ordinary dishonesty. And we also agree with Ariely that dishonesty of this sort and the self-deception that enables it are not as harmless as people take them to be.

Albert Bandura's research has shown how widespread and multifaceted this rationalization process is.[11] Strategies for rationalizing include minimizing the act, creating specious moral justifications, evading moral issues by using euphemisms designed to disguise the true nature of what one did, comparing oneself with others whose behavior is even worse, blaming others, denying one's particular responsibility to act for the good since others are failing to do so, distorting or denying the consequences of one's actions, and dehumanizing one's victims. These strategies, often deployed in combination with one another, enable even apparently decent people to perpetrate inhumane behaviors by morally disengaging—that is, by disconnecting the internal mechanisms of moral accountability, most notably avoiding self-blame for serious transgressions of their own moral beliefs by denying that these are genuine transgressions.

Moral disengagement of this sort often occurs in response to situational temptations or pressures. These pressures can be powerful enough to shape the behavior of the majority who experience them. This is the sort of contextual pressure that was documented by social psychologist Philip Zimbardo in his famous prison experiment. Pressures of a more ordinary variety also exert strong influence, in part because people often look to others to gauge what kind of behavior is acceptable in any particular context. This is why social pressures and temptations to cut corners can undermine a commitment to truthfulness and other ethical standards, especially in the absence of engaging models that represent compelling positive ideals. The ensuing moral disengagement can be gradual; but once mechanisms of moral self-deception are employed, they are usually self-perpetuating. The result can be a downward moral drift that is cumulative and very hard to reverse.

But Bandura also pointed out that, while social forces do exert powerful influence, people are producers as well as products of social forces. As we noted in Chapter 3, thoughtful sociologists have pointed to the reciprocal influences of individuals and institutions: People create social situations, which in turn create them. This circularity suggests that people who remain strongly attached to their convictions have the power to resist and even, ultimately, to change their social contexts.

Bandura's perspective, like ours, acknowledges not only people's vulnerability to moral disengagement, self-deception, and corrosive situational pressures but also people's potential to resist such pressures in favor of proactive moral choices. Many people "act in the name of humane principles even in terrible situations," Bandura writes. In such cases, "the individual triumphs as a moral agent."[12] This kind of fortitude, which Bandura calls moral heroism, is evident in the behavior of the subjects who disobeyed Milgram's authoritative experimenter in the white coat, refusing to go along with his demands to shock the helpless victim. It's evident in the work of journalists from our own studies who resist their organizations' pressures to sensationalize and commercialize the news. It is dramatically evident in the six moral leaders we describe in this book. A prerequisite for this kind of resolute and proactive moral commitment is inner truthfulness, the unrelenting struggle to find and stay true to the best within themselves.

HOW SIX TWENTIETH-CENTURY LEADERS RELIED ON TRUTHFULNESS IN THEIR PURSUIT OF WORLD-CHANGING MORAL GOALS

In the rest of this chapter, we focus on the virtue of truthfulness as it's revealed in the lives of the six twentieth-century leaders we studied. For each of the leaders, we analyzed a great number of documents, including biographies and the leaders' own published letters, diaries, speeches, books, and autobiographical accounts. To learn about the roles that truth, humility, and faith played in the lives of these extraordinary people, we developed a coding scheme meant to capture the range of themes expressed within each of the three virtues we were investigating.[13] Several independent raters then coded the case material using the thematic coding manual. For each of the three virtues, several themes emerged as especially salient in the lives of the leaders. For the virtue of truthfulness, we identified six important themes, the five most prevalent of which we discuss in the remainder of this chapter. Those five themes are discernment, resolve, truth as a public obligation, open-mindedness, and the evolving nature of truth.

The virtue of truthfulness was central to the lives and work of all six leaders. They were keenly aware of how important it is to be truthful—and how hard it is to avoid deception, especially self-deception.

Abraham Heschel was bold and unconventional in both his theological work and his politics, and for this he was often severely criticized, his actions and even his motives called into question. He had to wonder whether his critics might be right when they accused him of overreaching when he tried to influence the Vatican's position on the conversion of Jews, for example, or self-promotion when he marched with Martin Luther King, Jr. His response was a depth of self-examination that tried to take account of human beings' natural tendency toward rationalization. As he wrote: "Nothing is easier than to deceive oneself. As the mind grows more sophisticated, self-deception advances.... Who can trust his own motivations? His honesty?"[14]

An explicit commitment to both private and public truth was so salient in Abraham Heschel's life that it even figured prominently in his funeral service. He had died suddenly and still quite young, and his wife and daughter were devastated, as were his many friends. A consolation was their admiration for the way he had lived. At Heschel's funeral, the grieving congregation understood that the Biblical text for the service, Psalm 15, was a telling description of their friend: "He that walketh uprightly...speaketh truth in his heart."

As we examined the private and public documents of the six leaders, we found similar concerns in each case. They tried to pay attention to errors and learn from experience. They were also committed to truthfulness in their public pursuits, believing that their causes were best served by cultivating strong public trust, which would be severely damaged by deception. Although they were all immensely effective and goal-driven, they resisted the common temptation to use dishonest means to pursue noble ends. They saw this choice as both moral and practical: Honesty, they believed, is in every way the best policy.

The six lived in different contexts and cultures, in different times and circumstances, and they held different ideologies and religious beliefs, but they shared a commitment to truth in all its guises, not the least of which is inner truthfulness, or scrupulous honesty with oneself. All six described regular practices of self-reflection through which they scrutinized their own behavior and motivations with a searching frankness. These practices included prayer, self-reflective diaries, honest discussions with friends and intimate partners, requests to colleagues and staff for candid feedback, and conscious efforts to take seriously criticism from opponents. They all expressed the belief that honesty with others starts from honesty with oneself, and that one is not really possible without the other.

Nelson Mandela once commented, somewhat wryly, that being locked in prison gave him many opportunities for careful self-reflection. Not many would have seen it this way. At Robben Island, Mandela's days were spent hacking out seams in a lime quarry that was blindingly white in the sun. There was no shade, and prisoners were denied sunglasses to protect their eyes from the relentless glare. Political prisoners were forbidden to have radios or newspapers and were allowed only one letter every six months. The letters were usually so heavily censored that they were almost unreadable. Who would blame Mandela if he had been too consumed by rage, fear, worry, and desolation to see prison as a good chance for self-reflection? But for Mandela, honest self-reflection wasn't a luxury: It was part of what kept him on track and able to function brilliantly even with no assurance that his imprisonment would ever end.

As we noted, Albert Bandura called people who see through their own temptations to deceive themselves and succeed in maintaining integrity in the face of challenges "moral heroes." Some certainly do qualify for that designation, but ordinary people also know about the human tendency to give priority to their own interests and are capable of monitoring their thinking for self-serving biases. In a study of how people interpret situations, sociologist Janet Walker interviewed a racially and ethnically diverse group of workers in an auto parts factory.[15] Among other things, she found that many of the workers showed a clear awareness that people's views of moral situations, such as fairness in job assignments and in pay, are driven at least partly by a desire to legitimate their own self-interest in the situation. The workers were especially likely to attribute self-interested motives to others, but they also realized that their own interpretations could be biased.

Walker quotes a Mexican-American woman in the study who acknowledged that "the blacks think the Hispanics are treated better, and we think the blacks are being treated better than we are..."[16] This understanding led the woman to question her frequent anger toward her boss, who was white. She wondered whether her anger might come from misinterpretation of his motives and her own possibly biased conception of fairness in task assignments. Although Walker doesn't use Jon Baron's terminology, this case is a good example of what he calls actively open-minded thinking (see Chapter 1). As such, it belies the new science claims that what appears to be moral reflection is usually closer to rationalization than rationality.

This tendency to question one's own interpretations and motives occurred frequently in Janet Walker's interviews. Based on these and other analyses, Walker concludes that the pursuit of integrity involves learning to recognize the many times that we fail to live up to our own moral standards and then changing our interpretive habits based on that increased awareness and self-understanding: "In undertaking this quest [for greater integrity], we gradually mold our experience of the world, taking advantage of the opportunities provided in the micro-occasions of our lives so as to build a reality more hospitable to the moral self we aspire to. Acting with integrity provides us with moments which are morally satisfying, and which many times bring well-being and happiness to others."[17] Ordinary people, despite the skepticism of public intellectuals, behave with integrity and experience well-earned moments of moral satisfaction on many occasions throughout their lives (and we should say "our lives," because we two authors are certainly ordinary people).

We believe that the lives of the six moral leaders we studied show how truthfulness can help both extraordinary and ordinary people pursue moral purposes and deal with great challenges. We draw on these extraordinary lives as examples of effectiveness and commitment. We're convinced that these examples offer valuable lessons for the rest of us. This doesn't mean that the converse is true: Genius, for example, may not be fully explainable with reference to normal intelligence. The famous art historian Edgar Wind once made the same observation: "It seems to be a lesson of history that the commonplace may be understood as a reduction of the exceptional, but the exceptional cannot be understood as an amplification of the commonplace."[18] We are not fans of reductionism of any type, but we agree that the strategies of extraordinary people are readily available for all to adopt. Here we describe the major ways that the six leaders we studied used truthfulness in pursuit of their goals, strategies that all people can learn to use.

DISCERNMENT

An overriding concern for truth means that individuals stand by their deeply held values, even in the face of pressure. But first they need to understand exactly what those values tell them to do in difficult situations where the right path isn't clear. Often, the right path is easy to see, and little inner struggle is needed. At other times, though, discernment of one's own moral truth requires advice from other people, significant wrestling with alternative choices, searching self-reflection, and sometimes prayers for guidance.

Dietrich Bonhoeffer's struggle to find his own deepest truth was especially dramatic. Bonhoeffer understood the dangers posed by Adolf Hitler's bid for power in Germany even before Hitler was appointed chancellor in 1933. Bonhoeffer began speaking out early and by 1934 was working with the Confessing Church, a coalition of churches that opposed Hitler's encroachment on the Protestant church establishment in Germany. Bonhoeffer, a handsome and charming young man, only 28 years old, was often called on to bolster his comrades' fortitude. This was a dangerous business.

There is no easy explanation for Bonhoeffer's striking courage at this young age. He was still finding his way in the world. He had not yet married and had only begun to settle into his career as a pastor. In many ways, it wasn't a good moment for him to risk everything. Dietrich had so far led a highly privileged life. He had grown up with his parents and seven siblings in a beautiful house filled with books and music, playing the piano for the family's regular Saturday night concerts. At university, he was a star student who also found time for the camaraderie of a fraternity and travels to Rome and Bologna. As a charismatic young pastor, he formed the center of a close-knit group of scholars and was in no way a reckless or impulsive person.

Yet, very early in Hitler's ascendency, Bonhoeffer saw how high the stakes were and pressed others to join him in bold action. In a letter to other leaders of the Confessing Church written in 1934, he urged them to be true to the Church's dangerous but historically critical mission: "Now is the time when we must be radical on all points [in opposing Nazism]..., without fear of the possible disagreeable consequences for ourselves. If we are untrue to ourselves in any way at this point, we shall discredit the entire struggle..."[19] This was a standard that he was prepared to follow as well as recommend.

As Hitler's power in Germany grew and the world moved toward war, it was clear to Bonhoeffer that he would be called for military service under the regime. He knew that to refuse would lead to imprisonment and likely execution, but he believed that taking part in Hitler's military would be terribly wrong: "Shouldn't one refuse to obey a government which was heading straight for war and breaking all the commandments of God?"[20] He felt that he should either declare his conscientious objection or leave the country. Bonhoeffer knew that once his inevitable conscription took place, he would not be allowed to leave Germany. He struggled with the question of whether to go before that happened. After talking with people whose wisdom he trusted, he decided in the spring of 1939 to accept an invitation to join the Union Theological Seminary in New York and take up residence there. On June 2, he left for New York.

When Bonhoeffer arrived in New York, he was welcomed by a talented and warmly engaging group of colleagues. His work there would deepen his theological scholarship and give him the chance to experience a fascinating and exotic culture that was entirely new to him. But, despite these riches, it wasn't long before Dietrich began to question his decision to leave Germany. His diary reveals how tormented he was by the thought that his departure amounted to running away.[21] On his second day in New York, he prayed in the home of Henry Sloane Coffin, the president of Union, and shortly afterward wrote: "I was almost overcome by the short prayer...in which we thought of the German brothers....I haven't been able to stop thinking about Germany. The whole burden of self-reproach because of a wrong decision comes back again and again."[22] For days, Bonhoeffer struggled, thinking of Germany all the time. "No news from Germany the whole day....I want to know what is happening to the work over there, whether all is well or whether I am needed."[23]

Soon afterward, he made the decision to return to Germany and take up once again the Confessing Church's struggle against Hitler. Bonhoeffer's American hosts were disappointed, upset, and worried for him when he refused to stay and complete the planned work at Union. He hated to let them down but didn't see how he could turn his back on his country. Bonhoeffer reflected on his decision in his diary: "It is remarkable that I am never quite clear about the motives for any of my decisions. Is that a sign of confusion, of inner dishonesty, is it a sign that we are *guided* without our knowing, or is it both?"[24] The decision was final, and Bonhoeffer entrusted it to God. Less than a month after his arrival in the United States, and against the pleas of his American hosts, Bonhoeffer sailed back to Nazi Germany on one of the last ships to make the trip from the United States before war broke out.

RESOLVE

It's not easy to search rigorously for the truest path, tolerating no self-deception that could falsely justify easier choices. It's even harder to stand fast in pursuit of that path when faced with criticism, isolation, financial risks, attacks on one's character, physical danger, and sometimes imprisonment and death. But the resolve that it takes to stand fast is the defining feature of extraordinary moral commitment. It's the six leaders' willingness to take these risks and endure these sacrifices that makes their commitment to truth so convincing and their stories so awe-inspiring.

In ways that were more or less costly, all of the moral leaders in our study aligned themselves with ideals that expressed moral truth as they understood it and maintained their resolve in pursuing that truth whatever the costs. For all these men and women, the ideals were compelling enough to shape their major behavioral choices and the directions of their lives. The leaders often confronted severe pressures to turn away from their ideals.

Abraham Heschel's position at the Jewish Theological Seminary was extremely important to him. He had started his teaching career in the United States at Hebrew Union College in Cincinnati, a Reform seminary. As a Conservative rabbi, he felt out of place and at sea, in part because the daily and weekly routines of Jewish life are so different in the two traditions. Heschel longed to move to a Conservative seminary, and the chance to teach at JTS was a godsend. Naturally, Heschel was eager to earn the esteem of his colleagues there. But, in ways that were acutely painful for him, Heschel was marginalized by his academic colleagues for his unconventional approach to Jewish thought, which they believed was too "poetic" and insufficiently analytical. Many also objected to his political involvement, believing that his public stands against racism and the Vietnam War detracted from his professional standing and might even contribute to the anti-Semitism of the time. Even after his writing had made him a celebrity in the larger world, Heschel's office at JTS was so small that it couldn't contain the books and files he needed for his work. When he asked for a larger, less suffocating office, he was given a bookcase in the hall and access to a cubicle in the library of neighboring Columbia University. To Heschel, this was a humiliating sign of the administration's lack of respect for his contributions. Still, Heschel drove himself to exhaustion, carrying on his intensive writing as well as his pursuit of social justice in spite of his colleagues' disapproval and his own serious health problems. Many who knew him believed that this relentlessness led to the fatal heart attack he suffered at age 65.

Eleanor Roosevelt's constant activism on behalf of civil rights, gender equality, and workers was widely admired, but not universally so. Throughout her terms as First Lady, she endured public ridicule, politically motivated FBI investigations, and even death threats. Often in FDR's White House, lively groups would gather in the evenings for cocktails, laughter, and sparkling conversation. This might have provided some relief from her pressures, but Eleanor seldom joined them: She had her writing and other work to do and was sustained more by the camaraderie and outcomes of her mission than by evenings of wit and glamor.

Dag Hammarskjöld led a lonely existence despite his public role. For reasons that scholars have speculated about, he felt that his work was inconsistent with a fully developed personal life. In addition, his work toward world peace meant that he was immersed time and again in dangerous zones of civil war and other conflicts. He died in a small plane crash en route to one of the most difficult and dangerous of these conflicts, a bitter internal war in the Congo.

For Jane Addams, the pressure to retreat from her convictions marked the entirety of her long career. These pressures reached their apogee when she announced her opposition to World War I. Addams had already been working for many years to create and put into practice her vision of a democracy based in community, collaboration, and fellowship among people of all classes and ethnicities. She thought hard about democratic citizenship and institutions and believed that the healthiest institutions were those that nurtured life and contributed to the good of society as a whole. To her, any unnecessary war was the antithesis of democracy's essence—and World War I, she believed, was pointless and wrong. History, we should note, has garnered Addams lots of company in this belief.

Addams worked with other advocates of peace to try to create a settlement for ending the war and to persuade the United States to maintain its neutrality. Early on, she urged President Wilson to convene a conference of neutral nations to negotiate an armistice. In the end, of course, the United States did enter the war. Addams had already faced an onslaught of negative publicity and censure for her opposition to the war. Once the United States declared war, this criticism escalated into vicious and sustained attacks by her opponents and abandonment by many of her former supporters. Addams went from being one of the most admired women in the country to one of the most reviled.

The war years were lonely and desolate for Addams. She subsisted in a state of spiritual alienation, self-doubt, and despair. But she found comfort and support where she could, and she endured the attacks. She later wrote of pacifists during the war: "We could not…lose the conviction that…the moral changes in human affairs…begin…with the one who…is designated as a crank and a freak…"[25] As Louise Knight noted, "She had grasped why the West admired the hero—not just because he stood alone but because he stood for the truth as he saw it, regardless of the consequences."[26]

For Nelson Mandela, getting the truth about apartheid out to the world was worth the price of his own life. This bargain was never clearer than during the Rivonia trial, in which he and his co-defendants were accused of conspiracy to commit sabotage and other crimes in connection with their organized resistance to the South African regime. Toward the conclusion of this tumultuous trial, it seemed certain that the defendants would be convicted and sentenced to death. But Mandela was more determined to use the trial as a showcase of the evils of apartheid than to gain release or leniency. With this in mind, he delivered an address that was sure to seal his conviction but that vividly drew the world's attention to the extreme injustice of South Africa's policies. Even more dramatically, Mandela announced that, if convicted, he would not appeal, because he believed an appeal would undermine the moral stand he and his colleagues had taken. In the end, in response to international protests, intervention by the United Nations, and testimony for leniency by distinguished Afrikaners (the dominant white group currently in power), the judge sentenced Mandela and his co-defendants to life in prison rather than death.

Mandela's courage in sticking to his convictions carried through his long imprisonment from start to finish. Martin Meredith, author of one of the most definitive biographies of Mandela to date, describes a telling incident at the beginning of his long prison stay:

> When Mandela landed at Robben Island [South Africa's most brutal prison], he was ordered to run but refused and walked at a leisurely pace. The warders yelled, "Look man. We will kill you, we are not fooling around. Your wives and children and mothers and fathers will never know what happened to you. This is the last warning." Mandela calmly replied, "You have your duty and we have ours."[27]

TRUTH AS A PUBLIC OBLIGATION

Throughout this chapter, we have explored the significance of truthfulness as a character virtue of a personal nature. The constant search for and adherence to inner truth was a defining quality of the six moral leaders. In addition, all six believed that truth is a critical public obligation as well as an essential personal virtue. By that, they meant that not only individuals but also organizations, states, and the populace of those states acting as citizens are bound by obligations of truthfulness. The six leaders were acutely aware that public trust is vital for democracy and the proper functioning of public institutions, and they stressed the importance of individuals' insisting on truthfulness from their governments and institutions.

Abraham Heschel was especially concerned about the overriding value of public truth. One of Heschel's most consuming roles was that of social critic. He believed it was important to publicly speak the truth about the world as he saw it. Heschel was a critic of his country's consumerism, uncaring treatment of the elderly, and public callousness in all forms. Even more centrally, he decried injustice and worked for black civil rights and peace in Vietnam. On the latter, he wrote: "The cruelties committed by our armed forces in Southeast Asia were made possible by an unprecedented campaign of deceiving the American people.... The hour may have come to realize that falsehood, deception, is at the root of evil."[28]

Heschel didn't limit his critiques to the United States: He was at least as critical of the Soviet Union for its policies restricting the rights of Jews to worship and to emigrate. He worked long and hard to press the Roman Catholic Church to change what he saw as its false teachings about the role of Jews in the persecution and crucifixion of Christ. According to Heschel's major biographer, Edward Kaplan, "For the sake of truth and compassion, [Heschel] jeopardized his health, compromised his writing and teaching, and undermined his prestige within the Jewish community."[29]

In Heschel's roles as social critic and activist, he was trying to hold nations (the United States and the Soviet Union) and institutions (the Catholic Church, the American popular media) accountable to moral truth. Dag Hammarskjöld, as leader of one of the world's most powerful institutions, was equally aware of the critical importance of institutional accountability and integrity.

Along with the goal of peace among nations, the ideal of truth as impartiality and integrity served as the foundation of Hammarskjöld's leadership. In his view, inner truthfulness and honest self-reflection were as important for institutions as they were for individuals: "I feel that an administration inspired by sound self-criticism, never blunted by conceit or false loyalties, and self-improving in that spirit, has a just claim to respect and confidence of the government and the public."[30]

Hammarskjöld, like Heschel, was troubled by the lack of truthfulness and objectivity in press accounts, an awareness increased by his global perspective. At the time, in the early 1950s, worldwide television coverage was in its infancy but was gearing up quickly. Hammarskjöld saw both the good and bad sides of the increased visibility this coverage brought to world events: "Has there indeed been any time when the troubles of all the world were brought so quickly and so fully into every home? Quickly and fully—but how rarely in a spirit of objectivity! How rarely in such a way as to make it possible for the common man to find what should be his proper reaction to world affairs in the light of his basic ideals!"[31]

In Hammarskjöld's view, the success of the UN depended not only on increased public demand for truthful accounts of conflicts but also on impeccable impartiality within the organization itself. In a message for UN Staff Day in 1953, he asked: "Why are the standards and the independence of the Secretariat [of the UN] so important? The more I see of the work in the United Nations, the more convinced I feel of this importance. Countries are arming in order to be able to negotiate from a position of strength. The Secretariat too has to negotiate, not only in its own self-interest, but for the cause of peace and a peaceful development of our world. The weight we carry is not determined by physical force or the number of people who form the constituency. It is based solely on trust in our impartiality, our experience and knowledge, our maturity of judgment."[32]

Hammarskjöld was convinced that the UN's success depended on its willingness to look honestly at the world the way it is and to start from there, no matter how chaotic and brutal the present state of the world, no matter how great the distance between present realities and goals of cooperation and harmony. A truthful grasp on reality must be the starting point. In a speech to the UN Correspondents Association in 1953, Hammarskjöld remarked: "I have repeatedly quoted a phrase coined by Paul Valery [translated as "Those who prefer to swim instead of drown should concern themselves with the conditions of the water]. It expresses the simple truth that, when trying to change our world, we have to face it as it is."[33]

Jane Addams, one of the founders of American Pragmatism, displayed this same concern. Historian Louise Knight described many instances in which Addams insisted on understanding the present reality clearly before attempting to act in the world. Knight commented that Addams was "able to imagine new possibilities while also seeing life as it is, to create a bridge between those things we desire and those things which are possible."[34]

The concern for truth as a public obligation takes us back to our earlier discussions of the relationship of cultures to individuals. Culture is not a fixed reality, outside the interpretation, evaluation, and control of its participants. In fact, moral leadership often entails making apparent the destructive norms embedded in some cultural traditions and then joining with other people to work for cultural change.

This is one way to understand Nelson Mandela and Desmond Tutu's remarkable achievement in creating the Truth and Reconciliation Commission (TRC) in South Africa, which we described in Chapter 2. When Mandela was released from prison, South Africa was in the grip of intense hatred and fear among several opposing groups, to the point of hideously violent attacks and other flagrant human rights abuses. The streets were full of burning tires, gunshots, and lifeless bodies. Dramatic action was needed if the country was to heal. The TRC helped many people find ways to rise above the searing pain of apartheid and their desires for vengeance. It accomplished this by affirming and actualizing a commitment to truth as a public value—in Mandela's view, the only value capable of forming the basis for reconciliation. It was an astonishing achievement, surprising onlookers the world over and setting a new standard, since then widely emulated, for societal reconciliation in the wake of severe human rights abuses.

Beyond the drama of postapartheid South Africa, even in quieter times and places, there is often a need to reshape the cultures of societies and their key institutions. The same kind of moral leadership is called for in those cases—leadership committed to truth as a public obligation. In our studies of Good Work and professional integrity, we have written about moral leaders in fields such as journalism, law, and medicine. Like the six twentieth-century leaders in this book, these present-day men and women eschew tradeoffs between effectiveness and honesty. They understand truth to be essential to the long-term advancement of their goals. Without truthfulness, the missions of their fields would lose credibility—as has occurred in journalism in recent years due to several highly publicized scandals concerning falsified news stories. As a public obligation, truthfulness promotes and safeguards the public trust, without which democracy cannot flourish.

OPEN-MINDEDNESS

In a previous book, *Some Do Care: Contemporary Lives of Moral Commitment*,[35] we analyzed the lives of twenty-three highly committed Americans—moral exemplars who were, in other ways, completely ordinary people. Every one revealed a particular combination of qualities that may seem incompatible at first glance. They were all characterized by what we called certainty—an unwavering conviction about moral principles and clear sense of personal responsibility to act—and also by open-mindedness. We concluded that one of the main qualities that distinguish moral exemplars from fanatics is moral exemplars' open-mindedness toward many different perspectives.

People who are open-minded seek out, listen carefully to, and take seriously opinions different from their own. Open-mindedness among citizens and elected officials contributes directly to truth at the social and institutional levels. How can people with a wide array of opinions and divergent visions come to a working consensus unless they have a respectful regard for each others' points of view? Yet because the issues under discussion are often emotionally charged and carry high stakes, tolerance and respect for political opponents is as fragile as it is important. It seems that in recent years regard for truth in public discourse has decreased hand in hand with a reduction in people's willingness to listen with a truly open mind to political opinions different from their own. Perhaps this shouldn't be surprising, because truthfulness and open-mindedness in public discourse are linked—each influences the other. Open-mindedness is equally important for creating communities of trust and respect in families, schools, neighborhoods, and workplaces. Open-mindedness also leads to better outcomes in decision making. When leaders carefully consider and sift multiple perspectives and look for ways to synthesize the truths embedded in each as they craft their own positions, a deeper and more creative wisdom will emerge.

This quality of open-mindedness is notable in the moral leaders of our current study just as it was in the moral exemplars we described in *Some Do Care*. The six leaders' willingness, even eagerness, to listen to others attests to their sincere regard for finding the truth as well as their humility, about which we will say more in Chapter 5. As strong-minded as they were, the six leaders didn't believe they had all the answers. They were genuinely interested in learning from others about the issues they confronted.

Eleanor Roosevelt had longstanding connections with workers and labor movements and, because she was known as fair, impartial, and open-minded toward conflicting perspectives, she was often asked to help mediate disputes. As Brigid O'Farrell notes in her book on Roosevelt's role in the labor movement, "As labor's internal problems were intensifying, Eleanor Roosevelt responded as she always did: by listening to what the opposing parties had to say..."[36] In Chapter 7, we describe how this capacity to listen open-mindedly played a decisive role in Eleanor Roosevelt's supreme accomplishment, the crafting of the UN Declaration of Universal Rights.

Jane Addams also was well known for her broad-mindedness, her eagerness to understand all points of view on every important issue. During her opposition to World War I, even many of her supporters deserted her. Addams was hurt by this but also made very clear that she respected their right to disagree. This attitude reflected her passionate belief in free speech, which she defended in many ways throughout her career.

Addams' commitment to free speech was consistent with her belief in the importance of impartiality and serious consideration of views different from her own. In the famous Pullman workers strike that shut down the railroads in 1893, Addams was acutely aware of the animosity and self-righteousness on both sides of the conflict, despite her longstanding concern for the rights and welfare of workers. Addams saw mutual understanding and the search for common ground as a better way toward the resolution of conflicts than force, and she decried the polarization that takes place when each side is convinced that it's completely in the right. Following the Pullman strike, Addams acted on this conviction by working with others to press for state and federal boards to arbitrate disputes on a voluntary basis.

THE EVOLVING NATURE OF TRUTH

An open-minded orientation toward discerning the truth in complicated situations was characteristic of the six leaders we studied. They didn't believe they had direct access to a single, absolute, unchanging truth. On the contrary, they understood that searching for truth is an ongoing, evolving process that never ends. Human beings at any one time have only partial access to the truth, and the progression of civilizations lies in large part in their capacity to continue discovering and refining truth.

Jane Addams was explicit in laying out her conception of moral truth as evolving through a social process in which open-mindedness and humility play important roles. Addams made it clear that, for her, the truth wasn't fixed and fully knowable: "Each generation needed to shape its own [moral truth], in response to the new circumstances it faced and the new hopes to which it aspired."[37] Addams was fully committed to finding and living by the truth as she saw it. But, for her, the process of discovering the truth was social and experiential as well as reflective. Her ideals emerged from her reflections on her experience of working with others toward the creation of a shared community based on common humanitarian values, and then bringing the main lessons of that community building to American democracy as a whole. Addams' search for new perspectives on truth came out of her openness to multiple perspectives. She believed that the views of any single interested party were bound to be narrow. For her, truth required a synthesis of many different points of view as they all evolve over time, informed by one another.

In her own writings and in biographical accounts, there are many descriptions of the ways Addams' own thinking evolved. When she established Hull House, her goal was simple benevolence—reaching across class lines to bring the arts, literature, and other sources of ideas about work, democracy, and family life to poor immigrants. She was committed to using the resources provided by her own affluence to help those less fortunate than herself. The goal of benevolence was central to her family as she was growing up. With experience, however, Addams came to see benevolence as condescending and disrespectful to the poor, and she became convinced in a very immediate and concrete way that her implicit assumption of upper-class superiority was unfounded. Out of this grew her recognition of the contributions of her Hull House constituents, and from that came a conception of democracy that was more fully interdependent and egalitarian.

TRUTHFULNESS IN ORDINARY AND EXTRAORDINARY LIVES

As inspiring as the six leaders were in their commitments to personal and public truth, their concerns may feel too lofty to apply to ordinary people. Certainly their battles took place on grand global stages that most of us can barely imagine. And the scale of the battles does matter, in part because the nature of the concerns differs in some important ways. Dietrich Bonhoeffer wrote from prison that "It is not the sins of weakness but the sins of strength that matter."[38,39] How, he asked, could the church in Nazi Germany concern itself with small personal failings of its parishioners—coveting their neighbors' wives or showing disrespect for their parents—in the face of a state regime of unparalleled evil? The lives of the six moral leaders, concerned as they are with the sins—and virtues—of strength, can seem far removed from the small, everyday transgressions that concern ordinary people. They also seem quite distant from the ruminations of journalists who recommend self-deception and seem to condone small-scale dishonesty. Surely we should consider such transgressions to be sins of weakness, if they are sins at all.

But perhaps sins of strength and weakness should not be so easily separated. Inner truthfulness, respectful attention to divergent points of view, and cultures of truth within public life can all succeed or fail in countless small and large ways. The cumulative effects of truthful habits and cultures are large and consequential. If we are to have trust in our schools, government, corporations, professions, and public institutions as well as in other people, we must promote truth as a public and institutional value. Wishing to believe in the basic truthfulness and honesty of journalists, lawyers, and insurance companies is not an otherworldly kind of idealism: It is a desirable state of civilized and secure existence. Nor is personal aspiration for honesty within oneself—or for trusting and trustworthy relationships with one's family, neighbors, and co-workers—a naïve or impractical dream.

Although there's strong evidence that most people lie, cheat, and steal in small ways on many occasions, the reasons for this behavior are still somewhat mysterious. One convincing explanation for the small magnitude of these offenses is that the pettiness of the crime allows offenders to retain their sense of themselves as good people. In addition, people may be less afraid of being caught or facing serious penalties for offenses so small. But the pettiness of the crimes raises another question: Why bother? Why is it worth taking any risk, even the risk of mild embarrassment, uneasiness, or a habit of self-deception, for such small gains? It hardly seems that free pencils and Post-it notes are worth the price.

We find ourselves wondering whether one reason people want to cheat is that, in many cases, although in a vague, unacknowledged way, the act of cheating is actually satisfying. Why would that be? One possibility is that some kinds of dishonesty are satisfying because people don't trust or truly respect the corporations, employers, or government offices that they are cheating.

Maybe on some deep level, many of the offenses that are so prevalent really do feel justified to people. Maybe the high prevalence of cheating is, at least in part, a result as well as a cause of low public trust. Perhaps a lack of trust in public or private institutions that are perceived to be pursuing self-interested goals at the expense of human welfare and regard makes cheating feel like a small act of rebellion or retaliation. This kind of interpretation is suggested by the finding that participants in Ariely's studies cheat much more if they're irritated with the experimenter for rude behavior, such as carrying on a personal cellphone conversation when he's supposed to be running the study. But what these rebels are failing to notice is that each instance of dishonesty contributes to a vicious cycle in which private and public disregard for truth creates cultures that stimulate and justify further dishonesty. The power and destructiveness of this vicious cycle may be the best argument against cheating as well as the most compelling explanation for its prevalence.

In this sense, the petty sins of ordinary people, as well as the integrity and commitment they can show, have large-scale, long-term implications. In these and other ways, the concerns expressed and lived out by the six moral leaders are our own more ordinary concerns writ large. Earlier in this chapter, we drew on Sissela Bok's classic book *Lying* in our discussion of truth. In a new book on another human fundamental, *Exploring Happiness*, Bok writes that many psychologists are too sanguine about the benefits of self-deception as a route to contentment.[40] We are two psychologists who share Bok's skepticism about the bliss of willful ignorance. In many ways, self-deception is a harmful practice even in nonmoral areas. This is not to say that people ought to berate themselves for their failings, whether of appearance, talent, or moral character; it's a mistake to think that self-delusion and ruthless self-criticism are the only alternatives.

Maybe, as Pastor Rick Warren suggests in the memorable opening sentence of *The Purpose Driven Life*, "It's not about you."[41] Popular accounts of the benefits of self-deception seem to assume a competitive race to be the best-looking, smartest, most talented person on the block—or at least to be well above average on every valued dimension. What if the focus were taken off this constant self-assessment? What if people cared more about what they were trying to achieve than about building a portfolio of assets and accomplishments? This would eliminate the supposed utility of self-deception. But this requires another virtue to complement honesty: It requires humility, a frequently misunderstood virtue that we explore in the next chapter.

NOTES

1. Sue Shellenbarger, "The Case for Lying to Yourself," *Wall Street Journal*, Aug. 2, 2012.
2. Ulrich Boser, "We're all Lying Liars: Why People Tell Lies, and Why White Lies can be OK," usnews.com, http://health.usnews.com/health-news/family-health/brain-and-behavior/articles/2009/05/18/were-all-lying-liars-why-people-tell-lies-and-why-white-lies-can-be-ok (accessed January 16, 2014).

3. Dan Ariely, *The (Honest) Truth about Dishonesty: How We Lie to Everyone—Especially Ourselves* (New York: Harper, 2012).

4. William Damon, *Greater Expectations: Overcoming the Culture of Indulgence in America's Homes and Schools* (New York: Free Press, 1995).

5. Carol S. Dweck, *Mindset: The New Psychology of Success* (New York: Ballantine Books, 2008).

6. Sissela Bok, *Exploring Happiness: From Aristotle to Brain Science* (New Haven, CT: Yale University Press, 2010), 170.

7. Sissela Bok, *Lying: Moral Choice in Public and Private Life*, Vintage Books ed. (New York: Vintage Books, 1978).

8. Bok, *Lying,* 31.

9. Bok, *Lying,* 25.

10. Bok, *Lying,* 25.

11. Albert Bandura, "Selective Activation and Disengagement of Moral Control." *Journal of Social Issues* 46, no. 1 (Spring, 1990): 27–46.

12. Albert Bandura, "Moral Disengagement in the Perpetration of Inhumanities." *Personality and Social Psychology Review* 3, no. 3 (1999): 193–209.

13. This coding manual is available upon request from the authors.

14. Quote from Heschel's "A Passion for Truth." Edward K. Kaplan, *Spiritual Radical: Abraham Joshua Heschel in America, 1940–1972* (New Haven, CT: Yale University Press, 2007), 258.

15. Janet S. Walker, "Choosing Biases, Using Power and Practicing Resistance: Moral Development in a World without Certainty." *Human Development* 43, no. 3 (May, 2000): 135–156.

16. Walker, "Choosing Biases:" 140.

17. Walker, "Choosing Biases:" 154.

18. Edgar Wind, *Pagan Mysteries in the Renaissance* (New Haven, CT: Yale University Press, 1958), 238.

19. Ferdinand Schlingensiepen, *Dietrich Bonhoeffer, 1906–1945: Martyr, Thinker, Man of Resistance* [Dietrich Bonhoeffer 1906–1945 eine Biographie. English] (London; New York: T&T Clark, 2010), 147.

20. Schlingensiepen, *Dietrich Bonhoeffer, 1906–1945,* 224.

21. Schlingensiepen, *Dietrich Bonhoeffer, 1906–1945,* 229.

22. Schlingensiepen, *Dietrich Bonhoeffer, 1906–1945,* 228–229.

23. Schlingensiepen, *Dietrich Bonhoeffer, 1906–1945,* 229.

24. Schlingensiepen, *Dietrich Bonhoeffer, 1906–1945,* 230.

25. Louise Knight, *Jane Addams: Spirit in Action*, 1st ed. (New York: W.W. Norton & Co., 2010), 219.

26. Knight, *Jane Addams: Spirit in Action,* 220.

27. Martin Meredith, *Mandela: A Biography*, 1st ed. (New York: Public Affairs, 2010), 240.

28. Kaplan, *Spiritual Radical: Abraham Joshua Heschel in America, 1940–1972*, 360.
29. Kaplan, *Spiritual Radical*, 297.
30. Dag Hammarskjöld and Wilder Foote, *Servant of Peace: A Selection of the Speeches and Statements of Dag Hammarskjöld, Secretary-General of the United Nations, 1953–1961* (New York: Harper & Row, 1962), 27.
31. Hammarskjöld and Foote, *Servant of Peace*, 57.
32. Hammarskjöld and Foote, *Servant of Peace*, 32–33.
33. Hammarskjöld and Foote, *Servant of Peace*, 31.
34. Knight, *Jane Addams: Spirit in Action*, xiii.
35. Anne Colby and William Damon, *Some Do Care: Contemporary Lives of Moral Commitment* (New York: Free Press, 1992).
36. Brigid O'Farrell, *She Was One of Us: Eleanor Roosevelt and the American Worker* (Ithaca, NY: ILR Press, 2010), 196.
37. Knight, *Jane Addams: Spirit in Action*, 101.
38. Schlingensiepen, *Dietrich Bonhoeffer, 1906–1945*, 353.
39. Schlingensiepen, *Dietrich Bonhoeffer*, 353.
40. Sissela Bok, *Exploring Happiness: From Aristotle to Brain Science* (New Haven, CT: Yale University Press, 2010).
41. Rick Warren, *The Purpose Driven Life* (Grand Rapids, MI: Zondervan, 2002), 17.

CHAPTER FIVE

HUMILITY

The virtue of humility lies at the heart of all major world religions. The recognition of the limited, transitory, and ultimately powerless nature of human activity in relation to God (or some other transcendent reality) is one of the core messages shared by spiritual teachings.

The Hebrew Bible and Christian New Testament both contain a multitude of references to humility—such as "Man is like a breath, his days are like a passing shadow" and "Blessed are the meek, for they shall inherit the earth." Hindu scripture (the *Bhagavad Gita*) urges its followers to "Be humble, be harmless. Have no pretension... Serve your teacher in true obedience"; Hindu teacher Ramana Maharshi tells his followers to "Take no notice of the ego and its activities, but see only the light behind." The Sioux tradition depicts spiritual seekers humbling themselves and remembering their nothingness in the presence of the Great Spirit.[1] Muslims often acknowledge their place in the order of things by attaching "Insha'Allah" (if God is willing) to their intentions and predictions. The Dalai Lama expresses a core idea of Buddhism in this way: "The common enemy of all religious disciplines is selfishness of mind—for it is this which causes ignorance, anger and passion, which are at the root of all the troubles of the world."

Despite its almost universal presence in religious teachings, humility is an uncertain and contested virtue. Philosophers have pointed out its inherently paradoxical nature, suggesting that "[humility] is a virtue that is constantly in danger of subverting itself."[2] What they mean, in part, is that humility is a virtue that requires cultivation, yet it seems to disappear as soon as it's attained.

Benjamin Franklin wrote, "In reality, there is perhaps no one of our natural Passions so hard to subdue as pride. Disguise it, struggle with it, beat it down, stifle it, it is still alive...For even if I could conceive that I had completely overcome it, I should probably be proud of my Humility."[3] As Franklin implies, a claim to being humble (or at least too much satisfaction in one's humility) feels as if it might be incompatible with actually *being* humble.

Psychologists attempting to study humility have had a similar problem in dealing with humility's paradoxical nature, especially when they try to devise self-report measures that will render an accurate assessment. Will truly humble people describe themselves as humble? And does humility require persons of talent and accomplishment to deny their abilities? Humility in highly talented people seems inconsistent with honest self-appraisal. Is it possible for accomplished people to have both humility and accurate self-awareness?

All virtues are likely targets for skepticism, but humility may be especially vulnerable to charges of hypocrisy.[4] Political philosopher Mark Button counts among the liabilities of humility that "it seems a quality particularly prone to false representation and human dissemblance," and apparent humility is especially questionable "when it is rhetorically invoked by political and social elites—[raising] a concern that humility is often little more than a transparent power play for self-interested domination."[5]

This accusation is surely true is in many cases. It's hard to know when humility is sincere; it often seems false and self-serving. Naturally, the challenge of telling real from false humility contributes to the skepticism surrounding its status as a virtue.

As if this weren't problematic enough, there's doubt in some quarters about whether even sincere humility is, in fact, a virtue at all. Some philosophers actually consider it to be a minor vice. Spinoza criticized humility as a desire for self-depreciation and therefore a vice rather than a virtue, much like any other uncontrolled desire.[6] The eighteenth-century philosopher David Hume also took a harsh view of humility, calling it a "monkish virtue" that serves no purpose for anyone outside the cloistered context of monasteries.[7]

Friedrich Nietzsche went even further: For him, humility was a contrivance used by the weak to prevent the excellent from asserting their strength and vitality.

Perhaps in reaction to these views, British novelist and philosopher Iris Murdoch wrote that "humility is a rare virtue, and an unfashionable one, and one which is often hard to discern. Only rarely does one meet somebody in whom it positively shines, in whom one apprehends with amazement the absence of the anxious avaricious tentacles of the self..."[8] In her view, humility is not a habit of self-effacement but instead "a selfless respect for reality and one of the most difficult and central of the virtues."[9]

Despite this and many other defenses of humility, it remains an unfashionable virtue. A slightly tempered version of Nietzsche's skepticism is still a strong theme in our contemporary culture, where many celebrities and public figures are sought after largely because their swagger appeals to mass media and a fawning public.

In Chapter 4, we wrote about the appeal of positive self-evaluation, through self-deception if necessary, and the contemporary reliance on competitive advantage for positive self-appraisal. The popularity of television competitions such as "American Idol" and the rapid spread of online social media sites such as Facebook and Twitter reflect the appeal of forums where people can make ego-building public presentations of self. In recent times, the desire to display personal achievement and celebrity seems stronger than any distaste for self-congratulation and arrogance.

Along with today's press to cultivate and display the self, we have seen in recent years a growing assumption that vigorous self-promotion is required for advancement in corporate and other stratified settings. Indeed, some of the business leaders most admired for their innovation and business success have been notably lacking in humility. The late Apple CEO Steve Jobs, for example, was known for his imperious will, despite his longstanding interest in Eastern religions that stress the need to overcome ego.[10] Other highly visible business leaders of our time also have been revered for their hard-hitting business success despite, or maybe because of, their outsized egos.

Oddly, our culture's rewarding of self-promotion coexists with its occasional admiration of humility. Public attitudes toward humility are marked by ambivalence. The apparent egotism of admired business leaders stands in sharp contrast to the much-beloved concept of "servant leadership," introduced by Robert K. Greenleaf's influential essay "The Servant as Leader."[11] This 1970 essay and Greenleaf's subsequent writings, including the book *Servant Leadership*, provided the inspiration for a huge movement at the center of which was the idea that the most effective—and most highly moral—leaders are those who see themselves as stewards of the institutions they lead and whose role it is to work collaboratively with others to contribute to the well-being of those who work in the institution and those the institution serves—the community and the larger society. Servant leaders, in Greenleaf's influential vision, are servants first and leaders second. They use their leadership to serve the organization and its constituencies, concerning themselves with larger goals than acquiring power, money, and acclaim. They nurture their employees' growth, practice reciprocal rather than top-down communication and decision making, and build community within the organization.

Is this idealistic management philosophy still valid in the increasingly competitive business climate of today, a climate in which short-term gains seem to trump considerations of service and long-term stewardship? Is business success still compatible with the humility implied by servant leadership, or does it require ego-driven personal power and charisma?

At least some influential research on management suggests that humility in business leaders is not outmoded. In a study that has achieved iconic status, Jim Collins and his colleagues found that humility in a company's CEO is a critical factor for enabling large companies to make the transition "from good to great."[12] Over a five-year period, Collins studied 1,435 Fortune 500 companies, trying to learn what made the top companies stand out. With sustained greatness defined as "garnering stock returns at least three times the market's for fifteen years after a major transition period," only eleven of the 1,435 companies moved from good to great. These eleven great companies shared several qualities, such as a "culture of discipline," a clarity of focus, effective use of technology, and strategies for engaging the right people in the right jobs.

In addition, every one of the great companies had what Collins calls Level 5 leaders, the highest step in Collins' ladder of leadership capacity. Level 5 leadership is "a paradoxical combination of personal humility and professional will." In contrast with comparison cases at good but not great companies, Level 5 leaders were reluctant to take credit for their companies' successes but quick to take responsibility for problems along the way. They attended closely to people they worked with and dealt honestly with the harshest facts of their current reality—while never losing faith that their companies would prevail in the end.[13] They valued open-mindedness and curiosity in their staff more than protecting their own point of view. They turned their attention away from their own egos, toward the greater ambition of something larger and more lasting than themselves. Work for them was less about personal ambition and glory than about what they could create, build, and contribute by working with others.

Collins' study and subsequent work on factors that help move companies "from good to great" has been influential even though it cuts across the grain of much received wisdom in popular and corporate cultures. Collins speculates that one reason great companies are so rare is because it is Level 4 leaders who are most often chosen as CEOs. In corporate leadership, humility remains largely an unfashionable virtue, despite the evidence of its usefulness beyond the walls of monasteries.

At the very least, public and professional opinions regarding humility are decidedly mixed. There are few human qualities as universally acclaimed by religion, as hotly debated by philosophers, and as simultaneously disdained and cherished by the public.

WHY STUDY HUMILITY?

Given such ambivalence about the utility of humility, and the associated ambivalence about its moral worth, why do we give it so much attention in our study of six twentieth-century leaders?

Our attention was first drawn to the importance of humility by our earlier research on moral commitment, presented in *Some Do Care: Contemporary Lives of Moral Commitment*.[14] That project began with a nominating process designed to develop criteria and compile a list of potential participants for our investigation of people who are exceptionally morally committed—"moral exemplars," as we called them. In the initial nominating phase, we interviewed twenty-two moral philosophers, historians, social scientists, ethicists, and theologians with a wide range of backgrounds and beliefs. This lengthy nominating phase yielded a set of criteria for selecting participants that included (1) a generalized respect for humanity, (2) the use of morally defensible means as well as ends, (3) a willingness to risk self-interest for the sake of one's ideals, and (4) the capacity to inspire others. In addition to these four, the fifth and final criterion concerned humility: a sense of realistic humility about one's own importance relative to the world at large, implying a relative lack of concern for one's own ego.

It's worth noting that the distinguished thinkers who served as nominators in our earlier study did not conceive of humility as meekness or a tendency toward self-deprecation, as many dictionary definitions suggest. Instead, they focused on a sense of perspective on the self and its importance within a larger context and on motives that might include a bit of ego but are not *centrally* concerned with self-aggrandizement or self-importance.

The most important purpose of the humility criterion, as formulated by our nominators, was to help distinguish between moral exemplars and fanatics. It was an effort to specify what kinds of qualities can prevent powerful, passionate, ideal-driven people from doing serious harm. Along with a commitment to ideals that respect human rights and welfare in a universal sense (as opposed to a willingness to sacrifice the rights and welfare of one group for the sake of another) and consistency between the moral standing of means and ends, the nominators were attempting to rule out individuals who pursue supposedly moral ends primarily to advance their raw self-interest or to gratify their egos.

With this in mind, we used the humility criterion in our earlier study of moral exemplars as a way of disqualifying any nominees who also were known for their arrogance. This does not mean that, for our study, we sought out exemplars who were known to be humble as their main distinguishing feature; rather, for inclusion in our study, an exemplar could not be notably *lacking* in humility. The humility criterion led us to eliminate several potential study participants whose work on social causes seemed to be ego-driven at the expense of the moral goals themselves. But aside from this role for humility in select-ing cases for that earlier study, we did not use the study to look directly at the role of humility in exemplars' lives. Nor in that study did we have a chance to look at variations in humility within the group, nor at the nature of humility itself as revealed by our study participants.

In our current study of six twentieth-century moral leaders, we set out to explore more fully several of the issues that were marginal in our previous study, including the nature of humility. All six leaders in the present study were strong and influential, stood up courageously against pressures and opponents, and were highly acclaimed. This made us believe it would be especially enlightening to see what roles, if any, humility played for such people. Because we were looking at *leaders*, we were especially interested in learning about the relation-ships between humility and more widely recognized characteristics of effective leaders such as strength, courage, sense of mission, influence, and will to prevail.

The six moral leaders we studied are well known for their strength and courage, yet their lives also reveal a particularly constructive kind of humility. As scholars in both philosophy and psychology have writ-ten, reclaiming humility as a virtue independent of its theological roots requires a redefinition. One goal of our study was to contribute to that definition through analysis of the qualities these leaders reveal.

Of course, judgments about what kind of virtue humility is (if it *is* a virtue) depend on how it's defined. In this chapter we outline a concep-tion of humility as it actually appears in the lives of people who have every objective reason to think very well of themselves. We began our study with only a very general sense of what humility means, and we used the cases of twentieth-century leaders to develop themes that represent the various aspects of humility that are important in their lives.

CONCEPTIONS OF HUMILITY, CONFLICTING AND CONGRUENT

Skeptics converge on two general conceptions of humility. The first, which shows up in dictionary definitions of the term, conceives of humility as meekness, modesty, self-deprecation, and submissiveness. But this conception of humility opens the door to several serious problems. As Hume, Spinoza, Nietzsche, and others suggested, meekness and submissiveness are not self-evidently virtuous. Why should self-deprecation be considered a virtue? Humility as self-deprecation seems to require talented, successful people to deny their assets and achievements, forcing them into dishonesty or disingenuousness. Submissiveness is even worse, seeming to require some less-privileged individuals to be subservient, accepting even unjust or demeaning treatment. If we also value equality and fairness, this definition makes it hard to consider humility a virtue. Finally, in dictionary definitions, humility is understood as the opposite of pride; yet when pride manifests itself as insistence on dignity and respectful treatment, it can be a character strength.

C. S. Lewis defended humility by redefining it away from such definitions. As he put it, "humility is not thinking less of yourself; it's thinking of yourself less."[15] In this, Lewis comes close to the views of Iris Murdoch, quoted above: seeing humility as "the absence of the anxious avaricious tentacles of the self."

According to Thomas Aquinas (as discussed by Mary Keys), "in checking pride [or ego], humility curbs a powerful motive of tyranny...and a clever defender of injustice."[16] Buddhist teacher Kate Wheeler notes that "humility implies an awareness that one is not omnipotent, that one's actions are embedded in a wider network of cause and effect."[17] Dismayed that humility as a virtue continues to be unfashionable among philosophers despite that field's resurgence of interest in virtues, Mark Button has tried to revive humility's reputation by reconceiving it as "an active civic virtue" that serves as a foundation for open-mindedness and an antidote to dogmatism. Button argues for the usefulness in contemporary life of "democratic humility" defined as "a cultivated sensitivity toward the limitations, incompleteness, and contingency of one's personal moral powers and commitments..."[18]

An overview of philosophical discussions of humility, therefore, makes it clear that philosophers who dismiss humility and those who defend it are operating with very different, almost nonoverlapping, definitions of the term. Where do ordinary people come down in their understanding and experience of humility? In the past decade, psychologists have begun to pay more attention to this heretofore understudied quality, trying to learn what people mean by humility, how they think and feel about it, and how it relates to other psychological outcomes of interest such as well-being and achievement.

After a review of the psychological and philosophical literatures on humility, psychologist June Tangney[19] proposed a definition that attempted to synthesize key elements identified in that literature. The conception of humility that she put forward includes six qualities: (1) accurate assessment of one's ability and achievements; (2) ability to acknowledge one's mistakes, imperfections, gaps in knowledge, and limitations; (3) openness to new ideas, contradictory information, and advice; (4) keeping one's abilities and accomplishments—one's place in the world—in perspective (e.g., seeing oneself as just one person in the larger scheme of things); (5) a relatively low self-focus, a "forgetting of the self"; and (6) appreciation of the many different ways that people can contribute to the world.

Eric Landrum,[20] drawing on the elements of humility outlined by Tangney (as well as more traditional definitions of humility such as meekness, shyness, and low self-regard), looked at how these elements, and items that represented qualities that seem to be the opposite of humility or unrelated to it, would cluster together when people rate each item. Respondents were asked to rate on a scale of 1 (strongly disagree) to 5 (strongly agree) each of sixty-nine items that finish the sentence "I like people who..." Items were diverse, including things like [I like people who...] are hard workers; have compassion for others; can admit their faults; are usually open-minded; take pride in their accomplishments; know that they are smart but not all-knowing; are meek or modest; have very little pride; act like they are the center of the universe; have no understanding of their imperfections.

Using factor analysis procedures to look at how the items tend to cluster together, Landrum found that the sixty-nine items reflect six underlying factors. One of these factors included the items on the list of elements that make up Tangney's definition of humility. These items concern a willingness to admit one's mistakes and faults, openness to new ideas or advice, recognition of the partiality of one's knowledge, and understanding or compassion toward others. A second factor, which was strongly related to this first one, drew together items that point to the ability to keep one's abilities and accomplishments in perspective, awareness of one's limitations, and accurate assessment of one's abilities. Neither of these two factors was correlated with the third cluster, which referred to people who are meek, shy, self-deprecating, or lacking in self-esteem.

In a separate section of the survey, Landrum asked respondents to say whether or not each of eighteen items describes a person who has high levels of humility. Items that were most likely to be rated as descriptors of humility were "knows he/she is smart, but not all-knowing," "has the ability to acknowledge one's mistakes and limitations," "keeps his or her talents and accomplishments in perspective," "has an open and receptive mind," and "has a sense of self-acceptance." Items such as "meek and modest" and "has very little pride" were much less likely to be selected as characteristic of a humble person. Not surprisingly, items that were least likely to be rated as descriptive of humility referred to things like "has no understanding of his/her imperfections," "tends to overemphasize the importance of his/her own accomplishments," "acts like he/she is the center of the universe," and "is closed-minded and shallow." It is significant that the items "has low self-esteem," "is low in rank and station," and "is of little worth" were just as unlikely to be associated with humility as were the items that refer to self-centeredness and arrogance.

It is perhaps surprising, given widespread public admiration for celebrities who seem anything but humble, that psychological studies of humility show that ordinary people have a more positive view of humility than do many philosophers who write about this quality. This is likely because most respondents in the psychological studies conceive of humility in ways that correspond with conceptions of humility as a virtue rather than definitions in which it is considered to be weakness, self-deprecation, or subservience. In addition, studies that attempt to measure humility in ordinary people show relationships between humility and other qualities that are generally seen as positive. These studies find that individuals who are more humble are also higher in self-esteem; introspective self-examination (also called "private self-consciousness"); achievement orientation;[21] sense of purpose (in adolescents);[22] job performance when caring for difficult clients;[23] and gratitude, forgiveness, spirituality, and general health.[24]

Another study[25] found that when asked to recall situations in which they felt humble, people reported experiences that were accompanied by positive emotion. Their attitudes toward humility were generally positive, and they associated humility with good psychological adjustment. Still, these respondents viewed humility more favorably in the religiously faithful and less favorably as a characteristic of leaders and entertainers. Those who were religious themselves, and those who were least narcissistic, had higher opinions of humility than did the other study participants.

EXPLORATIONS OF HUMILITY IN SIX TWENTIETH-CENTURY MORAL LEADERS

We chose the six twentieth-century leaders in our study in part because we were interested in the role of faith in moral leadership. For this reason, faith—in a range of variations and guises—was important in the lives of these leaders, as we describe in Chapter 6. It's not surprising, then, that for some of these six leaders, humility is partly a stance in relation to God or some other transcendent dimension of reality.

This emphasis is especially characteristic of the clergy in the group, Dietrich Bonhoeffer and Abraham Heschel. Speaking to a group that included many atheists, Heschel spoke of the intellect as overwhelmed in the face of mystery and humility as the proper acknowledgment of human beings' inability to fully grasp that mystery.[26] But a sense of humility in relation to transcendent reality was not limited to the clergy. Dag Hammarskjöld also spoke about experiencing feelings of humility in relation to the transcendent and his view of spiritual meaning as ineffable, beyond full comprehension in human terms.

Despite the important spiritual roots of humility as a virtue both historically and philosophically, most of the references to humility in the lives of all six leaders concerned human relationships. Many of the themes revealed in these cases address the special need for those in positions of leadership and privilege to temper their decisions and actions with humility.

Collectively, the many themes we identified within the larger category of humility are closely consistent with the multifaceted articulations of that virtue put forward by Tangney's and Landrum's psychological studies. The themes that emerged from our case material include several that the Tangney and Landrum studies also laid out: a sense of perspective on oneself and one's abilities and achievements, a willingness to admit mistakes and limitations, open-mindedness and openness to new ideas, an appreciation of the many different kinds of contribution people from all backgrounds can make to the world, and a relative absence of self-seeking as a driving motive.

In addition, humility as revealed in our study aligns with Jim Collins' accounts of Level 5 business leaders. The leaders in our study were more likely to take responsibility for their mistakes than to seek credit for successes. They stressed the importance of facing reality squarely instead of covering over problems. Their open-mindedness allowed them to continue learning and minimized the risk of dogmatism. They focused their ambition on their ideals and their missions of peace, justice, and truth instead of on their own personal advancement.

As for the more conventional conceptions of humility, the leaders were anything but meek or subservient. Mandela's brave and risky insistence that he and the other inmates at Robben Island be treated with dignity reveals pride as a virtue, not a vice. For years, he and the other political prisoners were made to wear shorts rather than long trousers, which signified adulthood. Mandela pressed the case, but when he was eventually offered long pants, he refused to accept them unless they were available to the others as well. This insistence on respectful treatment was not personal pride but rather a demand for basic human dignity for all.

Some of the six leaders did show harsh self-criticism at certain points in their lives. Dag Hammarskjöld, for example, felt a lifelong hunger for righteousness and freedom from ego. But as his career in Swedish public service advanced, he questioned its ultimate significance and the lack of purity in the motives that drove his distinguished career. His self-denunciation was made all the worse by his acute awareness that the recriminations were themselves symptoms of the self-absorption that he hated.

Jane Addams, too, was almost immobilized by self-criticism as she entered an adult life torn between loyalty to the ambitious dreams she had developed in girlhood and her family, who wanted to protect her and keep her close to them. It was only after Addams found a purpose that transformed her life that she began to focus on what she and others were trying to accomplish rather than her own weaknesses and fears.

In these and other cases, it's telling that both the leaders themselves and their biographers treated too much self-criticism as a character defect to be overcome rather than a virtue. In his foreword to Hammarskjöld's famous diary *Markings*,[27] W. H. Auden referred to the self-criticism that was incessant during periods of Hammarskjöld's life as "a narcissistic fascination with himself."[28] For moral leaders, it's clear that debilitating self-recrimination is a weakness, not a strength. For that reason, we considered material that exhibits this theme to be a *counter-indicator* for humility—that is, this theme is treated as indicating a limitation in the individual's constructive sense of perspective or humility.

HUMILITY IN MORAL LEADERS

To be as complete and specific as possible in describing the many ways that humility was manifested in the lives and words of the six moral leaders, we identified a number of themes connected with this virtue. Independent judges coding the same material could agree on eight themes depicting various aspects of humility, along with three counter-indicators. Some of these themes were evident in all or just about all of the cases. Others were important in only a few of the cases but, for those cases, were essential to a full understanding of the individual.

Naturally, the three virtues we studied are not practiced and revealed in human lives independently of each other. They are deeply interconnected, and some themes represent important intersections of two or all three of the virtues. Some features of humility, such as open-mindedness toward others' points of view or awe in relation to the transcendent, are as much about truth or faith as they are about humility. In addition to the eight humility themes, we identified three additional hybrid themes that lie at the intersections between the virtues we studied. To streamline our discussion of the eleven specific themes representing humility in the lives of six great leaders, we have organized them into six larger themes or clusters: humility as (1) a moral ideal, (2) a sense of perspective, (3) human solidarity, (4) material simplicity, (5) awareness of limitations and mistakes, and (6) open-mindedness.

Humility as Moral Ideal. The six leaders we studied were widely recognized for their work. They were beloved by millions and won many prizes and awards. Although it's clear that prizes and accolades didn't serve as primary incentives for them, the leaders appreciated the public response to their work as a validation and recognition of its importance. The goals of equality, human rights, and peace were what really mattered to them, and recognition was instrumental toward achieving those goals as well as a source of personal pleasure. Public recognition served partly as a resource—as strong public relations efforts do for any sustained movement or campaign—and partly as a source of support and energy when demands of the work were especially heavy, as they often were. Many, although not all, of the leaders were gregarious by nature, and for them positive public responses were also enjoyable and refreshing in a simple, straightforward way. In the end, though, the leaders' focus was squarely on the goals and the various strategies for achieving them, not on personal rewards those achievements might carry. The leaders were not fundamentally self-seeking. In fact, they were prepared to give everything they had to accomplish their moral goals, and, in one way or another, all gave their lives for them.

Just as rewards and recognition were treated mostly as instrumental to the leaders' moral goals, attention to self was also largely instrumental. In Chapter 3, we described the ways the six leaders used self-knowledge to reshape their characteristic behaviors and emotional reactions to better serve their ideals. Mandela's reckless overconfidence became the basis for his relentless stamina and courage. Eleanor Roosevelt's insecurities led to her compassion and desire to be always useful. Jane Addams' sometimes hopeless youthful idealism fed the brilliance of her creative rethinking of democratic community.

For the six leaders, a low self-focus, or forgetting of the self as Tangney has called it, was evident in the degree to which they lost themselves in their passions for human welfare, peace, and justice. But their passions were accompanied by self-reflection, in the spirit of inner truthfulness, as they checked and tried to curb their weaknesses to better align themselves with their ideals. Paradoxically, their self-reflection served the purpose of self-forgetting or release from ego, among other things, because humility was central among the ideals they pursued. As such, it shaped their perceptions of and feelings toward themselves and other people, organizations, and nations.

Many of the six spoke and wrote about the moral risks posed by the ego, the limits of social action based in an attitude of *noblesse oblige*, and the human problems that result from a lack of humility. We wrote in earlier chapters about Jane Addams' hard-won realization that an attitude of benevolence can ultimately be selfish, arrogant, and condescending toward its recipients. She believed that true democracy and community require equality based in humility. Dag Hammarskjöld and Abraham Heschel also wrote eloquently about the dangers of an ego-driven life. As Heschel said: "Freedom is the liberation from the tyranny of the self-centered ego...[which requires] transcending the self."[29] Dietrich Bonhoeffer saw Germany's lack of humility as a reason for World War I and for its destructive response to defeat in that war: "As a Christian, I see the main guilt of Germany [in World War I] in quite a different light. I see it in Germany's complacency, in her belief in her almightiness, in the lack of humility and faith in God and fear of God."[30]

To a remarkable degree, the six leaders achieved the ideal of humility. They were not driven mainly by self-interest or self-aggrandizement; they saw themselves as ordinary people, shared credit for their achievements, were quick to admit their mistakes and limitations, and were eager to learn from all kinds of people. But it hadn't always been that way. In their youth, Dietrich Bonhoeffer and Dag Hammarskjöld were serious, highly cultured young men, prone to impatience with the frivolity of their peers. Mandela's youthful confidence bordered on arrogance. Jane Addams and Dag Hammarskjöld had to overcome an intense negative focus on the self.

As we described in Chapter 2, a sense of purpose and commitment to ideals provided the foundation from which the leaders were able to redirect these initial tendencies to focus beyond the self. Despite the sometimes remarkable transformations in their lives, however, most of them retained some of their human vulnerability to egoism. As Ben Franklin pointed out, when it comes to pride (or ego), you can "disguise it, struggle with it, beat it down, stifle it..., [but] it is still alive."[31] For several of the six, the struggle was lifelong, as it is for most ordinary people.

Humility as Sense of Perspective on the Self. As we have said, in selecting participants for our earlier study of living moral exemplars, we looked for people who were not overly focused on themselves or arrogant in their use of power—people with a sense of perspective on themselves and their own importance in the larger scheme of things. We saw a variant of the same theme in our study of historical moral leaders as well. Most brought some kind of big-picture sense of perspective to their lives, expressing the feeling that they were just one part of a larger story. They used a number of different frameworks to express the sense that they were not all-important, that their own contributions needed to be understood within a larger context of forces that go beyond the self.

For some of the six leaders, the larger perspective they brought to bear included a sense of history. This doesn't mean that they felt like great heroes who turned historical events in a direction that would correspond to their own will; rather, they understood their own times and experiences as part of a long, evolving set of events. Dag Hammarskjöld often thought explicitly about his work and that of the UN in its historical perspective. In one of his talks, he described the seemingly thankless efforts toward peace and human rights of a Chinese philosopher living in 350 BC. Noting how much he and his listeners could learn from the philosopher's attitude, he spoke of the philosopher's "strong sense of proportion of a man seeing his own time in the long perspective of history."[32] There were many instances in which this same sense of proportion was evident in Hammarskjöld's own perspective.

Abraham Heschel also wrote about this sense of perspective as an ideal to strive for: "It's always important to look at things from horizons that range beyond the span of an individual life or even the life of a nation."[33] Describing Jane Addams, historian Louise Knight commented that her "reflections toward the end of her life showed her feeling of being part of a larger whole. Her life was only a chapter in some longer book...and there were many more chapters to be written."[34]

For some of the leaders, this humble sense of perspective on the self was expressed in a charming sense of humor. Bonhoeffer chuckled with delight when he heard his friends playfully imitate the quirks of his rhetorical style, as they sometimes did. Eleanor Roosevelt learned to laugh at the ubiquitous caricatures of her face. But the sharpest comic of the six was surely Nelson Mandela—biographies of Mandela are full of references to his self-deprecating humor. Often in his speeches, Mandela told stories about ego-deflating incidents that he had recently experienced. According to biographer Martin Meredith, Mandela loved to tell his audiences about an incident during a private visit he had made to the Bahamas, just prior to winning the presidency in 1994. "In the street he was approached by a man and his wife who appeared to recognize him. 'Aren't you Nelson Mandela?' the man asked. "'I'm often confused with that chap,' replied Mandela mischievously. The man was not convinced and whispered to his wife about their unexpected find. 'What is he famous for?' his wife inquired in a hushed tone. Not satisfied with her husband's mumbled response, the woman turned to Mandela and asked outright, 'What are you famous for?'"[35] Later, while president of South Africa, Mandela criticized his political opponents as running a "Mickey Mouse organization." But when one of the leaders of that organization was sick in the hospital, Mandela went to visit him, alerting the patient to his presence outside the door by saying loudly: "Hello Mickey Mouse. This is Goofy. Can I come in?"[36] On his eightieth birthday, Mandela married Graca Machel (former minister of education and first lady of Mozambique) in a private ceremony at his home. When they announced their marriage, Mandela's wife, who was known for her independence, said that she had no intention of changing her name. With a sweet smile, Mandela responded to the same reporter: "I'm not going to change mine either."[37]

Humility as Human Solidarity. Although widely admired, even revered, and commanding in their leadership, the six were well known for not seeing themselves as special or separate from people of less privilege or power. They consistently acted in ways that revealed their sincere solidarity with and acknowledgment of what they had learned from people all across the social scale. In general, the leaders were known for their warm and deeply respectful connections with people from all sorts of backgrounds and their beliefs that anyone can make important contributions, because people's most important qualities have little to do with social position.

Despite her wealth, patrician background, and position as first lady of the United States, Eleanor Roosevelt was famous for her sympathy and solidarity with ordinary workers. Instead of making her feel superior to people with less distinguished backgrounds, Roosevelt's sense of personal and family history showed her the fragility and superficiality of social position. Reflecting on the up-and-down financial fortunes of generations of Roosevelts, she wrote, "It always amuses me when any one group of people take it for granted that, because they have been privileged for a generation or two, they are set apart in any way from the man or woman who is working to keep the wolf from the door. It is only luck and a little veneer temporarily on the surface, and before very long the wheels may turn and one and all must fall back on whatever basic 'quality' one may have."[38]

Roosevelt's solidarity with workers was not just sentimentality: It led to many powerful interventions that contributed to the effectiveness of unions and to changing conditions for working people. Brigid O'Farrell, in her book about Eleanor Roosevelt's part in the labor movement, recounts many incidents that reveal the depth of her connections with workers. On one such occasion, Roosevelt was the keynote speaker at the first Southern Conference on Human Welfare. A delegation from the Textile Workers Organizing Committee attended the conference, telling Roosevelt directly about their struggles with textile mill management, including their eviction from company-owned housing during an impasse in contract negotiations. An observer at the meeting recalled: "I'll never forget that sight. Mrs. Roosevelt, tall, lovely, gracious, shaking each work-hardened hand and bending her head to catch what each man said."[39] After Eleanor had urged her husband to do something about the situation, FDR asked the National Labor Relations Board to send investigators, and, ultimately, the evictions were stopped, relief was made available, and, in the end, a contract was secured.

Similarly, Nelson Mandela made a point of the personal moral qualities that are within reach of all and that he believed, ultimately, are the only qualities that really matter: "In judging our progress as individuals, we tend to concentrate on external factors such as one's social position, influence, and popularity, wealth and standard of education.... But internal factors may be even more crucial in assessing one's development as a human being. Honesty, sincerity, simplicity, humility, pure generosity, absence of vanity, readiness to serve others—qualities which are within easy reach of every soul—are the foundation of one's spiritual life" [40] Mandela's behavior toward individual people reflected exactly this kind of regard for the value of each human being. As one of his biographers noted, "Mandela was courteous and attentive to every individual, no matter what his or her status. At parties, he spent most of his time talking to maids, gardeners, domestic staff. At formal events, he always shook hands with the staff."[41]

Mandela also stressed how much he had learned from his activist partners, many of whom had very little formal education: "I was really very nervous...I didn't know politics, you see. I was backward politically and I was dealing with chaps who knew politics, who could discuss what was happening inside and outside South Africa. Chaps, some of whom had very little education, academically very humble qualifications, but they knew *far* more than I did."[42]

Humility as Material Simplicity. Conceptually, material simplicity can't be considered an essential feature of humility. There are surely many humble people who drive expensive cars, live in big houses, and are cared for by household staffs. And there are, no doubt, plenty of arrogant or self-centered people who are not concerned with material wealth or have no access to it. Still, it's striking how prevalent simplicity of style, surroundings, and protocol was in these six leaders, all of whom had opportunities for opulence or at least for the trappings and rituals of eminence. Yet they often refused to accept the special privileges offered by their positions of power and influence.

Eleanor Roosevelt, for example, was known for the simplicity of her dress and manner, annoyed her husband and his White House guests by serving exceedingly plain and humble food, and refused the special treatment due to the first lady, opening the door for visitors herself, learning to operate the elevator, and refusing Secret Service protection much of the time. Mandela was the same. As president of South Africa, he had the use of two grand state mansions but preferred to stay at his own modest house and donated much of his salary and prize money to charity. Bonhoeffer refused the special privileges offered to him in prison, choosing instead to live like his fellow inmates. And Jane

Addams spent her entire inheritance on Hull House and the rest of her life living in the midst of a Chicago slum. She believed in culture and beauty, so Hull House was designed to be a lovely environment within its low-income setting. But it was a lovely environment open to all.

Along with this simplicity of setting and style, the leaders believed that being appointed to high-level positions didn't make them special, didn't change the fact that they were still the same persons they had been before the appointment. Looking back on his career after his retirement, Mandela said, "I was not a messiah, but an ordinary man who had become a leader because of extraordinary circumstances."[43] In comments to reporters shortly after his appointment as Secretary General of the UN, Dag Hammarskjöld stressed that the position did not make him a different person, remarking that "personal views of mine are not or should not be of any greater interest to you today than...a couple of weeks ago."[44]

These qualities of simplicity and a sense of their own ordinariness derive, in part, from the leaders' belief that maintaining their deep connections with ordinary people would help them stay focused on the true nature of their goals, avoiding distraction by the extrinsic rewards of power. They also believed that the success of their missions would benefit from their willingness to live in accord with the values that informed those missions—unreserved respect for each individual and priority of peace and justice over less central goals.

For Jane Addams, living alongside and working closely with people from very different social circumstances formed the heart of her mission and philosophy. For Eleanor Roosevelt, intentional simplicity symbolized her equality and kinship with the American populace. As she wrote: "If we do not allow our high American officials and their families to live a usual American life, I wonder how long we will really have a representative type of American in official life."[45] Mandela's relatively austere lifestyle was, in part, a self-conscious rejection of a "fat cat" mentality that had plagued African life with corruption for years. Dietrich Bonhoeffer understood simplicity as inherent in Christian values. Hammarskjöld and Heschel may not have deliberately sought out material simplicity, but achieving wealth and ease was of little interest to them, given their single-minded focus on more important goals.

Humility as Awareness of One's Limitations. The leaders were very aware of their own limitations, not least the limitations in their capacity for humility. They seemed to be on the lookout for the kinds of ego-inflation that are occupational hazards in the positions they held and used humor, sense of perspective, honest feedback from friends, and the other themes we've outlined to keep their egos in check. This process, which is best described as inner truthfulness in the service of humility, requires accurate self-awareness but stops short of self-absorption. The ego-controlling disciplines they practiced, which kept the leaders focused outside themselves, bolstered their spirits rather than deflating them. As Abraham Heschel commented: "The austere disciplines of unremitting inquiry and self-criticism are acts of liberating man from the routine way of looking only at those features of experience which are familiar and regular and open his soul to the unique and the transcendent."[46]

The leaders' awareness of their own limitations, along with their feelings of kinship with the frailties of others, made them reluctant to pass judgment on other people, especially in simplistic or moralistic terms. Writing in her *My Day* column about the importance of cooperation, even with one's opponents, Eleanor Roosevelt said: "I don't believe that greed and selfishness have gone out of the human race. I am quite prepared to be considerably disappointed many times in the course of cooperation. I shall probably be disappointed in myself as much as in other people, but I want to try for a peaceful world."[47] Jane Addams also pointed to the complicated mix of good with bad, expressing humility in regard to her own moral judgments: "Life itself teaches us nothing is more inevitable than that right and wrong are most confusedly mixed,...that the blackest wrong is by our side and within our own motives, [and] that right has to be found by exerting patience, discrimination and impartiality."[48]

Dag Hammarskjöld, as leader of the UN, was acutely aware of the risks of making judgments about nations or groups of people. His words paralleled Addams' warning about judging individuals when he said: "Let us not get caught in the belief that divisions of our world between the righteous and the wrong-doers, between idealism and materialism, between freedom and slavery, coincide with national boundaries. The righteous are to be found everywhere, as are the wrong-doers..."[49]

For the six leaders we studied, clarity about the limitations of their knowledge, power, and wisdom informed their views of their leadership as well as their personal sense of themselves. For them, humility was an institutional as well as a personal ideal. Although Robert Greenleaf's *Servant Leadership* was not published until the end of the 1970s, Dag Hammarskjöld articulated the concept of leader as servant throughout his tenure at the UN. In one of many statements on this issue, he said, "The public servant is there to assist those who take the decisions that frame history; a leader is an instrument, a catalyst, perhaps an inspirer—he serves."[50]

One important feature of servant leadership as conceived by Hammarskjöld and others among the six leaders is an eagerness for frank feedback and criticism. Hammarskjöld often told his staff, in essence, "I am here to serve you all....It is for you to correct me if I fail."[51] Mandela conveyed the same message to his collaborators, staff, and the public. Referring to two close, long-term friends, he expressed his gratitude for their candor: "Walter [Sisulu] and Kathy [Ahmed Kathrada] share one common feature which forms an essential part of our friendship and which I value very much—they never hesitate to criticize me for my mistakes and throughout my political career have served as a mirror through which I can see myself."[52]

Also critical for leadership grounded in humility was the leaders' recognition that they were working as part of a team. For Dag Hammarskjöld, the team included not only UN staff but also volunteers. He told a group of volunteers early in his secretariat that "you and I are in the same boat together" in dealing with the opportunities and challenges of the UN.[53] Eleanor Roosevelt saw collective action as the only effective approach to the daunting social problems her country faced in the Great Depression—"I have no illusions that anyone can change the world in a short time...Yet I do believe that even a few people, who want to understand, to help and to do the right thing for great numbers of people instead of for the few can help."[54] For Mandela, being part of a tight-knit team gave him the stamina and spirit to go on: "What has sustained me even in the most grim moments is the knowledge that I am a member of a tried and tested family [of collaborators] which has triumphed over many difficulties. In such a large and broad family, opinions can be diverse on almost everything, but we have always succeeded in sorting things out together and going forward all the same. This fact endows my spirits with powerful wings."[55]

Humility as Open-mindedness. The leaders' awareness of their limitations is closely related to another aspect of humility—open-mindedness, a quality in which humility and regard for truth intersect. Open-mindedness as a key feature of humility has been highlighted in other studies and in philosophical writings as well. As Button suggested in his articulation of *civic humility*, a sense of humility about one's beliefs and points of view is essential for communication across religious, cultural, racial, national, and other differences in a diverse society and world.

As we reported in *Some Do Care*, open-mindedness was a key characteristic of the moral exemplars we studied at that time. This was intriguing, because the exemplars were also highly certain about their moral ideals and goals and about their personal responsibility for and commitment to those goals. The six leaders in the present study also exhibited this intriguing combination of open-mindedness and certainty. Many incidents in Jane Addams' life, for example, illustrate this same striking juxtaposition of humility and conviction. We've already described Addams' principled opposition to World War I and the assaults on her character that her position triggered. Her opposition to the war was very costly to her reputation and well-being, but she was willing to pay that price. Despite the certainty of her conviction, however, Addams didn't feel that she could impose her own views of the war on the other residents of Hull House. A majority of those residents, in a patriotic spirit, voted to let Hull House become a draft registration site. As Louise Knight describes it, "Addams could have used her influence to discourage the decision, and she spent 'a wretched night of internal debate' just before the [draft] board opened for business, wondering if she had done the right thing in allowing it. But she rejected the idea that Hull House was an extension of herself; she could not justify forcing her beliefs on the residents and neighborhood communities."[56]

A SYNTHETIC REDEFINITION

To extend the relevance of our observations about humility in moral leaders beyond that small, specialized sample, we generated a simple definition of humility that brings together the themes we've just described with the philosophical and social science literature on humility. To do this, we sifted through the themes, identified elements that were common to all six moral leaders as well as to ordinary people described in social science studies, and subsumed within these core elements the themes that represent more particularized emphases revealed by some but not all of these sources. The resulting definition includes four main elements and several thematic "corollaries" within two of these elements:

(1) A low degree of self-seeking or focus on the self

(2) A sense of perspective on the self—This includes several subthemes, which may not be present in every case: (a) expresses a sense of humor about the self, (b) doesn't see the self as special or superior relative to others in any essential sense, (c) appreciates others' contributions, potential, and inherent worth, and (d) does not show off special status with material or symbolic trappings of power, wealth, or social position.

(3) An awareness of one's limitations—Subthemes include (a) avoids overestimating or overstating one's talents, accomplishments, knowledge, virtues (beyond that, a thoroughly accurate assessment of all one's capacities does not seem to be essential), (b) welcomes constructive criticism and is willing to take it seriously, and (c) is reluctant to pass judgment on others.

(4) Open-mindedness

The cornerstone of this definition points to humility as locating the central focus of motivation and attention beyond the self. In this it recalls C. S. Lewis—humility not as thinking less of yourself but thinking of yourself less—as well as Rick Warren's telling statement that "It's not about you."[57] So, an essential element of humility refers to the habit of putting the focus of attention and energy on the tasks at hand, on other people and their welfare, rather than constantly assessing the implications of every event for the self. From the perspective of this element, the opposite of humility is not pride, at least in some definitions of that term, but excessive self-seeking, self-involvement, or self-congratulation, what some might call a narcissistic focus on self.

Based on our own and others' studies, it seems clear that a relative lack of self-seeking or self-focus is compatible with moderate degrees of self-reflection in the service of inner truth and moral growth. In fact, the third element of our definition, awareness of one's limitations, requires some degree of reflection on the self. And, if some people have actually achieved a degree of humility, consistency doesn't require them to deny it. Humility only requires, as Ben Franklin wrote, that a person not take inordinate satisfaction or glory in it.

Our research suggests, though, that many humble people set for themselves very high standards of self-forgetfulness, so they do often deny their own evident humility. This is not falsehood or misrepresentation; it is aspiration for ideals that still feel out of reach. In this definition of humility, paradoxes remain, but they don't make the concept self-contradictory. The paradoxes inherent in humility reflect the complexity of moral reality and human beings' efforts to make their way through it.

Humility as meekness or subservience is not represented in this definition. Quite the contrary: Those qualities are very different from and not closely related to the aspects of humility observed in the research literature or in our analyses of moral leaders. Our leaders' stories show vividly the compatibility of humility with strength.

HUMILITY FOR THE REST OF US

As the nominators in our study of moral exemplars warned, individuals who are driven by deep moral convictions, who feel a strong sense of certainty about their beliefs, and who demonstrate a powerful will to achieve their goals have the potential to do great harm as well as real, far-reaching good. This warning is even more important when applied to leaders who have public support and a wide scope of influence. What kinds of safeguards can mitigate the danger? In democracies, individuals in formal leadership positions can, to a large extent, be kept in check by the democratic process, assuming citizens are paying attention and thinking clearly.

But in the many situations when these democratic safeguards are weak, or leaders are operating outside democratic systems, the leaders' character and driving values are critical. Chief among the virtues that distinguish great moral leaders from tyrants and fanatics are humility and truth. This means moral leaders must have a sincere regard for truth and be driven primarily by prosocial rather than self-serving motives, have a sense of perspective on themselves, take criticism seriously, and be open to others' ideas.

Leaders have more reason than most to lack humility. They are faced with an endless string of opportunities to go astray, as expressed by the old adage "power corrupts." The struggle to gain some degree of freedom from ego is a difficult and ongoing process even for highly moral leaders. But even moderate success in that struggle can be a powerful force for keeping their development as persons, their lives, and their work on a positive track.

But is humility as important for ordinary people, who may have less potential to do great harm or great good? Both the challenges and the opportunities surrounding humility are different for powerful leaders than they are for the rest of us. Most of us don't have to decide whether to live mostly in the presidential palace or in our own suburban homes or whether to open our front doors to guests ourselves. The issue of servant leadership may feel like it applies more to our bosses than to us. Our limitations may be much too glaring to ignore or deny.

Still, all of us can benefit from keeping a sense of perspective ourselves, on both our trials and our triumphs. You don't have to be a
world leader to take yourself too seriously or inflate your impact or
importance. We all have the choice about whether to approach our fel-
lows with a sense of solidarity or cut-throat competition. It's hard for
most people to admit their mistakes, but equally important for ordinary people and leaders to do so, as anyone in a long-term marriage or
friendship can attest. We can all aspire to release from the avaricious
tentacles of self, however imperfectly we manage to escape their grasp.

There are many rewards to be had from developing a sense of perspective on the self and other elements of constructive humility. Seeing
oneself as part of a larger whole, keeping things in perspective, helps
lighten the suffering that's inevitable in human life and provides the
basis for meaning and purpose. A humble fellow-feeling provides the
basis for strong bonds with other people, which are a well-known
source of health, resilience, and well-being. Open-mindedness and an
honest sense of self are prerequisites for continuing growth.

Of course, a focus on our faults and limitations can be debilitating
if it's excessive or off the mark. If humility were to require extreme
self-deprecation, Hume would be right that it would be a monkish
virtue or no virtue at all. For constructive humility, genuine insight
about oneself and forthright responsibility for mistakes are needed,
and these require maturity and wisdom. Humility grounded in truth,
balance, and some degree of self-forgetting comes naturally to very
few people, whether moral leaders or ordinary folks. Developing this
and other virtues is a lifelong process, which requires not only honesty
with oneself but deeply truthful interactions with other people.

One of the main differences between the conception of morality
that we propose and the more reductionistic views we outlined in
Chapter 1 is that we believe that moral character is real, not illusory,
and that it can be supported by education, both formal education in
schools and colleges and informal education in many social institutions, including the family. Communication among members of a family can contribute to greater self-awareness, respect for humility as a
moral ideal, and a practice of considering others rather than habitually

putting oneself at the center. Formal as well as informal education that helps young people understand not only what they can contribute to the world but how their efforts fit into larger historical or global patterns is empowering and humbling at the same time, a singularly wholesome combination.

The examples provided by our six leaders make it clear that humility combined with strength is no oxymoron. Their lives illustrate the personal and societal benefits of humility as a moral and social ideal. These individuals understood that pursuing only the advancement of self is a never-ending, and ultimately self-defeating, enterprise. This is a central thread of world wisdom throughout the ages. Fulfillment and peace of mind come not from trying to create the most attractive possible self but from taking the focus off the self: not thinking less of oneself, but thinking of oneself less.

NOTES

1. Dr Andrew Wilson (Editor), "World Scripture: A Comparative Anthology of Sacred Texts, Humility." International Religious Foundation, 1991, http://www.unification.net/ws/theme128.htm (accessed January 22, 2014).

2. Wilfred M. McClay, "Vice or Virtue?" *In Character: A Journal of Everyday Virtues* 5, no. 3 (Winter, 2010): 6.

3. Benjamin Franklin, *The Autobiography of Benjamin Franklin (1906)* (Mineola, NY: Dover Thrift Editions, 1996), 72.

4. Judy Bachrach, "The Case for Lucifer: Pride Has Such a Bad Rap. Really, It's Unfair." *In Character: A Journal of Everyday Virtues* 5, no. 3 (Winter, 2010): 87.

5. Mark Button, "'A Monkish Kind of Virtue'? For and Against Humility." *Political Theory* 33, no. 6 (December, 2005): 845–846.

6. See Valtteri Viljanen, *Spinoza's Geometry of Power* (Cambridge, UK: Cambridge University Press, 2011).

7. David Fate Norton, *The Cambridge Companion to Hume* (Cambridge, UK, & New York: Cambridge University Press, 1993).

8. Iris Murdoch, *The Sovereignty of Good* (London: Routledge & Kegan Paul, 2013), 101.

9. Murdoch, *The Sovereignty of Good*, 93.

10. Walter Isaacson, *Steve Jobs* (New York: Simon & Schuster, 2011), 630.

11. Robert K. Greenleaf, *Servant Leadership: A Journey into the Nature of Legitimate Power and Greatness* (25th anniversary ed.). (New York: Paulist Press, 2002).

12. James C. Collins, *Good to Great: Why Some Companies Make the Leap, and Others Don't*, 1st ed. (New York: HarperBusiness, 2001), 304.

13. Collins, *Good to Great*, 87.

14. Anne Colby and William Damon, *Some Do Care: Contemporary Lives of Moral Commitment* (New York: Free Press, 1992).

15. C. S. Lewis, *Mere Christianity* (New York: Macmillan, 1958), 175.

16. Mary M. Keys, *A "Monkish Virtue" Outside the Monastery: On the Social and Civic Value of Humility*. Working paper submitted to the Religion and Culture Web Forum, University of Chicago (May, 2004): 1.

17. Michael Shermer et al., "Symposium: Can the Truly Humble Attain Greatness in Worldly Affairs?" *In Character: A Journal of Everyday Virtues* 5, no. 3 (Winter, 2010): 53.

18. Button, *"A Monkish Kind of Virtue"?*, 841.

19. June Price Tangney, "Humility: Theoretical Perspectives, Empirical Findings and Directions for Future Research." *Journal of Social and Clinical Psychology* 19, no. 1 (Spring, 2000): 70–82.

20. R. Eric Landrum, "Measuring Dispositional Humility: A First Approximation." *Psychological Reports* 108, no. 1 (2011): 217–228.

21. Landrum, "Measuring Dispositional Humility."

22. Kendall Cotton Bronk, *Purpose in Life: A Critical Component of Optimal Youth Development* (New York: Springer, 2014).

23. M. K. Johnson, W. C. Rowatt, and L. Petrini, "A New Trait on the Market: Honesty-Humility as a Unique Predictor of Job Performance Ratings." *Personality and Individual Differences* 50 (2011): 857–862.

24. Wade C. Rowatt et al., "Development and Initial Validation of an Implicit Measure of Humility Relative to Arrogance." *The Journal of Positive Psychology* 1, no. 4 (October, 2006): 198–211.

25. Jule J. Exline and Anne L. Geyer, "Perceptions of Humility: A Preliminary Study." *Self and Identity* (2004): 95–114.

26. Edward K. Kaplan, *Spiritual Radical: Abraham Joshua Heschel in America, 1940–1972* (New Haven, CT: Yale University Press, 2007), 90.

27. Dag Hammarskjöld and W. H. Auden, *Markings* (New York: Knopf, 1966).

28. Hammarskjöld and Auden, *Markings*, xiv.

29. Abraham Joshua Heschel, Jacob Neusner, and Noam M. M. Neusner, *To Grow in Wisdom: An Anthology of Abraham Joshua Heschel* (Lanham, MD: Madison Books, 1990), 156.

30. Ferdinand Schlingensiepen, *Dietrich Bonhoeffer, 1906–1945: Martyr, Thinker, Man of Resistance* [Dietrich Bonhoeffer 1906–1945 eine Biographie. English] (London; New York: T&T Clark, 2010).

31. Benjamin Franklin, *The Autobiography of Benjamin Franklin*, ed. John Bigelow (Boston and New York: Houghton, Mifflin & Co, 1906), 97 (as found on google.books).

32. Dag Hammarskjöld and Wilder Foote, *Servant of Peace: A Selection of the Speeches and Statements of Dag Hammarskjöld, Secretary-General of the United Nations, 1953-1961* [Speeches. Selections.] (New York: Harper & Row, 1962), 127.

33. Heschel, Neusner, and Neusner, *To Grow in Wisdom*, 134.

34. Louise Knight, *Jane Addams: Spirit in Action*, 1st ed. (New York: W. W. Norton & Co., 2010), 269.

35. Martin Meredith, *Mandela: A Biography*, 1st ed. (New York: PublicAffairs, 2010), xviii.

36. Meredith, *Mandela: A Biography*, 579.

37. Meredith, *Mandela: A Biography*, 576.

38. Eleanor Roosevelt, *This I Remember*, 1st ed. (New York: Harper, 1949), 267.

39. Brigid O'Farrell, *She Was One of Us: Eleanor Roosevelt and the American Worker* (Ithaca, NY: ILR Press, 2010), 70.

40. Nelson Mandela, *Conversations with Myself*, 1st ed. (New York: Farrar, Straus and Giroux, 2010), 211.

41. Meredith, *Mandela: A Biography*, 482.

42. Mandela, *Conversations with Myself*, 41.

43. Meredith, *Mandela: A Biography*, 599.

44. Hammarskjöld and Foote, *Servant of Peace*, 27.

45. Eleanor Roosevelt, Rochelle Chadakoff and David Emblidge, *Eleanor Roosevelt's My Day* (New York: Pharos Books, 1989), 8.

46. Heschel, Neusner, and Neusner, *To Grow in Wisdom*, 157.

47. Roosevelt, Chadakoff, and Emblidge, *Eleanor Roosevelt's My Day*, 23.

48. Knight, *Jane Addams: Spirit in Action*, 93.

49. Hammarskjöld and Foote, *Servant of Peace*, 59.

50. Hammarskjöld and Foote, *Servant of Peace*, 27.

51. Hammarskjöld and Foote, *Servant of Peace*, 29.

52. Mandela, *Conversations with Myself*, 211.

53. Hammarskjöld and Foote, *Servant of Peace*, 40.

54. O'Farrell, *She Was One of Us*, 6.

55. Mandela, *Conversations with Myself*, 177.

56. Knight, *Jane Addams: Spirit in Action*, 217.

57. Rick Warren, *The Purpose Driven Life* (Grand Rapids, MI: Zondervan, 2002), 17.

CHAPTER SIX

FAITH

Noted psychiatrist and author George Vaillant recently wrote that the absence of faith is nihilism, not atheism.[1] Faith means believing in something. Without faith *of some kind*, it isn't possible to have a sense of meaning, direction, or purpose in life. Without faith, it wouldn't make sense to expect (or keep) commitments. Some say that, without faith, even science is impossible[2] since science depends on a basic faith that "things lie together in a harmony which excludes mere arbitrariness."[3]

In Chapter 5, we described humility as a habit of placing one's central focus outside the self, a mitigation of ego and self-absorption. If the self is not the best place to put one's central focus, where does that focus belong? In trying to answer this question for themselves, individuals need to discern what they believe is most important during their deepest, wisest, most thoughtful moments. If they succeed, they are moving toward faith.

In an inclusive sense, we define people of faith as those who find something to believe in. People who maintain a regular (although not necessarily exclusive) focus on their deepest beliefs, and who behave as much as possible in ways that are consistent with those beliefs, may be said to be guided by faith of some kind.

When people grapple with questions about what really matters in life, they are engaging with what theologian Paul Tillich called *questions of ultimate concern*.[4] In Tillich's view, faith is intense engagement with questions about meaning and existence, purpose and value, what is good and true, and the nature of ultimate reality—all questions of "ultimate concern." Understood in this way, faith is something that offers at least a provisional solution to deep problems about the human situation.[5]

Building on Tillich's view of faith as ultimate concern, psychologist Robert Emmons has defined faith as living in accord with one's most searching and considered answers to questions of meaning and value. Religious belief and its secular equivalents provide "ultimate vision(s) of what people should be striving for in their lives...what makes life meaningful, valuable, and purposeful."[6]

Emmons begins, as we do, from the assumption that human beings are active, intentional, and goal-directed. This view has informed his many studies of the goals that people strive for and that shape and structure who they are and how they live. He has paid particular attention to goals that enable people to experience life as meaningful, valuable, and worth living. Emmons also has focused on the role that spirituality plays in investing personal goals with significance. Emmons calls *spiritual striving* the attempt to identify what is sacred or worthy of devotion. In Emmons' view, spiritual concerns pertain to the transcendent realm, which can mean God or the sacred in some alternative sense. A spiritual search is an attempt to identify what is sacred or worthy of devotion.

Such language may seem to suggest that what Emmons calls spiritual strivings or ultimate concerns are always religious in some way, but Emmons' view is broader than this. In his theory, spiritual strivings and ultimate concerns include fundamental moral principles or values (such as equality, justice, and compassion) as well as a sense of unity with a larger whole (including the cosmos, humanity, or nature). Such strivings and concerns also may include an awareness of the sacred or divine, such as connections with God, a higher power, or a sacred dimension of reality.

In studies of the range of personal goals that people actually work toward in their everyday lives, Emmons and his colleagues have found that ultimate concerns are rated as more important, and that they are engaged in for more intrinsic reasons, than are other kinds of strivings. Moreover, when people express a high proportion of spiritual strivings relative to the total number of other strivings they mention, this

predicts their well-being better than any other indicator the researchers found. All in all, "when people orient their lives around the attain-
ment of [ultimate concerns, including] spiritual ends, they tend to
experience their lives as worthwhile, unified, and meaningful."[7]

Emmons' research is consistent with the research on *purpose* that
we have been conducting for the past ten years. In Damon's studies
of adolescents and young adults, he and his colleagues have defined
purpose as a stable and generalized intention to accomplish something
that is at the same time meaningful to the self and consequential for
the world beyond the self.[8] Most young people lack a well-established
sense of purpose, but once they become purposeful they become
deeply engaged in challenging activities that contribute to the world,
and they show resilience in the face of challenges as well as high levels
of well-being and meaning in life.

Meaning in life, which infuses studies of both ultimate concern and
purpose, has been a relatively recent focus for psychologists. In the
past few decades, psychological research has shown what had already
been conjectured in literature and philosophy: Happiness in the sense
of a meaningful life is quite different from the happiness gained by
hedonic pleasures, and over the long haul, people's sense of what constitutes a life worth living (or "the good life") is based more on meaning than on the vicissitudes of hedonic pleasure.[9]

Departing from a long tradition of almost exclusive focus on
so-called subjective well-being, psychologists now have begun to distinguish between simple *happiness*, which refers to pleasure and positive emotions, and *meaning*, which refers to purpose, connectedness,
and growth. Martin Seligman, for example, has identified a pattern
that involves developing one's capacities and talents in the service of
something larger than the self, which he calls the *Meaningful Life*.[10]
This contrasts with the *Pleasant Life,* in which happiness is based only
in pleasurable experiences. Consistent with these labels, research has
shown that what individuals experience as a meaningful life is one
that's shaped by purpose and commitment, which provide a stable
sense of significance even when current life circumstances are difficult and aversive. One intriguing finding that illustrates the difference

between meaning and pleasure is that the experience of raising children predicts meaning in life, but not the type of happiness that's based mostly in pleasurable experiences.[11]

The capacities to find meaningful "ultimate concerns" and to engage productively with questions about the nature of human existence are so important that Howard Gardner, who created the theory of multiple intelligences, considered whether this capacity, which he calls *existential intelligence*, might constitute a domain of intelligence equivalent to the seven he had already documented (logical, linguistic, visual-spatial, bodily-kinesthetic, musical, interpersonal, and intrapersonal). Although Gardner isn't quite ready to grant existential intelligence this status, he acknowledges its uniqueness and significance. Gardner defines existential intelligence as the ability to "locate oneself with respect to the farthest reaches of the cosmos and...such existential features of the human condition as the significance of life, the meaning of death...and profound experiences as love of another person or total immersion in a work of art."[12]

Although the world's religions all have developed elaborate systems for dealing with existential issues, people also can connect with these issues through secular experiences such as immersion in the beauty of nature or music. Deep immersion in art, nature, or other moving experiences is existential when it becomes a felt encounter with the deeper truths of these realms. Such engagements can lead one to feel "enriched, ennobled, and humbled by the encounter,"[13] as do experiences that are more specifically identified as religious or spiritual.

This description of existential intelligence sounds intellectually demanding and abstract, but Gardner's description points also to the emotional nature of many transcendent experiences of meaning. The emotional dimensions of meaning and faith are undeniably important. Based on studies of lives over long periods of time, George Valliant has concluded that a sense of meaning is strongly bolstered by the positive emotions of love, compassion, hope, awe, inspiration, and gratitude. He points to the emotional dimensions of faith as well, especially a sense of trust, and he connects faith and meaning through the concept of trust. In his view, faith involves trusting that, in some important sense, the world has meaning, and that loving kindness or some other type of goodness exists. An absence of faith conveys a nihilist sense that no meaning is possible. In the coding scheme for our study of the six moral leaders in the present book, we include as a "counter-indicator" for faith (that is, as an indicator of the *lack* of faith) "evidence of immobilizing nihilism, meaninglessness, alienation, or spiritual despair."

A focus on the emotional dimensions of faith speaks also to the implications of faith for morality. The relationship of faith to morality is in part a function of the guiding significance of deep belief in ideals, as we described in Chapter 2, but it also can be found in the positive moral emotions that characterize faith and meaning. Jonathan Haidt[14] has described these inspiring emotions as *elevating*, and he has found them to be present in all the cultures that he and his colleagues have studied. Haidt's research describes elevation as a response to moral beauty, which involves not only a judgment that an action is morally right or good but also an emotional response of being moved or inspired by witnessing that action, which is accompanied by a desire to act morally oneself. Haidt points to physical concomitants as well, noting that people associate elevation with bodily warmth and a "tingling" kind of sensation.

Despite the clear importance of the emotional dimensions of faith that Vaillant, Haidt, and others have pointed out, feelings of inspiration, elevation, trust, and the like (what Haidt literally identifies as warm feelings) aren't a sufficient basis for a life of meaning. If they were, spending all day watching YouTube videos of kittens could constitute a meaningful life. Meaning requires not just feelings but some appreciation of their significance, some sense of the moral causes they connect us with and the moral possibilities they call up in us.

What many experiences of elevation or inspiration have in common is that, through appreciation of a particular moral action or object of beauty (such as a breathtaking sunset or powerful ocean), we can feel a deep sense of connection with transcendent truths, some sense that these truths are real. As Peter Benson, a visionary leader of programs for the well-being of youth and families, once pointed out, spirituality means creating a link between one's own life and *all* of life, and between one's own particular experience and some more transcendent reality.[15]

This may be why so many people experience human relationships as among the most meaningful aspects of their lives. Nathaniel Lambert and his colleagues[16] found, for example, that young people describe relationships with their families as the greatest single contributor to meaning in life. Others (see, for example, McAdams, *The Stories We Live By*[17]) have reported that generativity, which is a concern for nurturing the next generation and a desire to leave a positive legacy, is a common source of meaning for adults. Relationships not only carry great emotional significance, but at their best they provide a lived personal connection to timeless moral values—love, compassion, and altruism—that people not only enjoy but also *believe in* as fundamental to harmony among people and civilization at its best.

From a psychological perspective, it's important to know that having faith or living with a sense of purpose provides not only— by definition—conviction and direction to life, but also high levels of well-being, resilience, fulfillment, and sense of meaning. Ultimately, though, the value of faith does not depend on its useful consequences. A sense of personal well-being is not inherent in the concept of faith and doesn't serve as its ultimate justification. As Emmons points out, the Christian writer C. S. Lewis, when asked which religion makes people the happiest, said, "I didn't go to religion to make me happy. I always knew that a bottle of Port would do that."[18] Instead, faith is of value because (or insofar as) it helps one respond to the deepest questions of human existence, which are, at heart, moral as well as metaphysical questions.

A definition of faith as finding meaning and living accordingly is broad enough to include both religious and secular convictions and commitments. But it does not ensure that faith is a virtue. Faith as a consistency of focus on one's most important values, purposes, or convictions does represent a kind of integrity, but it leaves open the possibility of harmfully misguided faith commitments.

In religious terms, placing one's faith in an unworthy object, having faith in "false gods," or finding meaning in morally false values, all are known as idolatry. In a metaphorical sense, idolatry can signify anything that is treated as an ultimate concern when its dominant value is questionable. For many in the world today (or in past "gilded ages," for that matter), idolatry means an overriding concern for material and social success or other crude versions of the advancement of self. In some cases, the driving goals around which a life is organized can be wholly destructive. The question of whether having faith and living it is a good thing depends on whether the faith's ultimate concerns are themselves worthy and humane.

This qualification of faith's value points to the inescapable importance of reflection and judgment. If we are to avoid misplaced faith and false idols, faith and reason can't be treated as opposing forces. Faith, certainly, extends beyond reason: As we have noted, even the seemingly straightforward faith in the efficacy of science does this. But faith need not be *in opposition* to reason. To commit to worthwhile goals, ideals, and values, a person needs to *think about* them—not just accept whatever one's culture or role models provide, but give some independent thought to what one believes in and why. Moral and spiritual emotions and intuitions, along with the metaphors and narratives through which they're expressed, may seem to operate without any cognitive mediation. But if these emotions and intuitions, these beyond-rational experiences and attachments, are to be prevented from veering destructively off track, they need to rest on good judgment, reflection, and wisdom.

One way to think about faith that is true and good, as opposed to false and destructive, is to say that true faith is grounded in wisdom. Wisdom, like living a life of faith or meaning, requires *understanding* what's truly important in the larger view and being guided by that understanding. As philosopher Robert Nozick put it: "Wisdom…is knowing the deepest story, being able to see and appreciate the deepest significance of whatever occurs; this includes appreciating the ramifications of each thing or event for the various dimensions of reality, knowing and understanding not merely the proximate goods but the ultimate ones, and seeing the world in this light."[19] This is not entirely a cognitive capacity, but it centrally engages the thinking mind. Without wisdom, it's hard to ensure that faith and meaning constitute not only answers but, in some sense, good and true answers, to the big questions of human existence.

Distinguishing between real and false gods, true and false moral values, wise and foolish pursuits, is not a job for psychologists or other social scientists. These are *prescriptive* (philosophical and theological) rather than *empirical* questions, as we discussed in Chapter 2. For our purposes, the best we can do is to select moral exemplars and moral leaders who meet criteria laid out by philosophers and theologians— consistency between moral ends and means, behavior that appears to conform with moral principles that are universalizable, that include a generalized respect for humanity—and then describe the nature of the faith, meaning, or wisdom they exhibit. This is what we have tried to do. The questions that concern us are these: Do the moral exemplars and leaders we've studied in this and our previous research seem to exhibit faith—a deep belief in guiding values that organize their lives and give meaning and direction to their existence, even in the face of suffering? If so, what does that faith look like or entail, in both its religious or spiritual and its secular variants? Whether spiritual or secular, what roles does faith play in guiding moral actions and maintaining commitment, stamina, and focus?

Faith is of special interest to us because of its unexpected importance for the moral exemplars we described in *Some Do Care*.[20] Religious faith was not among the study's selection criteria. Given this, we were startled by the frequency with which religious or spiritual matters were central to the exemplars' lives: Almost 90 percent attributed their core moral commitments to their religious faith. This group was diverse in age, race, social class, and field of contribution as well as in religious denomination. It included Roman Catholics, mainline Protestants, Evangelical Christians, Quakers, Jews, and Buddhists.

For all these religiously grounded moral exemplars, faith contributed to their sense of certainty about central driving values such as honesty, fairness, charity, and harmony among people. It also played a role in their courage in the face of personal risk and in the positivity—enjoyment, realistic optimism, and hope—that sustained their commitment over the long haul. The exemplars for whom religious faith was important were more likely to forgive themselves and others and to express gratitude for their lives. The only people in the study who expressed bitterness about the difficulties of their work (three of the twenty-three) were all strictly secular in their beliefs. What's more, the exemplars' insights about faith emerged spontaneously during the interviews. None of our standard interview questions asked about religious faith, because we (foolishly, in hindsight) had not expected it to matter.

The clear and spontaneous salience of the theme led us to ask more explicitly about the role of faith in our present study of moral leaders. For this study, we chose two religious leaders, both members of the clergy—a Lutheran pastor and a rabbi. The other four leaders were included based solely on their moral leadership. We didn't consider the religious or spiritual beliefs of these four, or their orientations toward faith more generally, until we began the analyses of case material. As we discovered during our analyses, the four secular leaders—Addams, Hammarskjöld, Mandela, and Roosevelt—varied in the extent to which and the ways in which their moral values and goals, and their faith in a more secular sense, were connected with religion or spirituality.

The inclusion of both religious and secular leaders in the study reflects our desire to explore the place of faith in the lives of moral leaders from a broad conception of faith, not limited to religious affiliation. Although religion is important for many morally committed people, it is not essential for either moral leadership or moral commitment more generally. It's not hard to identify highly moral people who are nonreligious. Our concern is to understand the ways that deep moral convictions, as well as religious or spiritual faith, can support and direct moral commitment and action. Still, as in the study of living moral exemplars, we were struck by the important place of religious faith even in the secular leaders of the current study. This is no doubt partly due to the historical times and places in which they lived.

In our analyses of what faith meant to the six leaders, religion came up often for all six. This is important to note; but by noting such religious manifestations of faith, we don't mean to imply that religion is always necessary for the faith that informs and sustains moral commitment. Still, a full exploration of strictly secular faith and its role in moral leadership will require a different sort of study than the ones that we present in this book, a new study that selects its sample with that particular goal in mind.

FAITH AMONG SIX MORAL LEADERS

In Chapter 2, we discussed how the life choices of the six moral leaders in this book were organized by their moral ideals. Living in accord with deeply held ideals is part of what we mean by faith. For all six of the leaders, justice, truth, peace, harmony among people, and the worth and sacredness of all persons were foremost in their consciousness, even when current realities overwhelmingly violated these moral truths or values. Having faith meant that circumstances that might appear to negate the possibility of justice, truth, and peace did not lead to cynicism and despair but rather to a determination to bring the world closer to its proper moral orientation.

FAITH AND INTEGRITY

In our earlier study of living moral exemplars in *Some Do Care*, we found that they all shared a quality we called *certainty*. By *certainty* we meant that each had developed a core set of moral beliefs or principles that, once adopted, were not again called into question. Typically, these exemplars maintained a lifelong commitment to their central beliefs once they had established them. This commitment did not rule out openness to reexamining other, less central moral opinions they held: On the contrary, their value commitments encouraged such a reexamination. But their belief in moral principles such as equality and fairness didn't flag.

Crucially, the certainty of the exemplars' faith in these moral truths was accompanied by a strong sense of personal responsibility for working toward realizing these truths in the world. Characteristically, the exemplars felt they had no real choice in whether or not to work toward peace, racial equality, or equality of opportunity among rich and poor, despite the costs and risks. They said they wouldn't have been able to live with themselves if they had turned their backs on these issues, which they cared so much about.

In this way, the moral exemplars were displaying what we called "unity of self and moral goals." In some more recent studies, unity— defined as consistency among values, commitments, ideal selves, life goals, and life stories—has been shown to be a strong predictor of meaning and purpose in life.[21] Expressed in the language of faith, people with the kind of internal coherence that is organized around moral goals lead lives that are aligned with their ultimate concerns.

Whether through a conscious search for purpose or in a more evolving process, the six leaders in our present study found their own answers to the questions of what is worth living for, what is of ultimate importance and concern, what constitutes a worthwhile purpose, and what can be counted on as good and true. This kind of faith was a defining feature of all six of these moral leaders.

SPIRITUAL EXPERIENCE

When we describe faith as an engagement with questions concerning the nature of reality, the significance of life and death, and the nature of goodness and the sacred, it might seem that faith could be accessible only to philosophers, theologians, and other great intellectuals. But this seeming implication would be misleading. Within all of the world's major religions, engagement with ultimate reality is less likely to be described in terms of complex systems of belief than as spiritual *experiences*, often referred to as experiences of transcendence. Transcendent experiences have been described by many theologians and spiritual teachers throughout the millennia, and we will not attempt that task here except to say that they often involve a sense of unity, radiance, and overwhelming peace and love. They also have what is called a *noetic* quality—the sense that one *knows* a dimension of reality through the experience, although what one knows is not truth of the usual propositional sort.[22]

Throughout history, people who have had transcendent experiences report that these have changed them. From that time onward, limiting their perceptions and experiences to the mundane or material world seemed to have left out what's most important: a sacred dimension that had as much reality for them as material objects did. For many people, transcendent experiences are a major source of inspiration and the basis for their conviction that goodness, truth, and beauty are real. In this sense, transcendent experiences form the foundation for their faith.

Often engagement with the transcendent has been framed in terms of connection with a personal God, but this has not always been the case. For Paul Tillich, one of the most influential Christian theologians of the twentieth century, the concepts that represent God are symbols of ultimate reality but can never adequately represent that reality, which exceeds human understanding in its conceptual form. Because ultimate reality transcends any attempt to describe it adequately, it can be represented only by symbols or concepts that point to, but can't really capture, its nature. As Buddhist teachings have articulated, concepts are more like a finger pointing to the moon than a true representation of the moon (or ultimate truth) itself. In Tillich's view, the central spiritual question is not whether one believes that God exists but whether one is concerned with the nature of ultimate reality in this transcendent sense.[23] We include this reference to Tillich's conception of faith here not because his particular theology represents the views of the leaders we studied, but rather to illustrate that a faith in sacred dimensions of reality that transcend human understanding doesn't necessarily entail belief in a personal deity.

Faith that included experiences of transcendence was important to three of the six moral leaders we studied—Bonhoeffer, Heschel, and Hammarskjöld. These three men spoke of feeling direct connections with God and the sacred. The other three—Addams, Mandela, and

Roosevelt—were influenced by Christianity, especially Christian ethics, but did not express a strong sense of the transcendent.

For Heschel, awareness of and connection with the sacred was a critical element of faith and, in his opinion, ought to be the primary concern of religious teaching and experience. In this, he was pressing back against a set of religious traditions in which scholarship, analysis, and other intellectual functions were preeminent. Heschel's dean at Jewish Theological Seminary, for example, took a more cultural view of Judaism, rejecting "supernaturalism" and treating God as an abstract idea meant to serve human needs and aspirations. Heschel's attraction to a more mystical, joyful spirituality went back to his early childhood growing up in the small Polish town where Baal Shem Tov had founded the Hasidic movement. Heschel was greatly influenced by a grandfather for whom he was named. His grandfather Abraham was an illustrious rabbi who revered his Hasidic forebear so much that, when he died, he was buried next to Baal Shem.

For his entire life, Heschel never lost the sense of awe, beauty, and radiance conveyed by this approach to Judaism. He urged the "sociologically" oriented Jews of his time to recognize that religious practices are meant to connect individuals with the sacred as it is revealed in everyday life: "To sense in the small things the beginning of infinite significance...the ultimate in the common and simple...;[24] the ineffable inhabits both the magnificent and the common....Acts of worship counteract the trivialization of existence."[25] For him, this kind of spiritual experience involved an attitude of awe and wonder that infuses a life of faith: "Mystical encounter—at least caught a glimpse of the beauty, peace, power, that flow through the souls of those who are devoted to Him. Cultivate awe...a sense of wonder in the face of all existence. Intellect is overwhelmed in the face of mystery. Jewish education should unlock the reverence and awe. Replete is the world with spiritual radiance...[To miss this is to] dim all wonder by indifference."[26] Heschel's poetic writing on this subject was inspiring to many Christians as well as Jews.[27]

Dag Hammarskjöld was an exceptional student when in university, and after graduation his career advanced quickly: By age thirty-one, he was Sweden's Under-Secretary of State for Financial Affairs, and by thirty-six was chairman of the National Bank of Sweden. His ambitions were grounded in a commitment to social contribution that went back generations in his influential and highly distinguished family. But despite his privileged upbringing and personal success, as a young man he often felt spiritual distress. Albert Schweitzer exemplified the ideal of service that Hammarskjöld revered, but Schweitzer's ethical commitments didn't answer his spiritual emptiness. For that, Hammarskjöld turned to Christian mysticism, along with the teachings of Hinduism and Buddhism. Through this mystical spirituality, Hammarskjöld experienced a larger reality, a sense of transcendence, radiance, and awe. As he wrote in his diary, *Markings*, "...we die on the day when our lives cease to be illuminated by the steady radiance, renewed daily, of a wonder, the source of which is beyond all reason."[28] In keeping with this perspective, he spoke of the UN meditation room that he had created as a "center of stillness surrounded by silence; the sense in a vessel is not in its shell but in its void."[29]

THE TRANSCENDENT AND THE HUMAN

As compelling as these accounts of transcendence are, rooting one's faith entirely in this kind of spiritual experience may carry moral risks. The mundane human level of reality can lose its significance in the contemplation of a much larger cosmos. In this way, mysticism sometimes leads to disengagement and retreat from the world of human affairs.

All six moral leaders we studied led lives of action. None of them believed in retreating from the real world into an otherworldly existence of monasticism or disengagement. Dietrich Bonhoeffer was explicit in his writing about this, referring to his search for the place between the ultimate and penultimate (sacredness or God as ultimate and this human world as penultimate). As a pastor and devout Christian, the challenge for him was more in remaining connected to the world than in losing sight of the transcendent. He needed to remind himself and his students that "We need to stay in touch with this-worldliness. It is only by living completely in this world that one learns to have faith."[30]

Heschel too was concerned with the need to live at the intersection of "the human and the ultimate, the natural and the holy."[31] He believed that a central purpose of religious practices was to strengthen the connection between these two realms. Some of his most inspiring images deal with this connection, for example: "To feel in the rush of the passing the stillness of the eternal."[32] Despite their differences of nationality, life experience, and religious tradition, this same quality was evident in Dag Hammarskjöld. His biographer commented that "eternity for [Hammarskjöld] is to be experienced in the midst of this life."[33]

It is in this sense of connection between the human and the transcendent that Heschel's political activism was part and parcel of his Jewish faith. As one of his biographers noted, Heschel's life was marked by an "astonishing unity...the contemplative and the active, the mystic and the ethicist."[34] Combining almost constant political activism with the solitude and concentration needed for serious writing created stressful conflicts in time management for Heschel but no conflict in aspiration or identity. A fully integrated unity of action and reflection was inherent in Heschel's perspective on the relationship between ethics and ultimate concerns of a transcendent nature. In his view, "the answer to evil is not the good but the holy. It is an attempt to raise human beings to a higher level of existence where we are not alone when confronted by evil. Our ability to overcome evil comes through the power of love and holiness given us by God. Our deeds are the divine in disguise."[35]

RELIGIOUS THEMES AS MORAL GUIDES

We have pointed to both religious and secular versions of faith as foundations for moral action. Faith means not only conviction that moral goods such as justice, peace, and compassion are real but also efforts to align one's life with these goods. But how does this work? In what ways can faith provide *guidance* in one's moral and spiritual journey, apart from the sustenance it can provide?

In the cases we examined, we saw four ways that the leaders drew moral guidance from their religious faith traditions:

1) They prayed for guidance from God.
2) They drew on their faith tradition's moral rules.
3) They referred to religiously based moral images, models, and stories.
4) They drew on faith-related moral values that were encompassing enough to serve as touchstones in many realms of life.

We're well aware that each of these mechanisms can be used for good or ill. This speaks to the point we made earlier: Faith can be misguided, and judgment is needed to contain or avoid its destructive potential. Like any other moral practice, religious traditions are subject to ethical scrutiny using the same criteria and modes of analysis that apply when evaluating ethical claims or acts of a secular nature. In this sense, religious rules do not provide moral guidance that stands entirely apart from secular ethical considerations, although religious traditions do include unique cultural symbols, practices, and rituals.

This is not to say that difficult ethical questions can always be resolved through reason. Ethical argumentation, which takes place within faith traditions and also between faith traditions and their critics, often leads to ambiguous results. Many ethical questions have more than one plausible, justifiable answer. Universally cherished moral values often conflict with each other, and resolving those conflicts can involve setting one's own personal priorities, choosing among several possible orderings, each of which meets criteria of moral legitimacy.

Both the religious and secular leaders we studied drew guidance for these choices from their religious traditions. The lessons they drew were consistent with moral truths derived from nonreligious sources, and they could be justified in secular as well as religious terms. But the religious traditions that informed the leaders' moral thinking, feeling, and action provided both new insights and eloquent statements of timeless truths, as well as powerful representations of those truths. These served as valuable resources for the leaders, providing a different kind of guide for living than do references to abstract ethical principles.

While looking for guidance in gray areas, some of the moral leaders felt the need to pray for moral clarity. Dietrich Bonhoeffer faced difficult and consequential moral choices more than once—whether to return to Germany from New York at the start of the war, and whether to take part in efforts to assassinate Hitler, to take two dramatic examples. Bonhoeffer's struggles to find his way through these dilemmas show how deeply the search for moral guidance through faith is entwined with the challenges of maintaining inner truthfulness.

Questions of moral confusion, discernment, and self-deception interested Bonhoeffer throughout his life, especially once he had become an active conspirator in plots to kill Hitler. At Christmas 1942, Bonhoeffer wrote a letter reflecting on his experience living in Nazi Germany for the previous ten years and on his fateful decision to become involved with the coup. A copy of the letter, which he sent to several friends who were also involved in the resistance movement, was hidden under the shingles of his parents' roof and later recovered. The question he addressed in the letter concerned what it takes to stand fast against evil, and his reflections on this question lay out the many kinds of self-deception that entrap even well-intentioned individuals struggling to see how they can act in the face of overwhelming evil. After dispensing with the "reasonable person" and the moral fanatic, he goes on to discuss the person of conscience:

> Then there is the man with a conscience, who fights single-handed against heavy odds in situations that call for a decision. But the scale of the conflicts...tears him to pieces. Evil approaches him in so many respectable and seductive disguises that his conscience becomes nervous and vacillating, till at last he contents himself with a salved instead of a clear conscience, so that he lies to his own conscience in order to avoid despair....Here and there people flee from public altercation into the sanctuary of private virtuousness. But anyone who does this must shut his mouth and his eyes to the injustice around him. Only at the cost of self-deception can he keep himself pure from the contamination arising

from responsible action. In spite of all that he does, what he leaves undone will rob him of his peace of mind. He will either go to pieces because of this disquiet, or become the most hypocritical of Pharisees. Who stands fast? Only the man...who tries to make his whole life an answer to the question and call of God.[36]

In the end, Bonhoeffer believed that people confronting evil on the scale of Nazism need faith if they are to accept responsibility for the terrible choices required in that kind of battle. Otherwise, the way will be unclear and the many subtle ways of self-deception will overcome the individual trying to stand fast.

Sometimes the Biblical framing of a moral rule provides for inspiration, communication, justification, and coherence rather than offering a solution to an open question. The Golden Rule—do unto others as you would have them do unto you—lies at the heart of both Christianity and Judaism and has inspired people from all religious traditions and none at all to take the perspective of others before acting. It's not that people need a rule to tell them this is important; it's more that the Golden Rule makes it easy to keep a memorable formulation of the intention in mind as a constant reminder to do what they already know is right.

Jane Addams drew on another Christian rule as a key to living. She had known Jesus' injunction to turn the other cheek since childhood, but it took on new power when she read Tolstoy's explication of this moral rule in his book *My Religion*. Tolstoy wrote that Christ called his disciples to "observe the rule of non-resistance to evil." This meant "never do anything contrary to the law of love." This idea captured Addams' imagination and informed her life and work from that moment forward.[37]

Images, including especially images of people, such as Jesus Christ or the Hebrew prophets, serve somewhat the same function: providing a mental image to cling to in living out moral choices that may be harder to sustain than to discern. They provide a way of incorporating moral values and convictions into the self that's richer and more personally meaningful than abstract ethical principles can be.

All six of the leaders referred to Christ or to the prophets of the Hebrew Bible as ethical guides and exemplars of the right way to live. Bonhoeffer referred repeatedly to the Sermon on the Mount (Matthew, verses 5–7) as a guide to Christian discipleship, which he took as a central inspiration in decisions large and small. The serious implications of this commitment are evident in the fact that Bonhoeffer's decision to refuse military service was animated by the emphasis Jesus put on peace as an overriding human value. Bonhoeffer also had ethical, in addition to religious, grounds for conscientious objection to serving in the German military under Nazi rule. But his sense of absolute personal obligation, despite the very high risk of dire consequences to himself, was rooted in his religious faith and his commitment to live in the spirit of Christ.

The secular leaders among the six also drew on Biblical references, including prominently the Sermon on the Mount. Several cited this text, which is generally seen as representing the central tenets of Christian moral teaching, including the values of love, compassion, humility, peace, and reluctance to sit in judgment on others. In an address to the World Council of Churches, Dag Hammarskjöld referred to the Sermon on the Mount as a source of wisdom on which he could draw in his leadership of the United Nations, sometimes in surprising ways:

> In the Sermon on the Mount, it is said that we should take no thought of the morrow....Can anything seem further from the planning, the long-term considerations of political life? And yet is this not the very expression of the kind of patience we must all learn to show in our work for peace and justice? Mustn't we learn to believe that when we give to this work, daily, what it is in our power to give and when, daily, we meet the demands facing us to the best of our ability, this will ultimately lead to a world of greater justice and good will, even if nothing would seem to give us hope of success or even of progress in the right direction?[38]

Abraham Heschel also stressed the importance of following a guiding example rather than relying entirely on Biblical knowledge and analysis. Although Heschel was steeped in scholarship and Talmudic analysis, he also urged a more personal and emotional connection with the sacred: "God is not only the object of knowledge, he is the example one is to follow."[39] According to his biographer, Edward Kaplan, "for Heschel, a strong and consistent purpose was 'living in the sight of god'."[40]

Another way the moral leaders were guided by their religious traditions was by incorporating into their thinking and moral motivation some encompassing moral goods or values that seem to shine with truth and inspiration. For Heschel, this often involved references to justice, connecting this overarching value with the examples of the prophets. A passionate concern for justice informed and enlivened his lifelong activism as well as his theology, and this shared concern formed the basis for his close friendships with Martin Luther King, Jr., Daniel and Philip Berrigan, and others.

Christian love or compassion was the "essential truth" most often used as a touchstone of direction and purpose for the Christians among the six. Christian love was a prominent, even decisive, theme in the lives and work of Jane Addams, Dag Hammarskjöld, and Eleanor Roosevelt. Hammarskjöld organized his life around the Christian message that one ought to "Love thy neighbor as thyself; live together in peace; pursue universal brotherhood."[41] For Jane Addams, the whole of the settlement house movement represented a renaissance of the early Christians' joyous love and "the joy of finding the Christ which lieth in each man."[42] Eleanor Roosevelt, although acknowledging the religious diversity that pervaded the United States even during her lifetime, went on to suggest that some Christian values might be broad enough to apply to a multicultural democracy: "We are a mixed nation of many peoples and many religions, but most of us would accept the life of Christ as a pattern for our democratic way of life, and Christ taught love and never hate."[43]

SERENITY, HOPE, AND COURAGE

Faith can provide moral guidance, or at least images and stories that help articulate more inchoate moral intimations. But guidance is of limited value without motivation and sustenance. Among the most frequent and vivid references to faith, by both living moral exemplars and these six twentieth-century moral leaders, have been descriptions of the many ways that faith gives people patience, strength, serenity, hope, and courage.

All six of the leaders faced difficult and painful experiences; some faced hardships of the most dramatic possible nature. But they did not succumb to helplessness, despair, or nihilism even in the face of real evils like Nazism and apartheid. Both Eleanor Roosevelt and Nelson Mandela, from very different vantage points, believed that their faith offered a way to transform suffering into something worthwhile. Roosevelt believed that the suffering she had endured through the loss of her parents while a young child, and in the course of her husband's infidelity, had increased her ability to understand the suffering of others. Mandela, who endured imprisonment and abuse for decades, said: "Indeed, the chains of the body are often wings to the spirit. It has been so all along, and so it will always be. Shakespeare in *As You Like It* puts the same idea somewhat differently: Sweet are the uses of adversity; Which, like a toad, ugly and venomous; Wears yet a precious jewel in its head."[44]

Much like the moral exemplars we studied earlier, the six moral leaders also experienced their faith as a source of serenity and courage in the face of extreme circumstances, danger, and death. They spoke of surrendering themselves to God or to their faith and the peace they found in doing this. This is a form of courage that requires not powerful protection of the self, but "letting go" of a self-protective attitude.

Dag Hammarskjöld spoke of "letting go" in terms drawn from the Hindu text, the *Bhagavad Gita*, which teaches that release from suffering requires an attitude of nonattachment. Hammarskjöld's work at the UN was relentlessly intense and demanding, requiring him to manage several high-stakes global crises at any one time. The right course of action was seldom clear-cut, and the outcomes were uncertain. In dealing with these stressful demands, Hammarskjöld found that an approach grounded in nonattachment allowed him to make decisions and take action despite his acute awareness that he couldn't fully control the outcomes of his choices: "The Bhagavad-Gita echoes somewhere an experience of all ages and all philosophies in these words: 'Work with anxiety about results is far inferior to work without such anxiety, in calm self-surrender. [These words] express a deep faith. We will be happy if we can make that faith ours in all our efforts."[45]

Dietrich Bonhoeffer remains for us today an iconic example of serenity and courage during extreme circumstances. He was calm when, already in prison, he heard about the failure of the final and very promising coup attempt against Hitler, a failure that ensured his own impending execution. Bonhoeffer attributed his serene response to the fact that he had already "thrown himself completely into the arms of God."[46] This realization that he could rely on his faith to endure confinement in an SS prison led him to feel that "now there was nothing in life of which one need ever be afraid."[47] This fearlessness derived from "the calm of the mystic, which comes from the experience of the ultimate."[48] Bonhoeffer wanted to share his realization that faith provides peace when we see through "the human illusion that we can organize our lives so as to make ourselves safe from all strikes of fate."[49] It is part of his legacy that, even at the end, when his execution drew closer, he emanated calm and was cheerful, ready to respond to a joke, and apparently carefree.

Mandela cited a story about Christ's crucifixion to convey his experience that faith can provide courage and even peace in the midst of terrifying chaos. As Mandela said:

The story is as meaningful today as it was at the height of the Roman Empire. After Jesus' trial, Pilate writes to a friend in Rome to whom he makes remarkable confessions. Briefly, this is the story as told by him and, for convenience, I have put it in the first person. "As governor of a Roman province I have tried many cases involving all types of rebels. But this trial of Christ I shall never forget! One day a huge crowd, literally shivering with rage and excitement, assembled just outside my palace and demanded that I crucify Christ, at the same time pointing to a man whose arms and feet were heavily chained. I looked at the prisoner and our eyes met. In the midst of the excitement and noise, he remained perfectly calm, quiet and confident as if he had millions of people on his side."[50]

Dag Hammarskjöld knew well the peace and courage that comes from faith. As one of his biographers commented: "His commitment ultimately depends on his commitment to God...To be united with God, to be in his hands, means to rest in his stillness, to receive strength and inspiration from him, to be liberated by him and to live in freedom.... [This] union is to be realized in the service of men."[51] Hammarskjöld himself said: "[Establishing world peace requires] the courage to meet others with trust.... [H]e who fears God will no longer fear men."[52] Similarly, Jane Addams believed "that if a person trusted his own conscience, he would experience Christ's secret of peace, calm, a sense of restful centeredness."[53]

Along with a strong sense of peace and fearlessness, the moral leaders also drew on their faith as the primary source of the positive and sustaining emotions of gratitude and hope. This is much like the quality we called *positivity* in the living moral exemplars we studied. Mandela was in what could have seemed like a hopeless situation— separated from his family; unable to attend his own son's funeral; powerless to prevent the harassment, anguish, and eventual alienation of his beloved wife; and aware that his imprisonment and separation from his loved ones might never end. Yet he spoke often and eloquently about the power of hope to sustain him:

"In spite of all that has happened I have, throughout the ebb and flow of the tides of fortune..., lived in hope and expectation. Sometimes I even have the belief that this feeling is part and parcel of myself. It seems to be woven into my being. I feel my heart pumping hope steadily to every part of my body, warming my blood and pepping up my spirits. I am convinced that floods of personal disaster can never drown a determined revolutionary nor can the cumulus of misery that accompanies tragedy suffocate him. To a freedom fighter, hope is what a life belt is to a swimmer—a guarantee that one will keep afloat and free from danger.[54]

THE DEMANDS OF FAITH

The belief or hope that spirituality can provide a sense of meaning as well as comfort and strength in adversity is familiar to people facing ordinary circumstances as well as the extraordinary challenges faced by the moral leaders we studied. In fact, Princeton sociologist Robert Wuthnow observes with dismay that the desire to use faith as a source of comfort has, in contemporary American life, overtaken all its other roles. He observes that, unfortunately, most people who profess religious faith go about their lives in pretty much the same ways as those who have no faith at all.[55] Based in the many empirical studies he has conducted, Wuthnow concludes that "When we are influenced by our faith, we are more likely to say we *feel* better about what we do than to do anything differently.... Our spirituality is often little more than a therapeutic device.... Faith is a way of massaging our feelings. We pray for comfort but do not expect to be challenged."[56] Writing at an earlier time and in a different country (the United Kingdom), C. S. Lewis pointed to the same phenomenon when he followed his comment about the happiness to be had from Port wine with a remark that refers implicitly to the demands of faith: "If you want a religion to make you really comfortable, I certainly don't recommend Christianity."

Despite their reliance on faith as a resource, the six leaders considered the demands of faith, whether religious or secular, to be at least as real as its comforts. Bonhoeffer's concept of *cheap grace* is among his most influential legacies. The book in which he articulated this view, *The Cost of Discipleship*, is a classic of Christian thought.[57] In part due to his frustration at the unwillingness of the church to take the costly step of opposing Hitler, Bonhoeffer decried a kind of cheap grace in which forgiveness is offered without any real repentance or commitment to discipleship. "Grace is sold on the market like a cheapjack's wares...The consolations of religion are thrown away at cut-rate prices."[58] In his view, true grace is costly "because it calls us to follow."[59] He was speaking partly of himself when he said, "When you are faithful to the earth for the sake of things above...it dashes any hope for a comfortable life."[60] For Bonhoeffer, the moral imperative of the fight against Hitler dashed any hope of the comfortable life of a pastor, a life spent with the woman he loved, living long enough to marry, have children, and enjoy the many simple pleasures of an ordinary life.

Abraham Heschel was equally demanding in his view of faith's requirements. As his biographer commented, "He saw the role of religion as challenging people, making demands on them rather than as comforting them. Religion must challenge the status quo....[In Heschel's view] the prophets had disdain for those to whom God was comfort and security; to them God was a challenge, an incessant demand. Tranquility is unknown in the soul of a prophet. The miseries of the world give him no rest."[61]

Speaking in more secular language, Mandela expressed the same kind of impatience with those who disengage in the face of injustice. His passionate call for engagement in the fight against apartheid mirrors Bonhoeffer's frustration with individuals and institutions that stood by as Nazism took over Germany. As Mandela said:

> For one thing, those who have no soul, no sense of national pride and no ideals to win can suffer neither humiliation nor defeat, they can evolve no national heritage, are inspired by no sacred mission and can produce no martyrs or national heroes. A new world will be won not by those who stand at a distance with their arms folded, but by those who are in the arena, whose garments are torn by storms and whose bodies are maimed in the course of the contest. Honour belongs to those who never forsake the truth even when things seem dark and grim, who try over and over again, who are never discouraged by insults, humiliation and even defeat.[62]

These messages of demand and moral strength are incomplete, however, without the accompanying sentiment of forgiveness that is evident in all six leaders. It is characteristic of the generous spirit of Nelson Mandela that a former warder at Robben Island prison was among the guests honored to sit on the dais during his inauguration as president of South Africa. But Mandela's forgiveness went far beyond the personal when he and Bishop Tutu established the Truth and Reconciliation Commission. He knew that democracy could not go forward without forgiveness and reconciliation, so he not only forgave his enemies himself, but he set in motion a nationwide effort to bring about a more far-reaching forgiveness.

FAITH AS PRACTICE

Maintaining faith, responding to the demands of faith, is not easy. It doesn't happen by itself. In every religious tradition, faith is developed and sustained through spiritual practices. In this, it may have an advantage over secular faith, for which regular practices that keep it fresh and salient are less well developed and rarely institutionalized or pursued collectively. Both religious and secular leaders in our group of six spoke of the importance of prayer, meditation, Bible reading, or other spiritual practices in their lives. In part these were the mechanisms through which they achieved the calm that faith brought; in part they were reminders of the demands of faith. For the six leaders, prayer and other spiritual practices were a means to express, affirm, and share the convictions that lay at the heart of their faith.

Bonhoeffer maintained his equanimity in the worst of circumstances through a practice of daily meditations on Bible passages. And, sometimes, in her *My Day* column, Eleanor Roosevelt shared prayers that expressed her hopes for the country. On Flag Day in 1942, in the midst of World War II, she wrote:

The President read Mr. Stephen Vincent Benet's beautiful prayer, which I am giving [here] in part in the hope that all will cut it out and keep it with them. "God of the free, we pledge our lives and hearts today to the cause of all free mankind. Grant us victory over the tyrants who would enslave all free men and nations. Grant us faith and understanding to cherish all those who fight for freedom as if they were our brothers. Grant us brotherhood in hope and union, not only for the space of this bitter war, but for the days to come which shall and must unite all the children of earth. Our earth is but a small star in the great universe. Yet of it we can make, if we choose, a planet unvexed by war, untroubled by hunger or fear, undivided by senseless distinctions of race, color or theory. Grant us that courage and foreseeing to begin this task today that our children and our children's children may be proud of the name of man... Yet most of all grant us brotherhood, not only for this day but for all our years—a brotherhood not of words but of acts and deeds. We are all of us children of earth—grant us that simple knowledge. If our brothers are oppressed, then we are oppressed. If they hunger, we hunger. If their freedom is taken away, our freedom is not secure. Grant us a common faith that man shall know bread and peace—that he shall know justice and righteousness, freedom and security, an equal opportunity and an equal chance to do his best, not only in our own lands, but throughout the world. And in that faith let us march toward the clean world our hands can make. Amen."[63]

Part of the power of religious practices to sustain a life of faith comes from the collective nature of some of these practices. This was critical to Bonhoeffer, who spoke of the strength provided by a community of the faithful, which he felt applied to the collectivity of the Confessing Church through which he and his colleagues tried to resist Nazism. Jane Addams and Mandela expressed the same confidence in the value of a community of the faithful, although they used secular terms to identify the nature of that community. A community working together to achieve justice was at the heart of the settlement house movement and provided Addams with strategy, direction, and support in her lifelong commitment to democracy, compassion, and justice. Mandela's knowledge that he worked as part of a "tried and tested family" of freedom fighters endowed his "spirits with powerful wings."[64]

The six leaders also understood the potential for positive contributions by religious institutions in social as well as individual terms. For

Mandela, his association with Christianity derived from the role of the church in providing education for the native people of Africa, as it had for him. He saw the church as, by and large, a positive force, which held a position of some power in relation to the state and used that power, in part, to insist that African children receive an education. In his view, "All the progress my people had made...was all the product of missionary schools."[65] He went on to urge the church to play an active role in the fight against apartheid—"Just as the [individuals with political power] use their pulpit in order to propagate their views, our priests should do exactly the same."[66] And certainly, his good friend Bishop Desmond Tutu did just that.

Heschel felt the same way, arguing that clergy had important parts to play in public life, serving as "authentic biblical voices for social change."[67] But Heschel was also a frequent critic of institutionalized religion. Contemporary Judaism (like other institutionalized religions) had, in his view, become dull and irrelevant. He had little regard for the thoughtless performance of rituals, arguing that religious practice needs to "be a living fountain instead of an heirloom."[68] Heschel believed that "Religion has often suffered from the tendency to become an end in itself, to seclude the holy, to become parochial, self-indulgent, self-seeking; as if the task were not to ennoble human nature but to enhance the power and beauty of the institutions or to enlarge the body of doctrines."[69]

Heschel was hopeful about the possibility of bringing fresh life to religious ritual and practices. The spiritual practices of Judaism were central to his life from childhood onward. As a rabbi, his reflections on these practices were among his most important contributions. His book *The Sabbath*[70] is a classic. In his view, the Jewish practice of honoring the Sabbath by treating it as a day of rest and reflection calls attention to time rather than space as the critical dimension of spiritual practice. Setting aside specific times during the week and during the day for prayer and connection with the sacred were, for him, even more important than visits to sacred spaces, like the synagogue or (for Christians) a church.

FAITH TEMPERED BY HUMILITY AND TRUTH

We have alluded throughout this chapter to the destructive potential of misguided faith. Some would say that any faith informed by religious or spiritual perspectives is misguided. Books by the so-called new atheists (Richard Dawkins, Christopher Hitchens, and others) argue that religiosity of any sort—not only within organized religions but also personal attachments to spiritual beliefs and pursuits—is foolish, irrational, and dangerous and should be exposed and militantly opposed in public discourse and policy. Among other things, their books articulate in vehement ways the undeniable truth that organized religion, down through the ages, has inflicted great harm in the name of faith.

Whether or not one agrees with the full range of these authors' antireligious messages—and most people, especially in the United States, do not—it is hard to discount their warnings about the risks of faith. Dramatic incidents of religiously identified terrorism have brought up to date the truism that religious faith can lead to terrible violence against the innocent. This is no place to take on the larger issues raised by critics of organized religion, but we can't move on without some comment on the urgency of safeguards against the faith of fanatics.

A major point of this book is that irrational moral intuition and unthinking inculcation into moral cultures are inadequate bases for mature and trustworthy morality. This goes for spiritual intuitions and the cultures of organized religions as well as personal intuitions and ethnic and national cultures. Wise judgment need not involve deductive analysis, but it is always a form of understanding and reflection. As such, moral understanding, as expressed through wisdom, is an essential safeguard against the ill effects of turning one's life choices over to an unthinking faith.

One of the well-known risks of passionate faith, whether religious or ideological, is intolerance. Disdain, discrimination, and even violence, against nonbelievers are undeniable realities, and it is in part these realities that fuel the popularity of the new atheism. The only antidote for intolerance is open-mindedness and respect for differences (a principle that the new atheism does not itself always seem to honor). This is why we believe that faith must be closely linked with the other two virtues we've highlighted, *truthfulness* and *humility*, if its destructive potential is to be avoided.

Open-mindedness is a critical feature of moral character that lies at the intersection of truth and humility. This quality was evident in the faith of all of the leaders in our study. All six were known for their ecumenical work or their deeply pluralistic approaches to religious belief.

Dag Hammarskjöld's reflections on life were shot through with Hindu and Buddhist as well as Christian influences, and one of the last acts of his life was to arrange for the publication of Martin Buber's *I and Thou* in Sweden. He had previously met with Buber in Israel to discuss the project and took a copy of the book on his final journey to the Congo. Eleanor Roosevelt was able to unite the world's full range of faith traditions in support of the Universal Declaration of Human Rights. Abraham Heschel worked closely with the Catholic Church as well as with clergy from Protestant denominations. He reached out to Muslim leaders and was beloved by well-known Christians of his time, including Thomas Merton, Reinhold Niebuhr, and Daniel and Philip Berrigan.

Another signature weakness of religious faith is that it can lend itself to hypocrisy, along with its close cousin, self-righteousness. Clearly, scrupulous habits of searching self-examination, inner truthfulness, and humility are the most potent checks on these familiar religious vices. In our view, faith cannot stand alone: It must be combined with truth and humility; otherwise, faith can contribute to the worst kind of tyrannical leadership rather than preventing it.

NOTES

1. George Vaillant, *Spiritual Evolution: A Scientific Defense of Faith* (New York: Broadway Books, Random House LLC, 2008), 66.
2. Charles Taylor, *A Secular Age* (Cambridge, MA: Belknap Press of Harvard University Press, 2007).

3. Alfred North Whitehead, *Science and the Modern World*, Vol. 1925 (New York: Macmillan, 1926), 18.

4. Paul Tillich, *Dynamics of Faith* (New York: Harper & Row, 1957).

5. John Bishop, "Faith," http://plato.stanford.edu/archives/fall2010/entries/faith/ (accessed January 27, 2014).

6. Robert A. Emmons, *The Psychology of Ultimate Concerns: Motivation and Spirituality in Personality* (New York: Guilford Press, 1999), 3.

7. Emmons, *The Psychology of Ultimate Concerns,* 104.

8. William Damon, *The Path to Purpose: Helping Our Children Find Their Calling in Life* (New York: Free Press, 2008).

9. Laura A. King and Christie K. Napa, "What Makes a Life Good?" *Journal of Personality and Social Psychology* 75, no. 1 (1998): 156–165; Ian McGregor and Brian R. Little, "Personal Projects, Happiness, and Meaning." *Journal of Personality and Social Psychology* 74, no. 2 (1998): 494–551; Carol D. Ryff, "Psychological Well-being Revisited: Advances in the Science and Practice of Eudaimonia." *Psychotherapy and Psychosomatics* 83, no. 1 (2014): 10–28.

10. Martin E. P. Seligman, *Authentic Happiness: Using the New Positive Psychology to Realize Your Potential for Lasting Fulfillment* (New York: Free Press, 2002).

11. Roy F. Baumeister, "Some Key Differences between a Happy Life and a Meaningful Life." *The Journal of Positive Psychology* 8, no. 6 (2013): 505–516.

12. Howard Gardner, *Intelligence Reframed: Multiple Intelligences for the 21st Century* (New York: Basic Books, 1999), 60.

13. Gardner, *Intelligence Reframed,* 65.

14. Jonathan Haidt, "The Moral Emotions," in *Handbook of Affective Sciences, Series in Affective Science,* eds. Richard J. Davidson, Klaus R. Scherer, and H. Hill Goldsmith (New York: Oxford University Press, 2003), 852.

15. Peter Benson, "Spirituality and the Adolescent Journey: Reclaiming Children and Youth." *Journal of Emotional and Behavioral Problems* 5, no. 4 (Winter, 1997): 206–209, 219.

16. Nathaniel M. Lambert et al., "Family as a Salient Source of Meaning in Young Adulthood." *The Journal of Positive Psychology* 5, no. 5 (September, 2010): 367–376.

17. Dan P. McAdams, *The Stories We Live By: Personal Myths and the Making of the Self* (New York: Guilford Press, 1997, 1993).

18. Emmons, *The Psychology of Ultimate Concerns,* 137.

19. Robert Nozick, *The Examined Life: Philosophical Meditations* (New York: Touchstone, Simon & Schuster, 1989), 275.

20. Anne Colby and William Damon, *Some Do Care: Contemporary Lives of Moral Commitment* (New York: Free Press, 1992).

21. McGregor and Little, *Personal Projects, Happiness, and Meaning,* 494–551.

22. Marcus J. Borg, *The God We Never Knew: Beyond Dogmatic Religion to a More Authentic Contemporary Faith*, 1st ed. (San Francisco: HarperCollins, 1997).

23. Tillich, *Dynamics of Faith*.

24. Abraham Joshua Heschel, *The Wisdom of Heschel, Selected by Ruth Marcus Goodhill* (New York: Farrar, Straus and Giroux, 1975), 135.

25. Heschel, *The Wisdom of Heschel*, 193; Abraham Joshua Heschel, Jacob Neusner, and Noam M. M. Neusner, *To Grow in Wisdom: An Anthology of Abraham Joshua Heschel* (Lanham, MD: Madison Books, 1990), 160.

26. Heschel, *The Wisdom of Heschel, Selected by Ruth Marcus Goodhill*, 132–133.

27. It was, however, a source of irritation for some of his rabbinic colleagues, who considered his work to be more literary than seriously theological.

28. Gustaf Aulén, *Dag Hammarskjöld's White Book; An Analysis of Markings* (Philadelphia: Fortress Press, 1969), 23.

29. Dag Hammarskjöld and Wilder Foote, *Servant of Peace: A Selection of the Speeches and Statements of Dag Hammarskjöld, Secretary-General of the United Nations, 1953-1961* [Speeches. Selections.] (New York: Harper & Row, 1962), 160.

30. Dietrich Bonhoeffer, *Letters and Papers from Prison* [Widerstand und Ergebung], American ed. (New York: MacMillan, 1972), 369.

31. Edward K. Kaplan, *Spiritual Radical: Abraham Joshua Heschel in America, 1940–1972* (New Haven, CT: Yale University Press, 2007), 188.

32. Heschel, *The Wisdom of Heschel, Selected by Ruth Marcus Goodhill*, 135.

33. Aulén, *Dag Hammarskjöld's White Book*, 154.

34. Heschel, Neusner, and Neusner, *To Grow in Wisdom*, 126.

35. Heschel, Neusner, and Neusner, *To Grow in Wisdom*, 209.

36. Bonhoeffer, *Letters and Papers from Prison*, 4.

37. Louise Knight, *Jane Addams: Spirit in Action*, 1st ed. (New York: W. W. Norton & Co., 2010), 54.

38. Dag Hammarskjöld and W. H. Auden, *Markings* (New York: Knopf, 1966), 61.

39. Heschel, Neusner, and Neusner, *To Grow in Wisdom*, 127–128.

40. Kaplan, *Spiritual Radical*, 124.

41. Hammarskjöld and Auden, *Markings*, 61.

42. Jane Addams, *Twenty Years at Hull-House* (New York: Macmillan, 1973, c.1938), 123.

43. Eleanor Roosevelt, Rochelle Chadakoff, and David Emblidge, *Eleanor Roosevelt's My Day* (New York: Pharos Books, 1989), 299.

44. Nelson Mandela, *Conversations with Myself*, 1st ed. (New York: Farrar, Straus and Giroux, 2010), 45.

45. Hammarskjöld and Foote, *Servant of Peace*, 40.
46. Ferdinand Schlingensiepen, *Dietrich Bonhoeffer, 1906–1945: Martyr, Thinker, Man of Resistance* [Dietrich Bonhoeffer 1906–1945 eine Biographie. English] (London; New York: T&T Clark, 2010), 356.
47. Schlingensiepen, *Dietrich Bonhoeffer, 1906–1945*, 419.
48. Schlingensiepen, *Dietrich Bonhoeffer, 1906–1945*, 356.
49. Schlingensiepen, *Dietrich Bonhoeffer, 1906–1945*, 356.
50. Mandela, *Conversations with Myself*, 225.
51. Aulén, *Dag Hammarskjöld's White Book*, 149.
52. Hammarskjöld and Foote, *Servant of Peace*, 60.
53. Knight, *Jane Addams: Spirit in Action*, 45.
54. Mandela, *Conversations with Myself*, 54.
55. Robert Wuthnow, *God and Mammon in America* (New York: Free Press, 1994), 5.
56. Wuthnow, *God and Mammon in America*, 5–6.
57. Dietrich Bonhoeffer, *The Cost of Discipleship*, 95th ed. (New York: Touchstone Books, 1995).
58. Bonhoeffer, *The Cost of Discipleship*, 43.
59. Bonhoeffer, *The Cost of Discipleship*, 45.
60. Schlingensiepen, *Dietrich Bonhoeffer*, 111–112.
61. Heschel, Neusner, and Neusner, *To Grow in Wisdom*, 153.
62. Mandela, *Conversations with Myself*, 175.
63. Roosevelt, Chadakoff, and Emblidge, *Eleanor Roosevelt's My Day*, 247–248.
64. Mandela, *Conversations with Myself*, 177.
65. Martin Meredith, *Mandela: A Biography*, 1st ed. (New York: PublicAffairs, 2010), 8.
66. Mandela, *Conversations with Myself*, 64.
67. Kaplan, *Spiritual Radical*, 179.
68. Heschel, Neusner, and Neusner, *To Grow in Wisdom*, 147.
69. Heschel, Neusner and Neusner, *To Grow in Wisdom*, 152.
70. Abraham Joshua Heschel, *The Sabbath, Its Meaning for Modern Man*, Expanded ed. (New York: Farrar, Straus, 1952), 136.

CHAPTER SEVEN

THE UNIVERSAL SEARCH FOR MORAL TRUTH

Moral ideals such as truthfulness, compassion, fairness, and honor seem widely admired. But *how* widely, really? Are such ideals merely the product of particular times and places, valid only in the social and cultural contexts that are familiar to us? Or are some moral ideals general to the human condition, admired everywhere by people who are trying to do the right thing? And how *compelling* are even the most widely cherished ideals? Do such ideals make a difference in the way we live? Do they guide our conduct? Or are ideals merely high-minded illusions that we trot out after we've gone about our usual self-serving, irrational, culture-driven, impulse-ridden ways? In the end, are moral ideals no more than fanciful inventions that we use in an effort to look virtuous in our own and others' eyes?

Whether influential or not, no moral ideal operates in a vacuum. At every moment, we act and react on multiple levels—physical, emotional, social, ideational. Responses of the "gut"—the physical and emotional—carry a felt authenticity that can give them special power. Some social scientists have taken this special power to mean that, in the heat of the moment, ideals can't make themselves heard over the noise of the emotional tumult. Accordingly, the claim that emotion rules the day has great appeal for present-day social science and mass media alike. One aspect of this notion's appeal is that it seems to take us off the hook of our hectoring consciences. In a world where ideals don't matter, the voice of conscience becomes irrelevant and might as well be ignored.

In this book, we argue that ideals, at least on important occasions, do influence people's moral choices. At critical times, "the still small voice" of conscience can and does make itself heard over the din of emotional forces. Although we recognize the role that gut responses can play, we reject extreme positions of biological determinism that characterize the entire human moral sense as driven by such nonconscious responses.

But determinism takes many guises, cultural as well as biological. Even if we convince the reader that ideals do matter in human behavior, we still need to address the question of where ideals come from. Do we pick them up from whatever cultural surroundings we happen to be exposed to, or do we ourselves play a decisive role in selecting, personalizing, and sometimes authoring the ideals we live by? Do cultural forces beyond our control determine our moral ideals, or do we have some power as individuals to select and shape them ourselves?

These are big questions that have intrigued philosophers and other scholars for ages, and all these questions lead to an even bigger question about the nature of morality: Does the human moral sense reflect merely the legacies of fixed powers—internal or external—that are capricious, irrational, and impervious to conscious choice? Or do they reflect active searches for moral truth, guided by every individual's capacity for moral understanding and virtue—a search that is shared by people everywhere and that leads in many distinct but interconnected directions?

There is a great deal at stake in how we answer these questions. Efforts to reason together to determine the correct moral path; to formulate laws and codes to increase moral outcomes for individuals and societies; to reflect on one's own moral choices and purposes; and to educate the young for the capacity to make sound moral judgments; all assume that ideas matter and must be taken seriously. It's hard to imagine how a society would be able to make moral progress without thoughtful reflection on the ideals that its people cherish and wish to live by.

Martin Luther King, Jr. once made the stirring claim that "the arc of the moral universe is long, but it bends toward justice."[1] One key cause of this progressive bending has been people's relentless reconsideration of the validity of their current beliefs, along with an assessment of how well their behavior matches ideals they admire. Such reconsiderations and assessments are the products of understanding, judgment, and learning, all of which are within a person's control.

In today's intellectual climate, we realize that our claim that moral ideals can be decisive is controversial, requiring explanation and empirical support. The purpose of this book has been to provide both.

We consider the heart of the matter to be *the universal search for moral truth*. Recent controversies in the field reflect three major tensions implicit in this central phrase. The first major tension pertains to the concept *universal*. This concept has often been placed in opposition to respect for *particular* beliefs, which vary across cultural contexts. The second tension pertains to *search*, which indicates an *active* quest for truth by people who are *moral agents*—in contrast to the now-prevailing view that people's choices are determined by their biological and/or social circumstances. The third tension pertains to the term *moral truth*, which has often been taken as a claim that there is one right answer to any moral problem—placing it in opposition to the more seemingly tolerant perspectives of pluralism and relativism. But the term moral truth need *not* mean that there is only one answer to any moral problem: Without believing that there is one and only one absolute moral truth, one can recognize that some moral claims are more valid than others and that moral errors and falsehoods are real possibilities in the moral universe.

The tensions between universalism versus particularism, moral agency versus determinism, and principled versus relativistic approaches to moral truth are serious issues that must be considered by any view of human moral choice that strives to be accurate and complete. The moral leaders profiled in this book consciously and publicly wrestled with these very tensions, seeking to find beneficial ways of resolving them in support of sound moral choices. In this final chapter we examine one especially revealing example of this defining quest.

THE TRIUMPH OF UNIVERSAL STANDARDS ON THE CULTURALLY DIVERSE GLOBAL STAGE

When viewed through the fractious prism of our current social and political epoch, it's almost impossible to imagine a set of moral ideals that could garner agreement across the world's ideological, religious, ethnic, economic, and cultural divides. Yet this is exactly what happened less than seventy years ago, when, in the wake of World War II, all the world's nations voted to endorse the shared moral ideals embodied in the *Universal Declaration of Human Rights*, passed by the General Assembly of the United Nations in Paris on December 10, 1948.

Then, as now, the global stage was rife with conflict. Cold War hostilities had become urgent, with the Soviet blockade of West Berlin; Jews and Arabs had taken up arms against one another in Israel; armed resistance to colonialism was springing up on every continent; and in the domestic affairs of nations everywhere, including the United States and Great Britain, religious and cultural divisions were becoming increasingly apparent and antagonistic. Nevertheless, the Universal Declaration of Human Rights was greeted with common moral accord among all these divided groups.

The Declaration began by proclaiming "the inherent dignity and the equal and inalienable rights of all members of the human family."[2] It went on to specify twenty-nine articles defining those rights. Article 1 states that "all are born free and equal in dignity and rights..." and that all people "should act towards one another in a spirit of brotherhood." Other articles proclaim all persons' rights to life, security of person, property, freedom of movement and religion, equality under the law, peaceful assembly, education, choices of employment, marriage, and family. Slavery, torture, and arbitrary arrest were prohibited. Along with these rights came duties to the community and responsibilities to respect and preserve the rights of others. Twenty-six of the twenty-nine articles (including Article 1) drew unanimous agreement. The remaining three were passed overwhelmingly, with just eight abstentions and no negative votes.

The Declaration was a significant victory for the advancement of liberty in the war-torn, largely oppressed world of the mid-twentieth century. Legions of people around the world had just witnessed, and in many cases suffered, horrifying abuses of human rights under the totalitarian regimes of the time. No doubt fresh memories of these abuses helped the UN's effort to craft a document that would create a global testament against such inhumane acts. Yet even in light of this dramatic background, the successful passage of a "universal declaration" detailing principles that obligate people everywhere must be considered a colossal, and unlikely, achievement in the history of human morality.

The driving figure behind this astonishing success was Eleanor Roosevelt, aided by a team of talented and dedicated collaborators from several diverse nations. The story, which has been told in glorious detail by Mary Ann Glendon in *A World Made New: Eleanor Roosevelt and the Universal Declaration of Human Rights*,[3] is instructive both for its portrayal of moral leadership and its insights about how to resolve the tension between universalism and particularism. The story's enduring legacy is a testament to the power of moral ideals, because the Declaration has wielded enormous influence over world events subsequent to its global approval. It is especially remarkable, and directly pertinent to the thesis of this book, that this enormous influence has occurred despite the Declaration's lack of enforcement provisions, sanctions, or incentives.

In her leadership of the United Nations committee that drafted the document, Eleanor Roosevelt was able to help forge a common voice from the diverse cultural and ideological perspectives of the nations represented. This achievement was largely due to the great respect for Roosevelt among world leaders and the public alike. She had earned this respect because of her lifelong commitment to goals that transcended her own personal interests, and also because of the marked humility of her demeanor.

A window into this dimension of Roosevelt's character was provided by a reporter who observed her at work during the framing of the Declaration: "In an era conspicuous for the self-interest of both nations and individuals, she has become more and more widely recognized as a person of towering unselfishness.... Mrs. Roosevelt never cares if there is nothing in it for herself. She has absolutely no pride of station and no personal ambition. [To many], she is the personification of the American conscience."[4]

This conspicuous role did not come easily to her. Despite her many years as the First Lady of what was to become the world's most powerful nation, she did not seek or welcome the limelight. Shy by nature, she abhorred both the glitz and clamor of political life. When thrust into the leadership role of this potentially contentious UN commission, she was beset with doubts. For one thing, although famous and revered, she was a woman in an age when few of her gender held leadership roles, and the commission she led was made up entirely of powerful male world leaders. She spent many uncertain hours, often late into the night, working though incredibly complex matters of ideology and state policy with these highly distinguished men. Her education and vocational experience paled in comparison to these male colleagues, another reason for her to feel insecure in the role. Yet she soldiered on, winning the enduring respect of the commission for her wise and quietly forceful leadership. As we describe below, her faith, expressed in a prayer that she wrote and said nightly, helped her maintain equilibrium during this emotionally trying period.

Above all, Roosevelt was steadfast in upholding the principles that she believed were essential for any document on human rights. Some of these principles—such as the prohibition of slavery—were widely accepted, but others set her at odds with significant coalitions of other national representatives. In the economic area, for example, Roosevelt had to resist Soviet calls for full employment mandates, because she realized that this could lead to the assignment of jobs to workers against their wills, which would be an abrogation of their freedom to choose their occupations. Roosevelt also believed that the rights of persons to basic freedoms are linked to their duties to act in a way that preserves the basic freedoms of others. Rights must be balanced by responsibilities if a society is to maintain its capacity to preserve rights for all. It's clear from the beginning to the end of the Declaration that the joining of rights and duties is a central principle of the document. Article 1 enjoins all people to act "in a spirit of brotherhood" toward one another, and Article 29 (the final article) asserts that "Everyone has duties to the community in which alone the free and full development of his personality is possible."[5]

In this sense, the Declaration reflected a tradition of republican democracy built around the assumption that liberty in a society requires civic virtue among its citizens. As the great twentieth-century leader John Gardner put it when writing about the basis of American democracy: "Liberty and duty, freedom and responsibility. That's the deal."[6] How were leaders from all the world's diverse cultures persuaded to endorse a statement of moral principles and civic virtues that stemmed in large part from the republican traditions of Western democracies? In an insightful commentary, Mary Ann Glendon points out that the multicultural group of framers led by Eleanor Roosevelt was determined to put aside lesser differences in favor of the essential moral principles that united them: "What was crucial for them...was the *similarity* among all human beings. Their starting point was the simple fact of the common humanity shared by every man, woman, and child on earth, a fact that, for them, put linguistic, racial, religious, and other differences into their proper perspective."[7] That "proper perspective" was the belief that certain rights and obligations—those that follow from essential moral principles and virtues—are indeed universal.

Moral universalism without the uniformity is a phrase coined by anthropologist Richard Shweder to indicate how the tension between universalism and particularism can be resolved in a constructive way.[8] This phrase closely captures Eleanor Roosevelt's approach. Her belief in universal human rights was balanced by her recognition that there are a variety of legitimate ways that nations can uphold such rights. It was this balanced view that enabled diverse nations with distinct cultural perspectives to sign on to the agreement.

For example, in Roosevelt's view, the rights to family could admit to wide variation in kinship or other arrangements; core economic rights could be addressed by political systems as divergent as capitalism and communism; the rights to education could be fulfilled by formal schooling or by informal teaching of any number of skills, crafts, bodies of knowledge, and so on. Within the crucial parameters of codes that ensure human dignity, societies must have leeway to establish norms of behavior that are adapted to their own particular cultural contexts.

This pluralistic view, which made agreement possible among the nations of the world, was consistent with Roosevelt's personal religious faith. In her own words, Roosevelt drew compelling connections between universalism, respect for individual rights, cultural pluralism, and her own understanding of God's plan: "It seems to me that there is the chance that we were given our intelligence and our gifts as part of God's plan...I believe that the Lord looks upon His children with compassion and allows them to approach Him in many ways."[9]

The anthropological community, which sets a high priority on respecting the particularities of all cultures, has generated widely varied responses to the Declaration. The American Anthropological Association's official statement on the matter was restrained, staking a middle ground between universal rights and cultural relativism. It affirmed its "commitment to human rights consistent with international principles" and noted its intention to "build upon" the progress made by the Declaration.[10] Yet the emphasis in the statement, not surprisingly, was placed on "respect for concrete differences, both collective and individual, rather than the abstract legal uniformity of Western tradition," and their document places "people's rights to realize their capacity for culture" above other rights.[11]

Other cultural champions have been more strident in their doubts about the validity of the Declaration. Glendon's account, for example, quotes a University of Buffalo law professor's 1998 statement that excoriated the Declaration's "arrogant" assertions: "Muslims, Hindus, Africans, non-Judeo-Christians, feminists, critical-theorists, and scholars of an inquiring bent of mind have exposed the Declaration's bias and exclusivity."[12] Another cultural scholar derided "the principle that all the nations of the world must recognize a basic set of transcendent moral facts despite the equally manifest fact of cross-cultural and historical diversity."[13] Such views represent extreme versions of cultural relativism that are still very much alive and well in the academy today.

But it is hard to imagine how such relativist views could serve to rule out cultural practices that violate "the inherent dignity and equal and inalienable rights of all members of the human family" (the Declaration's leading principle). As history and anthropological studies have taught us, there are many cultural beliefs that do not hold that "all are born free and equal in dignity and rights," as the Declaration's Article 1 puts it. Indeed, a number of authoritarian governments in recent years have leveled these same cultural critiques at the Declaration in order to justify their disregard of human rights.[14] Even scholars who are sympathetic with cultural perspectives in general have pointed out that unmitigated relativism can serve as "the invariable ally of tyranny."[15]

Shweder's useful framing, "moral universalism without the uniformity," strikes a sensible middle ground between culturally oblivious universalists and extreme relativists. Shweder warns the culturally oblivious "that one should be slow to make moral judgments about the customary practices of little-known others," and he warns extreme relativists "not to subvert the entire process of moral debate by denying the existence of moral truth."[16]

The point, Shweder writes—and we are on the same page entirely (along with, we believe, Eleanor Roosevelt and her UN Commission)—is "to provide insiders and outsiders, minority groups and majority groups (in other words, everyone), with a common frame of reference for engaging in genuine moral debates and for judging what is right and wrong in their society and in other societies as well."[17]

How compelling was the Declaration's statement of ideals? Because the Declaration contained no enforcement provisions (no policing, no sanctions for breaches), skeptics derided the effort as a philosophical exercise in idealism that could amount to little more than a sterile collection of pious statements. Without some threat of force, the skeptics believed, the Declaration would be ignored. Such an objection, of course, reflects doubts about the power of moral ideals to sway human behavior: it assumes that either pressures or incentives are required to shape real behavioral choices.

But post-Declaration history belies this assumption. As Glendon writes in her account of the Declaration's world impact, "The Declaration's moral authority has made itself felt...impressive advances in human rights—the fall of apartheid in South Africa and the collapse of Eastern European totalitarian regimes—owe more to the moral beacon of the Declaration than to many covenants and treaties that are now in force."[18] What's more, close to one hundred nations have adopted their own human rights provisions modeled on the Declaration. The movement of many nations toward democracy since the Declaration also owes a debt to the document's influence. Before the late 1940s, only 28 percent of the world's nations claimed to be democratic; by the early years of the twenty-first century, this figure had reached 62 percent. The advancement of liberty through the democratization of nations is a goal encouraged by virtually all of the Declaration's provisions.

Roosevelt anticipated another significant impact of the Declaration, educational in nature: "I like to think that the Declaration will forward very largely the education of the people of the world," she wrote.[19] Education, of course, centers on the transmission of ideas across people and generations; it would be an empty exercise if ideas didn't matter. In the case of moral ideals such as those contained in the Declaration, history has made clear that such ideas matter very much, both to the societies that uphold them and to the individuals who benefit from them.

INDIVIDUAL AGENCY, REFLECTION, AND ACTIVE MORAL CHOICE

The question of whether individuals act as moral agents with some control over their choices, rather than as passive objects of predetermined internal or external influences, must be at the heart of any effort to characterize the human moral sense. Biological predispositions, cultural influence, and the quick, seemingly automatic nature of many moral responses are well-documented features of morality. But none of these should blind us to the role played by *active reflection* in determining the ultimate shape of the moral sense—and indeed, of the significance that these and other factors ultimately have for our most important moral choices.

It's true that people experience gut-level inclinations to respond with emotions such as empathy and disgust when confronted with certain social signals. But it's also true that these emotions, and their action consequences, change dramatically as people acquire increasingly advanced modes of moral understanding. We also acknowledge the many ways that all cultures immerse their members in frameworks of beliefs and practices that guide their daily behavior. Still, people also have the capacity to interpret their cultural contexts in their own unique ways, leading to great variety in reactions to culture, including criticism of and resistance to prevailing cultural norms. It's also important to recognize that cultures change, often as a result of active individuals or groups who strive to alter cultural practices they find objectionable. On what basis would people try to effect such changes if their judgments had been entirely molded by their cultural contexts or other immutable factors?

The six leaders profiled in this book were all highly active in trying to change aspects of their cultures they believed needed improvement. As well-known leaders with extraordinary stature and influence, all six left indelible marks on their cultures and the world. Each changed history in ways that have been widely recorded. Such cases of extraordinary historical figures, whose impact can be clearly traced, demonstrate that people, both as individuals and as participants in social movements, can change their societies. In fact, citing such cases, one distinguished European social psychologist pointed out that history has been *more* a story of individuals shaping their societies than vice versa.[20] We might not go that far, but we do credit extraordinary individuals with decisive influences on their surroundings, effected by active interpretations, judgments, and choices made within their own particular cultural contexts.

Most of us, of course, are not in positions to leave such outsized impacts on our broader societies. But we ordinary people do have important influences on our social worlds, even if these influences are hard to separate from the many interacting streams of events that affect social change.

Of course, people's capacity to interpret and influence their environments doesn't mean that they operate in isolation from others or that they are always in complete control of their own thoughts and behavior. In addition to biological predispositions that come along with genetic codes, people acquire habits that, once learned, become highly resistant to change. Indeed, such habits become so much part of us that they are sometimes referred to as our *second nature*, a functional equivalent to the characteristics we're born with.[21] The prominent role that habits play in moral conduct is revealed in the automatic quality that many responses display. Because well-learned habits become routine, they launch with little hesitation. (In the moral domain, *virtues* are among the habits that ensure routine moral responding, with little hesitation or reflection in most cases.) One important question, then, is the relationship of moral habits and moral reflection.

The fields of moral psychology and education have long been torn by a division between those who emphasize habits (or virtues) and those who emphasize reflection (or reasoning). Back in an earlier period of these competing emphases, U.S. Education Secretary William Bennett, author of *The Book of Virtues*,[22] lobbied for the habit side of the debate, opposing psychologist Lawrence Kohlberg, who argued instead for the importance of reasoning and judgment, denouncing what he called a shallow "bag of virtues" approach based in a presumption of fixed and general personality traits, which didn't withstand research scrutiny. But in more recent years, the field of character education has taken a more integrated view of habit and reflection, finding value in both when it comes to the practical task of educating for prosocial behavior. A sound moral psychology must emulate the practical wisdom of this contemporary trend in character education and try to capture the distinct contributions to the moral sense of both habit and reflection.

It's clear that habit directs much of our everyday moral behavior. But reflection is the leading edge of habit, influencing (although not fully determining) which habits are acquired, when and how they're used, and which should be fostered or inhibited. And, at least in some cases, habits can be changed. People spend vast amounts of energy in their efforts to transform or eliminate habits they believe are dysfunctional.

These efforts to change habits don't always produce the desired outcomes, but they do indicate that many people try to control their destinies to the degree that their circumstances allow. They try to consciously regulate and re-regulate their habits in order to increase the degree to which their habits will serve their broader life purposes. Choice and some degree of self-determination are possible (within the limiting parameters of reality), as long as people keep making efforts to examine, modify, and employ their habits in ways that accord with their ideals.

There have been some intimations of this integrated position in moral psychology, but its visibility has been swamped by the predominant messages of the field. Proponents of the "new science of morality" have made some mention (although without much emphasis) of the notion that moral functioning may require both habit and reflection. But where the new science falls short is in its assumption that the beliefs that spur reflection are shaped almost entirely by culture, acquired through engagement with shared narratives that transmit examples of culturally valued or prohibited behaviors.

An example of this simplistic narrative perspective on learning goes as follows: A young person hears the Aesop's fable about a grasshopper who spends the summer dancing while an ant stores up food for the winter. The story's conclusion (the grasshopper goes hungry in wintertime while the ant thrives) provides the young person with a lesson on the virtue of hard work and the perils of improvidence. Young people supposedly absorb such cultural narratives like sponges absorb liquid, and their behavior is shaped by the examples they've absorbed through these narratives. To the extent that the young people think about what they're doing with reference to moral beliefs or ideals, it's only to rationalize the behavior they would pursue anyway based on cultural learning or biologically based impulses. This view, apart from its lack of grounding in psychological reality, leads to a cynical perspective on human morality.

The scientific problem with this view is that it doesn't fully recognize how diverse, even conflicting, the cultural messages of any society are or the degree to which people pay attention to some stories more than others. Nor does it take account of the fact that, at least some of the time, people actively think about the cultural narratives and other messages they do pay attention to. In these cases, they make their own sense of the stories and their own decisions about the values and moral lessons they put forward. Many people do this as a matter of course, forging unique personal perspectives from the examples they see and the stories they hear. The six leaders we studied all made a regular practice of creatively selecting and synthesizing ideals they admired. They didn't follow mindlessly the examples they were exposed to. Although they did incorporate narratives and other cultural traditions into their ideals, they did so through active probing and discernment.

As a rule, people are influenced by their cultural experience, but they're not at its mercy. Cultural socialization can be powerful, but individuals' evaluations and critiques of their cultures eventually determine their moral choices—and sometimes even the future direction of the culture itself.

THE SHARED, VARIED, AND NEVER-FINAL PURSUIT OF MORAL TRUTH

In an age when the possibility of establishing even scientific and historical truth has been questioned, it's not hard to see why the term *moral truth* makes people uncomfortable. Postmodernists have expressed doubt about whether there is any way to determine truth objectively in any area of human thought, and some cultural theorists have cast doubt on the truth value of any moral claim that crosses cultural contexts. Any reference to moral truth risks sounding absolutistic, closed-minded, or even imperialistic. It seems to be a kind of "moral monism," to use Jonathan Haidt's language: that is, an assertion that there is only one true morality, one and only one correct approach to any moral issue.

We're not claiming that there is one true morality for all people, times, and places. The meaningful pursuit of moral truth *doesn't imply that there's only one right way to live or only one morally right answer to any moral question or social problem.* But this doesn't mean that the ideal of seeking moral truth must be abandoned. Judgments and justifications can and must be made about the truth value of any moral claim, even though there is often more than one valid answer to the question at hand.

To take an extreme example, we can judge Nazi ideology, with its creeds of racial superiority and world domination, as morally false without endorsing any particular system or ideology as the one and only true alternative. It is also legitimate to declare that the political systems that followed Nazism in Germany were more just and moral than Nazism without holding that any of those systems represents the one true morality for all people, times, and places. The determination that a democratic political ideology has greater moral legitimacy than Nazi ideology can be made on nonarbitrary grounds by showing (easy to do) that Nazi ideology intended and delivered less fairness, liberty, human rights, honesty, and compassion than did any of the democratic states that preceded or followed it. We in the United States have home-bred examples of such judgments as well. Slavery is morally wrong wherever it is practiced. Arguments in favor of slavery, now and in the past, are devoid of moral truth.

The position within moral philosophy that moral truth is not relative, that it entails some specifiable criteria, but that contested issues may yield more than one justifiable position, has important parallels in *developmental* approaches to moral psychology. From a developmental perspective, advances represent progress toward greater functionality and adaptation but need not define a single end point that represents perfect adaptation, no matter what the life path. Most developmental approaches don't find it useful to posit a final, decisive end point of maturity in a variegated world where organisms are creatively evolving to adapt to continually changing sets of conditions.

Yet certain modes of behavior are more developed, and more adaptive, than other modes—as when a child learns to express needs by making verbal requests rather than by issuing high-pitched wails. As the child encounters new conditions throughout life, development produces new and more adaptive modes of functioning.

As we noted in Chapter 4, Jane Addams took this perspective when she wrote that every generation must forge its own understandings "in response to the new circumstances...and the new hopes..." that emerge in its time.[23] Addams believed that, although moral truth is never fully knowable, our understanding of it can improve through a process of open-mindedly listening to many points of views. With characteristic humility, she was worried that her own opinions might be uninformed and biased, so she made conscious efforts to absorb and synthesize other opinions as she became aware of them over time.

Indeed, none of the six leaders believed that it was possible for humans to discover one final, absolute, unchanging truth. On the contrary, they believed that truth evolves and that the search for truth is an ongoing, never-ending process.

But positive evolution and development are not the only changes that can unfold over time. In general, people do develop more advanced capacities as they age and deal with life, but of course the reverse can also happen, with regression sometimes following injury, disease, or other traumatic events.

The process of moral corruption unfolds over time as well. Like moral growth, corruption results from a particular interaction of character and circumstance. Societies, too, can regress in a developmental sense. For example, not only was the German state that followed the Nazis more morally true, but so too were the states that preceded the Nazis. The passage of time in the first half of the twentieth century failed to produce development in the moral quality of German governance—just the reverse. Accordingly, neither development nor moral truth can be assessed by chronology. We always hope that, because humans can learn from their experience, the passage of time will eventually lead to developmental advances in moral truth, but this can't be ensured unless individuals make good use of their experience as moral learning opportunities.

How can people make good use of learning opportunities? A large part of learning from experience in a general sense is becoming aware of and taking seriously the perspectives of others, especially when those perspectives diverge from one's own point of view. This is also an essential part of any quest for moral truth. That quest requires the humility to open-mindedly examine one's own beliefs in light of other perspectives and come to an informed, balanced resolution. The six leaders in this book shared a determination to learn from the perspectives of many disparate people with widely varying values orientations. They often revised their visions of moral truth after learning about concerns and insights that had previously been unfamiliar to them.

Dag Hammarskjöld's leadership of the UN in its early days required negotiating common ground in the context of deep divisions among member nations. In this context, it was clear that people from different parts of the world saw moral truth in very different terms. Hammarskjöld viewed moral truth as emerging from a process through which multiple viewpoints could interact—the process of considering seriously the full range of perspectives on a question, testing one's starting assumptions and beliefs against a well-informed understanding of other varied points of view, then reconsidering or revising one's own views based on that experience. Hammarskjöld described the process this way:

> In thinking about international service, how [can we] achieve unity (which might seem to require being empty of personal convictions) while also being true to our ideals—these should be those that we can endorse after having opened our minds, with great honesty, to the many voices of the world,...to represent frankly what survives or emerges as one's own after such a test;...let those ideals reach maturity and fruition in a universal climate....It will not permit us to live lazily under the protection of inherited and conventional ideas.[24]

This is the same process that Shweder recommends as a way of understanding moral truth from a pluralistic perspective. Shweder calls this perspective (which he contrasts with extreme cultural relativism on the one hand and extreme absolutism on the other) "the view from *many-wheres*." Shweder writes that "the knowable world is incomplete if seen from any one point of view, incoherent if seen from all points of view at once, and empty if seen from nowhere in particular."[25]

Although cultures are irreducibly different, some moral universals, such as impartiality, community, and harm avoidance, cut across all cultures. Unfortunately, these moral universals may conflict with each other, necessitating tradeoffs among them. For this reason, cultures and individuals may respond to moral questions very differently despite the existence of universal concerns. To come to a resolution of contentious issues across cultures, Shweder recommends serious and sustained efforts to understand moral concerns from culturally disparate points of view and holding off on coming to conclusions about what's right until one has achieved an understanding of others' perspectives that is as deep and valid as possible.[26]

For moral decision making in everyday life, this is far more than an academic exercise. In Dag Hammarskjöld's early leadership of the UN, the stakes were high, the conflicts fierce, and the looming cultural and political contentions daunting. The need to bridge these stark differences was essential to the UN's nascent mission. Hammarskjöld foresaw that without such bridging, progress in resolving international conflicts would be impossible. He approached this task in the tradition of Eleanor Roosevelt by advocating core moral convictions that all nations could accept and by honoring pluralism without succumbing to a cultural relativism that in the end could provide no moral compass to guide the way forward.

In drawing on Hammarskjöld's example in leading the UN to consensus and on Eleanor Roosevelt's example in organizing the Universal Declaration of Human Rights, we're aware that the language these two leaders used embodied the ideals of justice, rights, and other notions associated with the Western emphasis on the autonomous individual.

But these ideals are valued also in the cultures that emphasize communal and spiritual ideals, just as communal and spiritual ideals such as charity and hope are valued in Western societies. All of these cultural values have parts to play in the search for moral truth, and any claim to moral universals must take the entire range into account.

Both a commitment to widely shared cultural values and a pluralistic respect for diverse cultural perspectives are necessary in any search for moral truth—a search that can never be final. Eleanor Roosevelt and Dag Hammarskjöld fought for this perspective in the international realm, always seeking ways to balance universalism and pluralism across warring societies and diverse cultures. Jane Addams, Nelson Mandela, and Dietrich Bonhoeffer fought the same kinds of battles in their own countries, informed by their own particular visions of justice, community, faith, and divinity.

EDUCATION, HUMAN DEVELOPMENT, AND MORAL TRUTH

As we have written, Eleanor Roosevelt considered the greatest potential of the Universal Declaration of Human Rights to be the education of the people of the world. In saying this, she understood that education has an enduring power that can reach beyond coercive legislation. In its gradual, undramatic way, education can exert a lasting influence on the conduct of individuals and the moral atmosphere of societies. Education can elevate the minds of citizens, especially those still forming their moral orientations. As people come to understand and cherish moral ideals, they're more likely to act in accord with them. Nelson Mandela understood this when he famously said that "Education is the most powerful weapon which you can use to change the world."[27]

The psychological means through which education exerts long-term behavioral effects is the process of development toward more mature ways of functioning. It's relatively easy to assess development in realms of functioning that advance mastery of the physical world. For a child, walking is a developmental advance over crawling, and mathematical skills such as algebra are an advance over simple counting.

For a society, modern medicine is an advance over non–science-based practices such as leeching. In these cases, the more developmentally advanced skills, knowledge, and practices work better overall in coping with physical realities than did those they replaced.

In the moral realm, what constitutes a developmental advance is far less certain and more contentious. Many believe, for example, that the Golden Rule is a moral advance over the eye-for-an-eye ethic of revenge, but can this be demonstrated? If someone prefers revenge to forgiveness, who is to say this choice is morally inferior? The appeal of cultural relativism derives from the understandable wish to avoid taking a position on which values represent moral righteousness, especially when there is disagreement among people from different cultural backgrounds. What's more, even values that are widely endorsed—such as loyalty and fairness, for example—can conflict with one another in everyday life. It's not always clear when special obligations to friends or family members trump even-handedness or how to go about deciding such cases.

It is conundrums such as this that have led culturally oriented psychologists to decry what Jonathan Haidt calls moral monism. Haidt argues that people from different cultures will inevitably differ from one another in their moral preferences because their cultures don't share the same foundations of belief: Some cultures value purity above all, others justice, community, autonomy, and so on. In Haidt's view, following Shweder's formulation,[28] there are five distinct foundations of moral belief worldwide, each of which has intrinsic moral validity. So Haidt asks, quoting Rodney King's famous exclamation during the 1992 Los Angeles riots, although people make different moral choices, "Why can't we all get along?" In this relativistic vision, the primary obligation that people have—the sole value that, in effect, actually applies universally—is mutual toleration.

Haidt is by no means the first relativist to suggest that tolerance is one moral standard that everyone should accept. But what gives tolerance this unique status? And what does one do about practices that one believes must *not* be tolerated, when tolerance and justice conflict? In those cases, tolerating certain practices can mean overlooking oppressively brutal conditions, up to and including slavery and genocide. History is full of examples of this sort of misguided tolerance.

For a moral life, choices must be made, and no cultural prescription can provide a sound guide to moral choice in every situation. As new and changing events emerge, people must think both individually and together about which values and ideals to draw on in formulating a moral response. As psychologist Darcia Narvaez has written,[29] each of Haidt's moral foundations has a dark side if misapplied or taken too far: Zealous pursuit of purity, tyrannical pressure to conform to community, self-centered or irresponsible autonomy, and merciless implementations of justice all can cause great humanitarian harm, as history has shown. The only way to avoid harmful misapplications of values is to actively exercise one's best considered judgment and to work with others to search open-mindedly for the moral truth in every situation. Similarly, when basic moral values conflict—as, for example, when telling the truth could cause serious harm—the conflict must be resolved in a way that gives one of the values moral priority in that situation. Only judgment, guided by a never-ending search for truth, can provide principled solutions that offer hope for a moral resolution to such conflicts. Narvaez rightly points out that education requires taking normative positions about what is worthy of being passed on to the learner. For this reason, education must face the question of how to think carefully about establishing priorities among conflicting values while also promoting open-mindedness and mutual respect; otherwise, education teaches moral relativism rather than moral pluralism.

Human development and education support growth, not just change. For this reason, they require prescriptive, nonrelativist stances. Educational and developmental perspectives assume that ideas matter, that people can in fact make choices based upon their best judgments, and that individuals have the capacity to make moral choices that reflect their deepest values and highest ideals. Neither ignores the many nonideational forces, from biological to social-contextual, that influence human behavior: It's understood in the fields of human development and education that the most complex behaviors appear to be automatic, fast, and unreflective once they become habitual. But those who study human development, and those who practice education, know that habitual behaviors often begin as consciously driven choices, and at any time, people can decide to follow, question, refine, or oppose their own habits if their judgment leads them to do so.

If ideas and judgment didn't matter, there would be little point to the whole enterprise of education. Nor, by the way, would there be much point to writing books and media articles, even ones that try to convince readers that ideas, ideals, and judgments don't matter.

We have written this book to make the case that ideas and ideals do matter. We have used the lives and actions of six extraordinary moral leaders to make this case. But the case that we've made applies to all segments of the human population. Even criminals, as a recent *New Yorker* article documents, are sometimes moved by a yearning for justice, albeit in sometimes violent or dysfunctional ways. The *New Yorker* article describes how seasoned prosecutors often elicit confessions from the most hardened criminals by appealing to their desire to see themselves as fair-minded.[30] We are a truth-and-justice–seeking species, even if we don't always get it right—and although some people tend to get it more right than others, it's wise to remember that everyone will fall short at times.

Progress through human development and education means becoming better able to seek moral truths and more willing (and thus more likely) to align our choices with those truths. And, even for the most inspiring people in our midst, progress inevitably will be slow, uncertain, and never final.

It is the same with human societies. In any society, moral progress takes place in fits and starts over many centuries, three steps forward and two steps back. As Martin Luther King, Jr.'s arc bends toward justice, it takes lots of detours along the way. But in the long run it describes the progressive expansion of human rights, in the manner envisioned by the UN Declaration that Eleanor Roosevelt organized. Admittedly the world has not uniformly risen to the challenge of the Declaration, and in parts of the world there have been dramatic reversals and violations of the Declaration's ideals. We could conclude that the Declaration's passage was an apogee of moral progress thus far and that subsequently the world has fallen away from this ideal. It could be that the falling away will continue for a long barren stretch of time. But the moral ideal is out there to educate and inspire future generations, people yet to be born who will bend the arc back in its right direction.

NOTES

1. Martin Luther King Jr., "Moving to Another Mountain." Baccalaureate sermon, Wesleyan University commencement exercises, June 8, 1964.
2. Mary Ann Glendon, *A World Made New: Eleanor Roosevelt and the Universal Declaration of Human Rights*, 1st ed. (New York: Random House, 2001), 310.
3. Glendon, *A World Made New*.
4. Glendon, *A World Made New*, 206.
5. Glendon, *A World Made New*, 314.
6. John W. Gardner and Francesca Gardner, *Living, Leading, and the American Dream*, 1st ed. (San Francisco: Jossey-Bass, 2003).
7. Glendon, *A World Made New*, 232.
8. Richard Shweder, "Relativism and Universalism," in *A Companion to Moral Anthropology*, ed. Didier Fassin, Vol. 20 (Chichester, West Sussex, UK, & Hoboken, NJ: Wiley-Blackwell, 2012), 85–102.
9. As quoted in Glendon, *A World Made New*.
10. American Anthropological Association, "Declaration on Anthropology and Human Rights," http://www.aaanet.org/about/Policies/statements/Declaration-on-Anthropology-and-Human-Rights.cfm (accessed June 4, 2014).
11. American Anthropological Association, "Declaration on Anthropology and Human Rights."
12. Glendon, *A World Made New*, 224.
13. Mark Goodale, *Surrendering to Utopia: An Anthropology of Human Rights* (Stanford, CA: Stanford University Press, 2009), 42.
14. Glendon, *A World Made New*, 224.
15. Goodale, *Surrendering to Utopia*, 43.
16. Shweder, "Relativism and Universalism," 88.
17. Shweder, "Relativism and Universalism," 88.
18. Glendon, *A World Made New*, 236.
19. Glendon, *A World Made New*, 236.
20. Serge Moscovici & Charlan Nemeth, *Social Influence: II. Minority Influence* (Oxford: Rand McNally, 1974), 999.

21. See: William Damon, "Nature, Second Nature, and Individual Development: An Ethnographic Opportunity," in *Ethnography and Human Development: Context and Meaning in Social Inquiry*, eds. Richard Jessor, Anne Colby, and Richard A. Shweder (Chicago: University of Chicago Press, 1996), 459–475.

22. William J. Bennett, *The Book of Virtues: A Treasury of Great Moral Stories* (New York: Simon & Schuster, 1993), 999.

23. Louise Knight, *Jane Addams: Spirit in Action*, 1st ed. (New York: W. W. Norton & Co., 2010), 101.

24. Dag Hammarskjöld and Wilder Foote, *Servant of Peace: A Selection of the Speeches and Statements of Dag Hammarskjöld, Secretary-General of the United Nations, 1953-1961* [Speeches. Selections.] (New York: Harper & Row, 1962), 81.

25. Richard Shweder et al., "The `Big Three' of Morality (Autonomy, Community, and Divinity), and the `Big Three' Explanations of Suffering," in *Morality and Health*, eds. A. Brandt and P. Rozin (New York: Routledge, 1997), 45.

26. Richard Shweder, *Why Do Men Barbecue?: Recipes for Cultural Psychology* (Cambridge, MA: Harvard University Press, 2003), 38.

27. Nelson Mandela, "Lighting Your Way to a Better Future: Presentation for Launch of Mindset Network." University of the Witwatersrand, Johannesburg, South Africa, July 16, 2003. http://db.nelsonmandela.org/ speeches/pub_view.asp?pg=item&ItemID=NMS909&txtstr=education%20 is%20the%20most%20powerful (accessed June 4, 2014).

28. Shweder et al., "The `Big Three' of Morality," 119–169.

29. Darcia Narvaez, "Integrative Ethical Education," in *Handbook of Moral Development.*, eds. M. Killen and J. G. Smetana (Mahwah, NJ: Erlbaum., 2006), 703–733.

30. Douglas Starr, "Do Police Interrogation Techniques Produce False Confessions?" *New Yorker*, 2013, December 9: 42.

INDEX